Plant Mineral Nutrition

Plant
Mineral
Nutrition

E. J. Hewitt, Ph.D., D.Sc., A.K.C.,
F.I.Biol.
Reader in Plant Physiology, University of Bristol

T. A. Smith, Ph.D., M.I.Biol.
Research Fellow in Plant Physiology, University of Bristol

The English Universities Press Ltd

ISBN 0 340 18498 1 Boards
ISBN 0 340 05086 1 Paperback

First published 1975

The English Universities Press Ltd
St Paul's House, Warwick Lane, London EC4P 4AH

Printed in Great Britain by
Fletcher & Son Ltd, Norwich

Contents

Preface

The study of the mineral nutrition of plants is a vast and complex subject, though it is also a subject which is rapidly growing in importance as the demand for food increases. In the present short book we cannot claim to review the subject in its entirety, and our presentation may even be criticised for placing too much emphasis on those aspects which are of greatest interest to the authors, especially on the interaction of mineral nutrition with plant biochemistry. We have endeavoured to consider aspects of animal and bacterial nutrition where these are of comparative interest. We trust that our work will serve in some small measure to complement the thorough and lucid treatises on plant mineral nutrition which have been published recently.

The authors are greatly indebted to Professor J. P. Hudson for his permission to write this book and for his encouragement in the course of the work. In addition, thanks are due to the Agricultural Research Council and to the University of Bristol for providing facilities which have allowed the fulfilment of this project.

Many members of staff of Long Ashton Research Station, both past and present, have given generously of their time in helping us to write this book. Of these, we are particularly grateful to Miss Jeanne Ogborne and Miss Alithia Goddard for typing the manuscript, to George Jones, Mrs Jackie Sadd, Peter Rushby and Richard Chenoweth for photography, to Miss Marilyn Banwell and Mrs Daisy Bickley for proof reading, and to Mrs Gedelita Wilshire for her help with the index. The assistance of the staff of our Library, Miss Peggy Keeton, Mrs Geraldine Collings, Mrs Joyce Hunwicks and Mrs Barbara Hooper, must also be acknowledged, and in addition we are greatly indebted to Douglas James for drawing the figures. Many authors have generously supplied illustrative material and to all these we are most grateful. No small part has been played by the editorial staff of the English Universities Press, in particular by Mrs Jennifer Bowe and Miss Karen Wilby.

Any faults or omissions in this book are entirely due to our own incompetence, and for these we take full responsibility.

I
Introduction

'If, for instance, by the year 2000, the developed countries were to reach the point at which couples replace themselves, and the developing countries were to reach that point by the year 2050, and both these achievements appear unlikely—the world's present population of 3500 million would not become stationary before the year 2120, and would then stand at 15 000 million.'

Robert S. McNamara
as President of the World Bank

It is only relatively recently that mankind has realised that this planet does not have inexhaustible resources, and one of the most important of these is agricultural land. Areas of unexploited potential agricultural land are increasingly difficult to find, and 10% of the earth's land area is now under cultivation. By current world estimates each person has at most 2 hectares of land surface which can be cultivated, and by the year 2000 this area will probably be reduced to 1 hectare (about 2·5 acres), due to the anticipated doubling in population over the intervening period. Moreover, at least 500 million people (i.e. one in seven) at present may be said to have a seriously inadequate diet. Although this is partly a problem of politics and food redistribution, there is no doubt that the efficiency of world agriculture must also be increased very considerably if the population continues to expand. Even now, probably fifty to one hundred thousand people die each week as a direct or indirect effect of hunger, although the overall population increase is about 1·5 million (births in excess of deaths) in this time.

The use of fertilisers

The application of fertilisers at present accounts for at least 25% of the yield of crops throughout the world; more in the advanced countries, less in the underdeveloped countries: a total of 60 million metric tonnes of nutrients is used each year, or on average nearly 50 kg applied per hectare of agricultural land.

The lodging (bending) of cereal stems when grown with high levels of nitrogen in the soil has until recently limited the grain obtainable with artificial nitrogenous fertilisers to a yield below the full crop potential. This problem has now been largely overcome by breeding strains of wheat and rice with short stems. The Nobel Peace Prize was awarded to Norman Borlaug in 1970 for his achievements in this work. The consequent yields, which have been doubled in some cases, have revolutionised agriculture in parts of the world. However, these increased yields are dependent on the application of additional nitrogen fertiliser, and artificial nitrogen fixation makes considerable demands on our scarce energy resources.

Certainly the world consumption of fertilisers is increasing very considerably, the amount applied doubling each ten years, and the fixation of nitrogen due to the activities of man is now said to equal that attributable to natural biological fixation.

However, the use of fertilisers is not without disadvantages and excessive use may be detrimental to the environment in several ways. For instance, fertiliser may be washed from the fields by rain into waterways, where it can cause large increases in the algal populations. This eventually changes a lake which was once a clear body of water into a thick algal suspension and leads to an increased rate of silting. Phosphate and nitrate containing fertilisers are mainly responsible for this process, which is called eutrophication. Eventually, marginal vegetation encroaches in the water and some inland lakes have been turned into swamps in this way. Nitrate applied in large amounts to agricultural land may also drain into well water where it can accumulate to such high levels that it becomes toxic, especially to very young children, causing methaemoglobinaemia. There is also some risk that impurities of certain elements in fertilisers can accumulate to toxic levels in fields after prolonged applications. It is therefore important that fertilisers are applied wisely and under conditions which guarantee the optimal returns.

A large proportion of the mineral nutrients applied to the land is lost in domestic sewage and in excreta from farm animals confined to intensive feeding lots. Sewage is frequently mixed with industrial waste before disposal and the possible benefits resulting from attempts to return the nutrients to the soil are offset by the toxicity due to heavy metals arising from industrial processes. There is a clear case for the segregation of industrial and organic wastes, and this is most important in view of the finite nature of our known phosphate reserves which may last only another thirty years.

The scientific study of plant nutrition in the past has greatly contributed to the effective use of the large amounts of fertilisers currently being applied to the land. However, there is still scope for considerable improvements in crop yields by an increased understanding of the mineral nutrition of plants. This is of paramount importance if we are to provide adequate nutritional standards for the underprivileged majority on this planet. The daunting increase in world population makes these efforts even more urgent.

The study of plant nutrition

The solution of problems arising directly from the large amounts of fertilisers used must depend on a sound knowledge of the science of plant nutrition. Similarly, the reclamation of the large waste areas resulting from industrial processes, such as power station fly-ash tips and mine tailings (Plate 64), and the elimination from the environment of radioactive elements arising from nuclear processes, fully justify the acquisition of basic knowledge of mineral uptake and function.

The study of plant nutrition may be viewed in several ways depending on our personal interest and the economic reasons for our employment. In practice our studies may seek answers to such questions as: How much of a particular element does a plant need? Which elements are in fact essential? Are some elements beneficial if not essential? How are mineral elements absorbed? Can one element replace the functions of another, and what are the specific functions of those elements already recognised as essential for plant life? What happens when there is a lack or an excess? How are these problems investigated? These are simple questions, but difficulties arise in providing unequivocal answers to some because of the experimental problems involved.

Before proceeding, it is necessary to define the term 'mineral nutrient'. Although by far the greatest proportion of an intact plant may usually be attributed to water, by general usage the elements hydrogen and oxygen are not termed nutrients; neither is the element carbon, on which the structure and metabolism of plants is based, considered to be a mineral nutrient. The importance of hydrogen, oxygen and carbon fully justifies their separate study. The elements at present considered to be mineral nutrients are listed in Table 1.1. They will be discussed individually and the way in which their essentiality was discovered will be described in Chapter 2. In general, these elements are absorbed through the roots of higher plants from the soil, which has a complex structure and is not merely an inert medium containing mineral elements in aqueous solution. A healthy soil has an important organic component, both living and dead, the effects of which are sometimes difficult to assess. The importance of soil microbiology must not be underestimated and the effects of nutrients on the balance of soil micro-organisms must be observed in order to gain a full understanding of the response of crop plants to fertilisers. The complications due to the organic compounds of the soil sometimes increase the difficulties of extrapolating the results of conventional culture techniques to the results obtainable in the field. Despite these problems, considerable success has been achieved by the use of water or sand culture methods in the elucidation of nutritional problems in agriculture.

Table 1.1   The status of the elements in the nutrition of plants

Essential* macronutrients	Essential* micronutrients	Beneficial*	Essentiality not demonstrated
Metals			
Potassium (1)	Iron (1)	Aluminium	Chromium (1)
Calcium (1, 2)	Copper (1)	Strontium	Tin (1)
Magnesium (1)	Manganese (1)	Rubidium	Nickel (1?)
	Zinc (1)		
	Molybdenum (1, 4, 5)		
	Cobalt (1, 5)		
	Vanadium (1, 6)		
	Sodium (1, 7)		
	Gallium (8)		
Non-metals			
Carbon (1)	Boron (3)	Selenium (1, 11)	Fluorine (1)
Hydrogen (1)	Silicon (1, 9)		Bromine (12)
Oxygen (1)	Chlorine (1)		
Phosphorus (1)	Iodine (1, 10)		
Nitrogen (1)			
Sulphur (1)			

Notes

(1) Essential for at least some animals.
(2) Not required* by *Azotobacter agile*.
(3) Not required* by *Aspergillus*.
(4) Essential for plants with nitrate as nitrogen source.
(5) Essential for nitrogen fixation in bacteria and algae.
(6) Essentiality shown for the alga *Scenedesmus obliquus*.
(7) Essentiality shown for *Atriplex vesicaria*, *Halogeton glomeratus* and some blue-green algae.
(8) Essentiality claimed for *Aspergillus*.
(9) Essentiality shown for the alga *Navicula*, the pteridophyte *Equisetum arvense* and for certain grasses.
(10) Essentiality shown for the seaweed *Polysiphonia urceolata*.
(11) Essential for *Escherichia coli* in nitrate medium.
(12) Beneficial for some animals.

* *See Chapter 2 (page 24) for definition.*

The research needed to widen our knowledge of plant nutrition involves the application of many new and sophisticated techniques. Early investigations were confined to growth measurements but later advances in analytical chemistry led to the development of tissue analysis which has been the basis of many of the classical experiments in the first half of the present century. More recently, the use of isotopes has contributed greatly to our understanding of translocation, metabolism and accumulation of the elements. Techniques for chemical analysis of the elements have now been augmented by atomic absorption spectrophotometry and activation analysis, while for the investigation of subcellular mineral distribution the potential of radio-autography and the electron beam microprobe X-ray analyser used in conjunction with a scanning electron microscope (Fig. 8.1, p. 242) has still to be realised.

Although it is possible that other essential elements will be found, the amounts needed will probably take the most sophisticated techniques to detect and monitor them.

Advances in mineral nutrition and biochemistry are frequently interdependent. Mineral deficiency experiments have demonstrated the existence of metabolic pathways which might otherwise be overlooked, and conversely the identification of a metal in an enzymic prosthetic group has provided confirmation of the essentiality of certain micronutrients.

Further Reading

Epstein, E. (1972) *Mineral Nutrition of Plants.* John Wiley: New York, London, Sydney and Toronto. 422 pp.

Gauch, H. G. (1972) *Inorganic Plant Nutrition.* Dowden, Hutchinson and Ross, Stroudsberg, Pennsylvania. 488 pp.

Scientific American (1970) An issue entitled 'The Biosphere' **223** (3).

Plate I Greenhouse for nutrient culture in sand media (*above*) and water de-ionising equipment (*below*) used at Long Ashton Research Station.

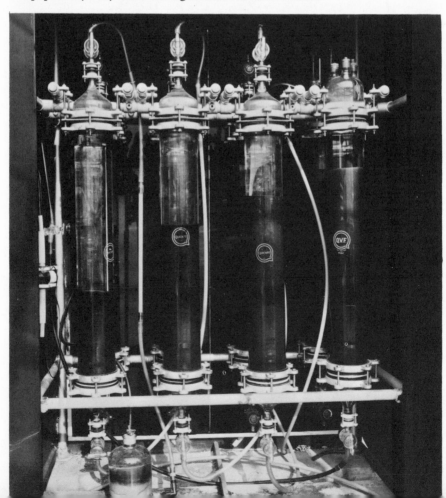

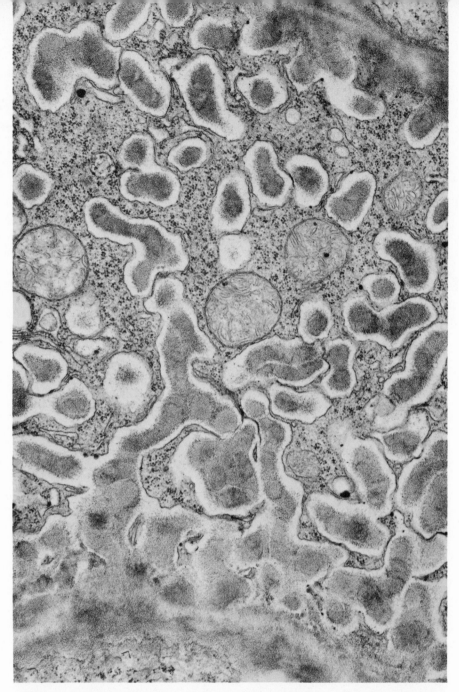

Plate 2 Transfer cells—plant cells with wall ingrowths, specialised in relation to short distance transport of solutes. Part of a transfer cell in the phloem of a minor vein of *Pisum arvense*, viewed in tangential longitudinal section to show the abundance of the wall ingrowths. Some ingrowths are several microns in length and are repeatedly branched; very few of them lack associated endoplasmic reticulum. ×20 000. From Gunning, B. E. S. and Pate, J. S. (1969) 'Transfer Cells'. Plant cells with wall ingrowths, specialised in relation to short distance transfer of solutes —their occurrence, structure and development. *Protoplasma* **68**, 107–33.

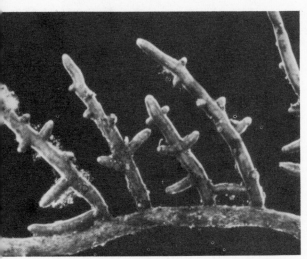
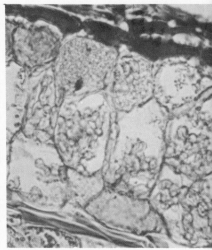

Plate 3 Mycorrhizae on roots of the pine *Picea abies* with a thick hyphal mantle. Southern Sweden. ×8. From Björkman (1970) *Pl. Soil* **32**, 589–610.

Plate 4 Longitudinal section of an ectendotrophic mycorrhiza on *Pinus silvestris* from Northern Sweden. The hyphal mantle is very thin but the intercellular hyphae are well developed. ×500. From Björkman (1970) *Pl. Soil* **32**, 589–610.

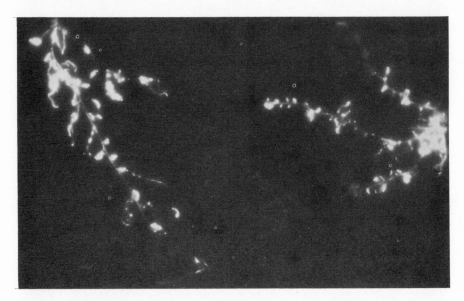

Plate 5 Autoradiograph of parts of diffuse mycorrhizal systems of beech. The relative intensity indicates the uptake of radioactive phosphate, ^{32}P. The long leaders and uninfected laterals are less active in uptake than mycorrhizal roots. Width of picture represents 15 cm. From Harley and McCready (1950) *New Phytol.* **49**, 388–97.

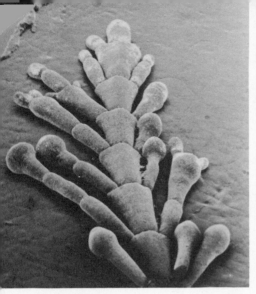
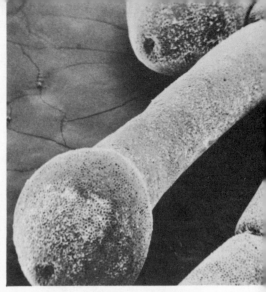

Plate 6 Scanning electron micrograph of part of a frond of *Corallina officinalis*, a marine alga (Rhodophyceae) with a skeleton of calcium carbonate in the form of calcite. *Left*—branching frond ×16; *right*—single segment ×78. Calcareous algae are important contributors to the reef limestone found in tropical seas. Photograph by Elizabeth Parsons, Long Ashton Research Station.

Plate 7 Photograph taken with the scanning electron microscope of stinging hairs in the nettle (*Urtica dioica*). According to Haberlandt (1914) the cell is silicified towards the apex and calcified towards the base. ×180. By courtesy of Elizabeth Parsons, Long Ashton Research Station.

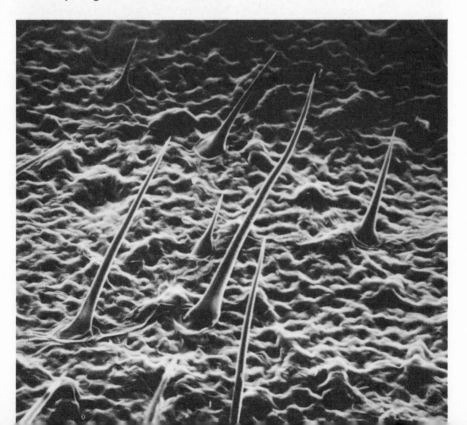

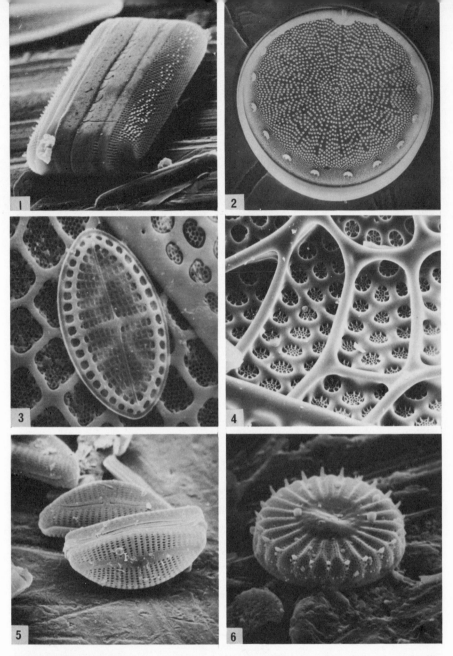

Plate 8 The diatoms form a group of algae in which the cell wall is of pectin-like material impregnated with silica.

(1) Whole cell of the marine diatom *Grammatophora*. ×2100.

(2) Inside view of single valve of the marine diatom *Actinocyclus*. ×780.

(3) A single cell of the marine diatom *Cocconeis*, epiphytic on another large diatom *Isthmia*. ×2600.

(4) Portion of the inside of the valve of the marine diatom *Isthmia nervosa*. ×1400.

(5) Cells of the freshwater diatom *Cymbella*. ×1600.

(6) Single valve of the freshwater diatom *Cyclotella*. ×3900.

By courtesy of Dr F. E. Round, Department of Botany, Bristol University.

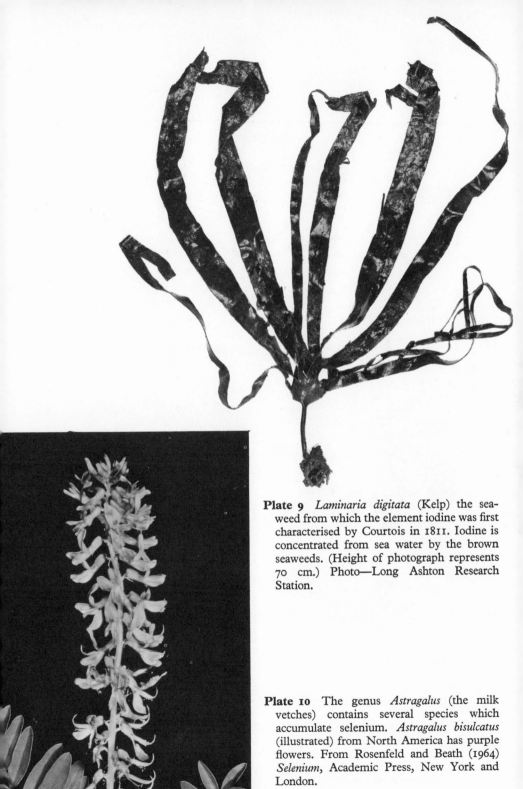

Plate 9 *Laminaria digitata* (Kelp) the seaweed from which the element iodine was first characterised by Courtois in 1811. Iodine is concentrated from sea water by the brown seaweeds. (Height of photograph represents 70 cm.) Photo—Long Ashton Research Station.

Plate 10 The genus *Astragalus* (the milk vetches) contains several species which accumulate selenium. *Astragalus bisulcatus* (illustrated) from North America has purple flowers. From Rosenfeld and Beath (1964) *Selenium*, Academic Press, New York and London.

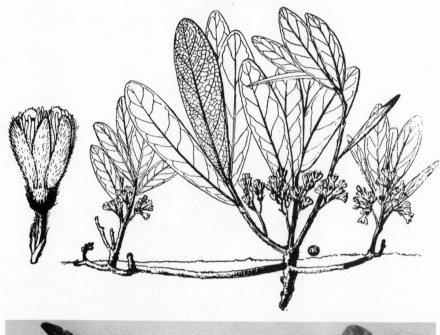

Plate 11 *Dichapetalum cymosum* Hook., Eng., the poisonous South African plant which contains fluoroacetate. The leaves are highly toxic, 25 g being sufficient to kill a sheep.

(*a*) Showing the underground stem system (Burt Hardy).

(*b*) Showing the fruit (reproduced by courtesy of Sir Rudolph Peters).

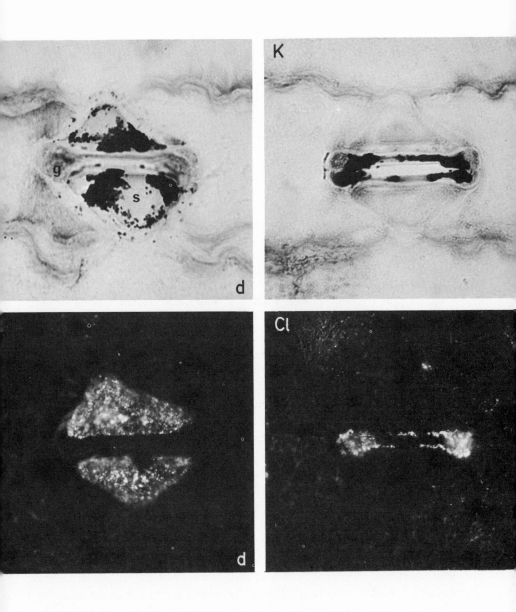

Plate 12 Distribution of potassium and chloride within guard cells (g) and subsidiary cells (s) in leaves of maize sampled from the dark (d) and from the light (l). Reactions with cobaltinitrite (K) or silver nitrate (Cl), the silver precipitates were photographed in incident light. On transfer from the dark to light the K^+ and Cl^- ions move from the subsidiary cells into the guard cells. On darkening, both elements return to the subsidiary cells and the stomata close. From Raschke, K. and Fellows, M. P. (1971) Stomatal movement in *Zea mays*: shuttle of potassium and chloride between guard cells and subsidiary cells. *Planta* (Berl.) **101**, 296–316. Springer: Berlin–Heidelberg–New York.

2
The History and Principles of Plant Nutrition

'Faith, imagination, and intuition are decisive factors in the progress of science.'

Max Born

History of plant nutrition

The experimental study of plant nutrition was first given serious consideration by Nicholas of Cusa (1401–46) who suggested that plants absorb constituents from the soil by some process related to water uptake. He appears to have anticipated, at least in a theoretical sense, the classical willow branch experiment described by Van Helmont (1577–1644) about 200 years later. Van Helmont is perhaps better known as the person who first used the word 'gas', derived from the Greek word 'chaos'. Van Helmont took a willow branch weighing 5 lb, planted it in a known weight of oven-dried soil and then added water only when required for a period of five years. The branch and the re-dried soil were then weighed again. The shoot had gained about 164 lb and the soil had lost 2 oz. Two experimental points should be noted; namely, he omitted to recover and weigh fallen leaves, but he covered the soil to exclude dust. This second point will be seen to have been particularly far-sighted in the light of problems discussed in the next chapter. His conclusion that the whole of the gain in weight of the branch was the result of water uptake was unfortunate, but the failure to take account of loss in weight of soil of much less than 1% was understandable. Robert Boyle criticised Van Helmont's principal conclusion, and in *The Sceptical Chymist* (1661 and 1680) described similar experiments carried out with squash and cucumber plants. As a result of careful work he observed a loss in the weight of the soil at the end of the experiments but unfortunately he attributed this to wastage rather than removal by the plants. However, Boyle did show that plants contained a mineral ash and he therefore questioned the idea that vegetable matter was derived solely from water. The origin of this ash component was first attributed correctly to the soil by Glauber (1656) and Mayow (1674) who recognised the importance of saltpetre (potassium nitrate) for plants and realised the significance of animal excreta in the soil-plant cycle. Mayow measured the 'nitro-aerial' factor (nitrate) in soils and found seasonal differences which he related to rapid uptake by plants during the spring. The existence in plants of other saline non-volatile components derived from the soil was also deduced.

Woodward (1699) described a water culture experiment which introduced several significant ideas. He grew mint, vetch and potato plants for up to seventy-seven days in water obtained from rivers, springs, rainfall and by distillation, and in some cases he added garden mould which resulted in increased growth. He concluded that water serves merely as a carrier of 'terrestrial matter' and remarked 'some waters are indeed so very clear and transparent that one would not suspect any terrestrial matter were latent in them: but they may be highly saturated with such matter, tho' the eye may not be presently able to describe or discern it'. The difficulties in obtaining and testing water of adequate purity for the investigation of mineral nutrition of plants are still with us.

Duhamel du Monceau (1758) performed rather similar experiments to those of Woodward by growing walnut, chestnut, oak and almond saplings, and beans in filtered water from the Seine but published no important conclusions. A much more intelligent study by Home (1762) was made independently for a competition for which he was awarded a gold medal. He grew barley in pots of soil and introduced plant analysis as a means of investigating uptake. He drew attention to the formation of nitre (nitrate) in the soil from organic waste nitrogen sources and concluded that even snow or rain water contained appreciable amounts of mineral nutrients. He also discovered the importance of providing potassium and magnesium (as the sulphates) thus adding the next two essential elements to the list.

The next important work was that of Theodor de Saussure (1804). He grew *Bidens cannabina* and *Polygonum persicaria* in distilled water to which were added various salts, and he included nitrates, which he found essential for growth. He also showed that roots absorbed both beneficial and toxic compounds; that different salts were absorbed to different extents; that uptake varied with species and plant age; and that accumulation could occur from very dilute solutions. Wiegman and Polstorff (1840) found that plant roots could absorb all the elements needed for growth and they were the first to draw attention to the fact that seed reserves may contribute to nutritional requirements. This observation is still most relevant to the study of the micronutrients or trace elements needed by plants.

An important practical aspect of water culture experimentation was anticipated by Senebier (1791) who found that plants died in stagnant water. De Saussure (1804) extended this by showing that if roots of chestnut saplings in water were exposed to carbon dioxide instead of air they died in seven days. The importance of adequate aeration of roots was first emphasised by Sachs (1887). Woodward and De Saussure were the originators of the water culture approach to studying plant nutrition. Boussingault (1851–6) and Count Salm-Horstmar (1849, 1851) introduced the idea of using sand culture or other inert rooting media to support the plants with their roots in a relatively normal environment.

The research of the great German chemist Liebig (1840) drew attention to the possibility that artificial fertilisers could be used to supplement the minerals present in the soil, and this work led to the development of a commercial form of soluble calcium phosphate, the superphosphate, by Lawes in England which was patented in 1842. The experimental appraisal of fertilisers originated by Lawes and Gilbert at Rothamsted has continued to the present day.

Sprengel (1839) is regarded as having first identified and listed the major nutrients (the macronutrients) required by plants in general, comprising nitrogen, phosphorus, sulphur, potassium, calcium and magnesium (Plates 13 to 22, 30, 31).

The basis of modern water culture techniques was developed by Sachs (1860) at the Tharandt School of Forestry, who showed that the normal growth of plants could be sustained without a solid rooting medium, thus avoiding the impurities carried by sand when studying nutrient requirements. He published a standardised formula for nutrient composition and introduced the ideas of changing solutions regularly, of relating culture volume to plant density and of using ammonium compounds as alternatives to nitrates.

Knop (1861, 1865) described a much improved nutrient formula based on molar ratios which has been widely used, even until recently, though appropriately supplemented with some micronutrients. The composition of Knop's solution is given in Chapter 3 (Table 3.2). Knop (1860) improved the techniques for seed germination by using muslin stretched over a shallow dish of solution. Many other nutrient solutions have been described since the time of Knop (see Hewitt, 1966), though only a few of these are now in general use (Table 3.2).

Identification of the micronutrient requirements

Iron

Gris (1844) found that iron was essential for curing chlorosis in vines and observed that specific cell inclusions now known as the chloroplasts became abnormal in shape and colour when iron was lacking. This was the first discovery concerning trace elements (the micronutrients) which are essential, but at much lower concentrations (less than 0·5 mM) than the major nutrients (the macronutrients) which are required at 1 to 10 mM levels (Tables 1.1 and 3.1). The terms micronutrient and macronutrient were suggested by Loomis and Shull (1937) and recommended as standard terminology by Arnon (1938).

Examples of iron-deficiency symptoms are shown in Plates 32 and 33.

Manganese

The experimental study of the micronutrients was initiated by the Count Salm-Horstmar in 1849–51 who used glass or wax containers and acid-washed sand and quartz as rooting media; he was probably the first to describe the preparation of purified nutrient reagents, including iron compounds and calcium nitrate. He described symptoms in oat plants when grown in the absence of manganese which we now know were those of grey speck disease caused by manganese deficiency and frequently observed in the field, though not identified until the work of McHargue (1922) and Samuel and Piper (1928). The experimental care and methods used by Salm-Horstmar are worthy of note even in the present time. He also showed experimentally the essential nature of iron deficiency as well as that of nitrogen, phosphorus, sulphur, calcium, potassium and magnesium which had already been observed by Sprengel in 1839. Sachs (1860) included both iron and manganese in his standardised nutrient solution.

The first clear demonstration of the essential nature of manganese as an element required in small amounts was achieved by Raulin in 1863 for a fungus, *Rhizopus* (*Ascophora*) *nigricans*, and the importance of zinc was similarly discovered by Raulin in 1869. Pfeffer contested these conclusions as merely evidence of beneficial effects of elements toxic in higher concentrations. However Raulin's work on fungi was confirmed beyond all doubt for manganese by the great physiologists Javillier and Bertrand between 1907 and 1912, working with *Rhizopus* and *Aspergillus niger*. The first experimental proof of the essential nature of manganese in higher plants was obtained by McHargue in 1922 for oat (*Avena sativa*), soybean (*Glycine max*), tomato (*Lycopersicon esculentum*) and other species. The importance of manganese was demonstrated beyond all doubt by Samuel and Piper (1928) using greatly improved techniques. In plants grown in culture they reproduced all the symptoms of grey speck disease of oats (Plate 42) known for many years in the field. Another field disorder long known as marsh spot of peas (Plate 43) was proved by Piper to be caused by manganese deficiency as recently as 1941, and analogous effects in certain species of beans (Plates 43 and 44) were found to be caused by the same deficiency.

Zinc

Following the work of Raulin (1869) and Javillier (1907) with *A. niger* the importance of zinc for a higher plant, maize (*Zea mais*) was observed by Mazé (1914) and shown beyond all doubt for several other plant species by Sommer and Lipmna (1926) and Sommer (1928) (Plates 45 to 49).

Boron

Agulhon (1910) observed that boron stimulated the growth of radish (*Raphanus sativus*), oat (*Avena sativa*) and wheat (*Triticum aestivum*) in water culture, and Mazé (1915) observed similar effects for maize. The essential nature of boron was proved convincingly by Warington in 1923 for broad bean (*Vicia faba*) (Plate 60) and this work was extended by Sommer and Lipman (1926) to include several other species (Plates 57 to 62). By contrast with the clear-cut results obtained with higher plants to show the importance of boron, experiments with fungi reported by Winfield (1945) have indicated that boron requirements, if any, are very small and may well not exist. On the other hand, blue-green algae studied by Eyster (1952) need this element, and *Azotobacter chroococcum* needs boron for nitrogen fixation in pure culture media. These contrasting results bring up for the first time the suggestion that different plant groups may have qualitatively differing needs and this viewpoint will be discussed later (page 28).

Copper

The demonstration of the importance and essentiality of copper for plants was less readily achieved. The first evidence was reported for fungi and other micro-organisms by Bortels (1927), Roberg (1928), Steinberg (1935) and Mulder (1939), and for plants including tomato (*Lycopersicon esculentum*), sunflower (*Helianthus annuus*), barley (*Hordeum vulgare*) and flax (*Linum usitatissimum*) by Sommer (1931) and Lipman and MacKinney (1931). Stout and Arnon (1939) and Piper (1942) introduced more specific methods of nutrient purification for the removal of copper and zinc and placed the evidence on a sound basis for several species (Plates 34 to 41, 45).

Molybdenum

Indications that molybdenum is essential were obtained first by Bortels (1930, 1936) in free-living nitrogen-fixing bacteria (*Azotobacter*), and quite clearly so for the root nodule bacterium *Rhizobium* by Anderson (1942) and Jensen and Betty (1943). Other micro-organisms for which requirements were shown by Bortels (1940) included *Nostoc*, *Anabaena* and *Clostridium butyricum* especially when dependent on nitrogen fixation. By analogy with the legumes, a molybdenum requirement was shown for nitrogen fixation by root nodule organisms (probably Actinomycetes) of the non-leguminous species *Casuarina cunninghamiana*, *Myrica gale* and *Alnus glutinosa* in the work of Bond and Hewitt (1961, 1962). Steinberg (1937) was among the first to show that molybdenum was required by a micro-organism when grown with nitrate as a source of fixed nitrogen.

The discovery that higher plants need molybdenum when grown with nitrate as the source of fixed nitrogen from the soil or culture medium is of interest in a number of respects. This was first observed accidentally by Arnon and Stout in 1939 because of the use of chemicals exceptionally free from molybdenum.

An unknown and hitherto unrecorded physiological disorder occurred in tomato plants growing in water culture when special precautions had been taken to eliminate copper and zinc (Plate 52). The condition was rapidly cured by giving a mixture containing thirteen elements, including molybdenum, which was shown specifically to restore normal growth when given at 0·01 p.p.m. The purification method used to treat the nutrient reagents was nevertheless most unlikely to have removed molybdenum and unusually pure salts were probably responsible for the initial observation.

Long before the importance of molybdenum was known, two important field disorders were clearly described, namely yellow spotting of citrus leaves in Florida recorded by Floyd (1908) (Plate 51) and whiptail of broccoli (*Brassica oleracea* v. *Italica*) (Plate 54) and cauliflower (*B. oleracea* v. *botrytis*) (Plates 55 and 56) recorded in Long Island, New York by Clayton (1924) and well known in many other parts of the world, particularly when the plants are growing in somewhat acid soils (pH 5–6). The former was identified by Stewart and Leonard (1952) as molybdenum deficiency by response to foliage sprays, and the latter was found to respond to molybdenum at rates as low as 1 kg/hectare (about 1 lb/acre) of molybdate in tests made by Davis (1945) and Mitchell (1945) in New Zealand. The condition was first reproduced experimentally by omission of molybdenum in sand culture by Hewitt and Jones (1947) and Hewitt and Agarwala (1951) using techniques newly developed for this purpose.

Chlorine

Although it was not until 1954 that chlorine was established as an essential element, prior to this several workers including Nobbe and Siegert in 1862, Mazé in 1919 and Lipman in 1938 had claimed to have found beneficial effects on adding chlorine. The final proof was provided during the course of very careful attempts to investigate the status of cobalt as a nutrient for tomato plants by Broyer, Carlton, Johnson and Stout. Significant growth responses were observed which were eventually traced to the addition of the element chlorine. The chlorine content of the deficient leaves was found to be 250 p.p.m. and the requirement was therefore not small. For example, by comparison molybdenum is needed at only 0·1 p.p.m. for the complete alleviation of deficiency symptoms. Later work by Ulrich and Ohki (1956), Johnson, Stout, Broyer and Carlton (1957) and Ozanne, Woolley and Broyer (1957) quite clearly showed that chlorine is essential for several species of plants and that bromine can partially substitute for chlorine. This second point regarding substitution is important in a general sense and will be discussed again later (page 29). The effect of chlorine deficiency in cabbage can be seen in Plate 63.

Iodine

There is at present no evidence to indicate that iodine is essential for higher plants when growing as entire organisms, although stimulation has been reported by Borst Pauwels (1961) in a variety of crop plants, and more recently this has been confirmed by Umaly and Poel (1970) for barley and tomato plants. Moreover, it has been shown by White (1938, 1943), Heller (1953) and by Hannay (1956) working in Professor Street's laboratory and confirmed by Dr A. J. Abbott at Long Ashton, that iodine is necessary for maximal growth rates of excised pea and tomato roots in sterile culture. The significance of these observations is not yet understood.

Cobalt

The status of cobalt as an essential micronutrient for plants is uncertain, but indirectly it has been shown to be of great importance. Cobalt is an inseparable part of vitamin B_{12} and its analogues (Fig. 7·3), and of all cobamide coenzymes. It therefore follows that any organism which depends on B_{12} or any cobamide derivative requires cobalt. It is immaterial here whether the organism (bacterium, plant or animal) is able to synthesise such compounds with a supply of inorganic cobalt or whether it is heterotrophic in this respect and depends on other organisms which produce B_{12} cofactors or precursors. Inorganic cobalt has been shown to be an essential component of the mineral nutrient solution used to grow both legumes and the root nodulated non-legumes when any of these is dependent on symbiotic nitrogen fixation (Plates 27 to 29). This fact was first most effectively shown by Ahmed and Evans (1959–61) for soybean and by Delwiche, Johnson and Reisenauer (1961) for lucerne (*Medicago sativa*) and by Bond and Hewitt (1963) for *Alnus, Casuarina* and *Myrica*. Although the importance of cobalt for ruminant animals was recognised from the classical work of Marston (1935) the significance of the element for plant life was not proved until the chemical composition of B_{12} derivatives was first shown independently by Smith (1948) in England, and Rickes and his co-workers (1948) in the USA, and the importance of compounds having B_{12} activity was reported for *Lactobacillus lactis* by Schorb (1948).

The earliest experimental reports concerning plant life indicating a requirement for cobalt in inorganic form appear to be those by Hutner and his associates (1950) for *Euglena gracilis* and for some blue-green algae including *Nostoc muscorum* and *Calothrix parietina* studied by Holm-Hansen, Gerloff and Skoog (1954). Reports that cobalt is required by other plant species or by those already mentioned when given fixed nitrogen, e.g. nitrate or ammonia in solution, are unsubstantiated and not convincing. The recent observations that there are two major routes of methionine synthesis in *Escherichia coli* of which one only is dependent on the presence of B_{12} is relevant to this point, since the B_{12}-independent mechanism is that now shown to operate in plants. Further studies by Evans and his associates on the biochemical aspects of cobalt metabolism would seem to substantiate the negative view and suggest that only cobalt-independent systems operate in higher plants. There is, therefore, at present no special reason for postulating a cobalt requirement when fixed nitrogen is given to plants and moreover, according to Darken (1952), there is no satisfactory evidence for the presence of appreciable amounts of B_{12} in plant tissues other than in root nodules. Reports by Maskell, Evans and Murray (1953) that omission of cobalt induced a leaf symptom in cacao, and by Bolle-Jones and Mallikarjuneswara (1957) of stimulated growth in *Hevea brasiliensis* in the presence of cobalt and by Wilson and Nicholas (1967) for wheat and non-nodulated clover, though valid, do not indicate conclusively at present that cobalt is required by higher plants, particularly as cobalt markedly antagonises incipient manganese toxicity at quite low concentrations. In root nodules of soybean and other legumes, and in those of *Alnus* and *Casuarina*, the amounts of B_{12} found by Ahmed and Evans, and Bond and Hewitt range from 519 ng/g to 0·13 ng/g in soybean given 0·05 p.p.m. or no cobalt respectively, and from 320 to 12 ng/g in *Alnus*, and 145 to 4 ng/g in *Casuarina*. The amount found by Fries (1962) in excised roots of pea (*Pisum sativum*) grown in sterile culture in the absence of *Rhizobium* but with a supposedly complete mineral nutrient was 0·1 ng/g and therefore very small by comparison. Her contention that this amount shows an essential role for cobalt in plants does not seem valid.

Vanadium

A curious discovery was made by Arnon and Wessel (1953) concerning the effect of vanadium on the growth of the green alga *Scenedesmus obliquus* in the presence of an otherwise complete nutrient medium which contained an adequate amount of molybdenum. They were concerned with the amount of iron needed for optimal growth of the alga and unexpectedly observed a great stimulation of growth by increasing the iron supply beyond limits regarded as likely to be necessary. This led them to believe that another element was being introduced in the iron compound, and the effect of higher concentrations of iron was entirely reproduced by giving vanadium at 10 μg/litre. When ferric chloride was extracted with ether in 6N HCl the purified compound was no longer stimulatory and vanadium had to be added for maximal growth rates. Vanadium does not replace molybdenum and is not itself replaced by molybdenum. This report is at present unique and has not been confirmed independently. The only other report of a separate requirement for vanadium was by D. Bertrand (1941) for *A. niger* but this too remains unconfirmed. The view of Arnon and Wessel that it is likely that vanadium is required by other green plants does not seem to be warranted at present, though it does occur at high levels in the blood of tunicates and it is essential for these organisms. The interchangeability of molybdenum and vanadium will be discussed later.

Sodium

There is now evidence for regarding sodium as an essential nutrient in certain species in addition to the need of potassium. Sodium is required by the blue-green algae, *Anabaena cylindrica, A. variabilis, Anacystis nidulens* and *Nostoc muscorum* studied by Allen and Arnon (1955) and Kratz and Myers (1955), and in some blue-green algae the sodium requirement may even exceed that for potassium. Among the higher plants Brownell and Wood (1957) have shown that sodium is required by the saltmarsh species *Atriplex vesicaria*, and Williams (1960) concluded that sodium is an essential element for *Halogeton glomeratus*, a toxic plant which accumulates large quantities of sodium in its leaves.

Aluminium

There are some other elements whose status as essential nutrients is still uncertain. In some cases the records are old and the methods used were inadequate at the time to prevent other interpretations being placed on the results in the light of more recent and complete knowledge. Thus in much of the early work by Mazé, Stoklasa, Sommer, Lipman, Raleigh and Wagner on aluminium, one or more of the micronutrients now known to be required were sometimes omitted. It is possible that these were introduced as impurities by the larger amounts of aluminium being tested. Some reports of the stimulation of growth by aluminium are quite impressive, notably that of Chenery (1955) who observed that aluminium was accumulated by the tea plant (*Camellia sinensis*). However, although this element appeared to be beneficial to the growth of several other species it could not be shown to be essential. The 'beneficial' effects of aluminium salts may find explanations in antagonism of excess copper, co-precipitation at higher pH values by aluminium hydroxide of excesses of other elements (e.g. phosphate) in an impure or unbalanced medium, and in acidification of somewhat alkaline media by hydrolysis of aluminium salts, thus improving availability of iron and manganese. A more interesting and plausible effect reported by Randall and Vose (1963) may be the stimulation of phosphate uptake by low aluminium concentrations (5 p.p.m.). At concentrations between 10 and 50 p.p.m. aluminium is usually severely toxic (see Chapter 5).

Silicon

Silicon is present in most plant ash and X-ray studies by Lanning, Ponnaiya and Crumpton (1958) have indicated the presence of structurally organised forms of silica in the cells of many plants (Plates 7 and 8). Jorgensen (1952) and Lewin (1955) have obtained good evidence that silicon is essential for the formation of the cell wall and growth of the diatom *Navicula pelliculosa* and *Nitschia palea*. More recently Chen and Lewin (1969) concluded that silicon is an essential element for the highly silicified Pteridophyte *Equisetum arvense* in which the ash has up to 16% of silica. Silicon may have some structural importance in cereal stems. Grasses, and in particular the rice plant, incorporate large amounts of silica and it seems that in higher plants the main function of silica is in providing rigidity to otherwise flexible cell walls. However, as with aluminium, silicon shows other relationships of an indirect nature. According to Vlamis and Williams (1967) soluble silicate in the nutrient medium antagonises manganese toxicity in barley and prevents the localisation of manganese in small areas of high concentrations which occurs in these circumstances. The addition of high levels of copper (0·5 p.p.m.) in the experiment of Wagner (1940) might similarly account for the markedly beneficial effects of silicate.

Selenium

Although it has been established for many years that selenium is an essential element for certain domestic animals, notably for poultry, sheep and cows, a similar requirement has not been demonstrated for any plant species. However, the leguminous indicator species for seleniferous soils *Astragalus bisulcatus* (Plate 10), *A. pattersonii* and *A. racemosus*, were shown by Levine (1925) and Trelease and Trelease (1938) to be benefited by selenium. In the bacterium, *Escherichia coli*, both selenium and molybdenum were required for the formation of the enzyme formic dehydrogenase. The metabolic aspects of selenium and growth of selenium-tolerant plants is considered further in Chapters 6 and 8. So much selenium may be accumulated by *Astragalus* plants that cattle eating them suffer from selenium poisoning, called 'alkali disease'.

Absolute requirements and quantitative effects

The examples of boron, vanadium, cobalt and sodium suggest an important feature or principle of nutrient requirements, namely that qualitative or absolute requirements for a certain element may be limited to certain species or groups. On the other hand, certain elements such as copper and zinc appear to be universally required where tests have been made by critical means.

It is convenient at this stage to consider by what criteria absolute or qualitative requirements for mineral elements can be determined. The most important contribution to our thought in this field has been made by Arnon and Stout (1939) and Arnon (1948, 1950). They suggested three criteria of essentiality by which the status of an element should be judged, as follows:

(i) Omission of the element must directly cause abnormal growth or failure to complete the life-cycle, or premature senescence and death.
(ii) The effect must be specific and not fulfilled completely by any other element.
(iii) The effect must be direct on some aspect of growth or metabolism and not indirect, as for example by antagonism of the effect of another element present in relative excess.

It is relevant to add that if the omission or inclusion of an element results in a significant change in metabolic activity or morphology without decrease in yield, interference in reproduction or longevity or the appearance of deformity, these metabolic or morphological effects do not provide valid reasons for regarding that element as essential.

Arnon and Stout pointed out that it is theoretically probably impossible to prove that a particular element is not essential merely because no response can be obtained when it is omitted from the growth medium. It is possible only to say that if negative results are obtained the requirements may either be nil, or if positive, the requirements are below those demonstrable by the limits of the methods used. When it is understood that only 10 000 molybdenum atoms per cell of *Scenedesmus obliquus* or perhaps 1000 cobalt atoms per cell of *Rhizobium meliloti* are *adequate* for growth and that 1 μmol contains 6×10^{17} atoms it is readily appreciated that the difficulties in attaining nil levels which alone can prove negative requirements are almost insuperable. It is however important to accept the probability, which equally cannot be disproved at present, that certain elements may not be essential for any species, that some may be required quite specifically by some species and not by others, and that some may be required only under certain conditions imposed by the nutrient environment.

This last concept leads to consideration of the status of essential elements under certain conditions. One may readily imagine that if an element is required in a single and specific metabolic reaction, its importance may be decreased or even wholly eliminated if that particular reaction is rendered superfluous or is by-passed by a change in metabolism. It has already been suggested that such a relationship may apply to cobalt in respect of differences between different organisms. The known role of molybdenum provides an interesting example of another aspect where changes in the metabolism in a particular individual organism may influence requirements. This is now considered in more detail.

When Steinberg (1937) investigated the molybdenum requirement for *Aspergillus niger* he also observed that this requirement was greatly decreased or possibly abolished if nitrate were replaced by urea or ammonium compounds. He also predicted that molybdenum might serve to activate the enzyme system now known as nitrate reductase because it could perhaps form an integral part of the reductase molecule. This suggestion was remarkable in foresight, since the enzyme was still unknown at that time. A similar function in plants was considered likely by Hewitt and Jones (1947). Mulder concluded in 1948 that when nitrogen was given to molybdenum-deficient pea plants as ammonium compounds in place of nitrate, there was no longer any restriction on the production of free amino acids in the tissues. There was therefore evidence even before the precise role of the element had been elucidated, which suggested that by circumventing the nitrate reduction step, the need for molybdenum was decreased or even abolished.

The reduction of nitrate to ammonia and the enzymes involved are described in Chapter 7. Brief mention is necessary here of the role of molybdenum. The investigations of Nicholas and Nason (1954–5), Nicholas and Stevens (1956), Evans (1956) and Taniguchi and Itagaki (1960) showed that molybdenum is a constituent of the enzymic protein, nitrate reductase. The metal atom is closely combined to the enzyme protein in higher plants, fungi and bacteria, and mediates the final electron transfer to nitrate. This is the only role so far identified in these species; the function in nitrogen fixation where activation of gaseous nitrogen occurs is still unknown and for the purposes of this discussion it need not concern us here. The reduction of nitrate is the first step in nitrate assimilation to ammonia and protein, but if nitrate is replaced by other nitrogen compounds, e.g. ammonia or glutamic acid in the nutrient medium, it might be expected that molybdenum would no longer be required under these new circumstances and that the 'Criteria of Essentiality' would not be applicable. What is the further evidence on this point?

The unusual but very characteristic symptoms known as whiptail in cauliflower (Plates 55 and 56) which could now be reproduced at will by careful control of the molybdenum supply, presented a useful opportunity to study the requirements for molybdenum when plants were grown with nitrogen given in forms other than as nitrate. Extensive investigations at Long Ashton by Hewitt and Agarwala (1951–6) showed beyond any doubt that molybdenum was required by cauliflower grown in non-sterile culture regardless of the compounds used to supply nitrogen to plants grown in sand cultures. Similar experiments by Hewitt and McCready (1954–6) indicated that tomato plants also required molybdenum when grown with urea, glutamate or ammonium compounds including ammonium nitrate or nitrite as nitrogen sources. Nicholas and Nason (1955) concluded similarly, contrary to the earlier deductions of Steinberg, that fungi still required molybdenum when nitrate was supplemented with or was wholly replaced by ammonium compounds. Following these results the view was generally accepted that molybdenum has either a multiple role in plants or that it is still essential in some manner for normal growth even when this process is not dependent on nitrate reduction. Two important observations have since cast doubt on the first of these simple interpretations for reasons summarised below.

Ichioka and Arnon (1955) decided, as the result of very careful experiments, that *Scenedesmus obliquus* did not require molybdenum at all when grown in

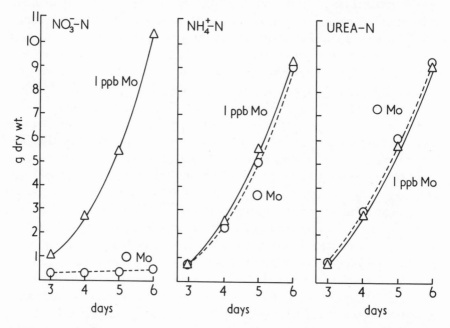

Figure 2.1 Effect of molybdate on growth of the alga *Scenedesmus* supplied with nitrate, ammonia or urea nitrogen (ordinate represents g dry weight per litre of nutrient solution). From Ichioka and Arnon (1955) *Physiologia Pl.* **8**, 552–60.

sterilised media containing pure recrystallised urea or ammonium carbonate prepared from ammonia gas and carbon dioxide (Fig. 2.1). This conclusion was reached without hesitation in spite of the philosophical limitations already discussed which Arnon had earlier pointed out are attached to such negative results. Nevertheless, both the critical examination of their results and the general background of experience gained at Long Ashton support this view and there is at present no evidence whatsoever to suggest that molybdenum is required by this alga under these special circumstances. In the presence of nitrate, molybdenum-deficiency effects are severe when the molybdenum concentration falls to a calculated value of $1 \cdot 5 \times 10^3$ atoms/cell. Experience with purified media in relation to growth stimulation obtained by progressive increments of molybdenum indicates with some confidence that the maximum concentration required would be as low as 100 or perhaps 25 atoms per cell, namely less than 0·000 000 1 p.p.m. in the medium when ammonia or urea are given as nitrogen sources.

The second point is that the enzyme nitrate reductase is inducible not only in fungi, as shown by Evans and Nason (1952) and in bacteria, but also in higher plants especially cauliflower, which has been studied by Hewitt and Afridi (1959–65) (see Chapter 7). It is also clear from this work, and that of Nicholas and Nason with fungi, that the enzyme is not detected in the absence of the prosthetic metal. Adding the metal to cell-free extracts cannot restore activity after cell rupture. When the metal is added to living cells nitrate reductase activity reappears over a period of several hours. There are thus two independent factors, the substrate and the prosthetic metal, which must be present during the life of the organism for the enzyme to be produced (see Chapter 7).

The results obtained at Long Ashton show that when cauliflower plants are grown in sand or water culture in the usual way in the presence of molybdenum but without precautions to maintain sterile conditions even though highly-purified media as described in Chapter 3 are used, some of the ammonia, urea, glutamic acid or other similar nitrogen sources is quite rapidly oxidised by micro-organisms (nitrified) to nitrite and to nitrate. Such plants normally contain nitrate reductase and the concentrations of nitrate in the culture media produced by nitrification have been shown to be sufficient to account for enzyme induction when absorbed by the roots during the growth of the plants. When glutamate or urea are used as sources of nitrogen for cauliflower in *sterile* culture no nitrate reductase is induced. Ichioka and Arnon obtained sterilised ammonium carbonate by preparation from ammonia and carbon dioxide gases while recrystallised urea was introduced through a bacterial filter. It is possible that in those instances where molybdenum requirements have been reported under the conditions of nutrition outlined above, there was still some inducer present during growth, and that only in complete absence of nitrate (and probably also nitrite) can the molybdenum requirement be dispensed with altogether.

It is not possible at present to say with certainty how nitrate induces whiptail in molybdenum-deficient cauliflower, but the relationships between enzyme formation, the inducer and prosthetic metal provide a possible clue. Adding molybdate ions to an extract of cauliflower leaves with whiptail symptoms does not regenerate the nitrate reductase, and apoprotein is either absent or is not reconstituted. It is possible that in the presence of nitrate, but in the absence of the metal, the inducing system causes the formation of an abnormal nitrate reductase apo-enzyme and this protein may have unfavourable effects on metabolism or cell growth; such abnormal protein formation is not without precedent.

In experiments by Hewitt and Gundry (1970) molybdenum-deficient cauliflower plants have been grown under sterile conditions. With nitrate as sole nitrogen source, whiptail symptoms were induced, while with the ammonium ion as nitrogen source no such abnormality was found. It seems likely therefore that when nitrate is completely absent there is no requirement for molybdenum and that the original observation of a molybdenum requirement when nitrogen was given in the reduced form was due to bacterial nitrification giving rise to nitrate. The reason why whiptail is uniquely associated with *Brassica* species is still unknown. The effects of molybdenum deficiency on other plants is illustrated in Plates 50 to 53 (see also pp. 166 and 204).

Alternative and beneficial elements

The criteria of essentiality outlined earlier have been considered in relation to circumstances where a change in metabolic needs may produce an absolute or qualitative difference in mineral nutrient requirements in the same individual. One element may replace another or an element may appear to be clearly beneficial when given at readily measurable concentrations. This may occur even though no evidence of essential properties can be obtained when attempts are made to decrease its concentration to a much lower value or to eliminate it. These possibilities raise interesting problems.

The relationships between elements that can replace one another in certain circumstances show series that range from quantitative to absolutely qualitative effects and support the suggestion above that requirements for a particular element may be positive or non-existent according to species. Thus in the nitrogen-fixing species *Clostridium butyricum* it has been shown by Jensen and Spencer (1947) that vanadium can substitute for molybdenum with equal effectiveness in certain strains while in other strains, partial replacement is possible and in yet others, vanadium cannot replace molybdenum at all. The replacement of molybdenum by vanadium for nitrogen fixation by *Azotobacter vinelandii* and *A. chroococcum* was originally demonstrated by Bortels. Vanadium being much less efficient was required at higher concentrations than molybdenum. A survey by Becking (1962) of the genera *Azotobacter* and *Beijerinckia* which now embraces *A. indicum* has revealed a similar range of interchangeability from a maximum of 84% to less than 1% replacement in *B. indicum* of the function of molybdenum by vanadium. Vanadium cannot replace molybdenum for nitrogen fixation by symbiotic rhizobia or in nodulated non-legumes, or for nitrate reduction in fungi or plants. The additional requirement for vanadium by *Scenedesmus* is therefore all the more remarkable and in urgent need of independent and unequivocal verification.

The relationships between calcium and strontium are comparable. These elements appear to be entirely interchangeable in species of *Azotobacter* studied by Burk and Lineweaver (1931) and Norris and Jensen (1957) and in *Chlorella pyrenoidosa* when grown with urea but not with nitrate according to Walker (1953). By contrast with this situation Becking (1962) and Norris (1957, 1959) have concluded that *Azotobacter agile*, rhizobia and species of *Beijerinckia* do not require calcium at all. In wheat, barley and oats, Walsh (1945) showed that only a very limited replacement of calcium by strontium was possible, but a substantial effect of strontium as a partial but not complete substitute for calcium has been shown to occur in maize by Da Silva (1964) (Plate 17). Similar differences in the degree of partial or total interchangeability between potassium and rubidium or sodium also occur for bacteria, algae and plants. An interesting effect of calcium is shown by its specificity for zoospore formation by *Protosiphon* while strontium can replace calcium for vegetative growth according to O'Kelley and Hearndon (1959).

In the presence of an adequate concentration of one of a pair of interchangeable elements, the other member of the pair will not usually appear to be required. In the presence of sub-optimal amounts of both of them, the addition of either will appear to be beneficial. However, if either is decreased in amount or even eliminated, it will not be found to behave as an essential element since growth will continue at a rate which is determined by the level of the other element. If both elements are severely deficient, each when tested alone in the absence of the other will appear to behave as an essential element. There is thus the possibility of a particular element (A) appearing to behave as a non-essential, beneficial or essential element, depending on the amounts present of an alternative element (B). If such an alternative element (B) has not been recognised in this context, let alone estimated in the experimental media, great confusion may arise regarding the status of the element (A), whose importance is under investigation.

Beneficial effects may be observed from the inclusion of an element that can only incompletely replace at decreased efficiency the physiologically essential element, when the physiologically essential element is present at sub-optimal concentrations. Such a response is frequently observed with sodium or rubidium when potassium supplies are inadequate. Here it may be assumed that either potassium is redistributed more economically between competing sites as a result of introducing sodium, or that potassium has multiple functions (see Chapter 8) one or more of which can be replaced by sodium or rubidium while yet others are specifically dependent on potassium. The absolute requirement for sodium by *Atriplex vesicaria* suggests that one or more of such functions here has come to depend specifically on sodium. The apparent vanadium requirement of *Scenedesmus* may be a parallel example.

Further Reading

Epstein, E. (1965) Mineral metabolism. Chap. 18, pp. 438–66 in *Plant Biochemistry* (Ed. J. Bonner and J. E. Varner). Academic Press: New York and London.

Frieden, E. (1972) The chemical elements of life. *Scientific American* **227** (1), 52–60.

Gilbert, F. A. (1957) *Mineral Nutrition and the Balance of Life*. University of Oklahoma Press. 350 pp.

Hewitt, E. J. (1966) *Sand and Water Culture Methods used in the Study of Plant Nutrition*. 2nd edn. Commonwealth Agricultural Bureaux; Farnham Royal, England. 547 pp.

Russell, E. J. Revised by Russell, E. W. (1961) *Soil Conditions and Plant Growth*. 9th edn. Longmans Green: London. 688 pp.

Russell, E. J. (1966) *A History of Agricultural Science in Great Britain*. George Allen and Unwin Ltd.: London. 493 pp.

Sauchelli, V. (1969) *Trace Elements in Agriculture*. Van Nostrand Reinhold: New York. 300 pp.

Stiles, W. (1961) *Trace Elements in Plants*. 3rd edn. Cambridge University Press. 189 pp.

3
Experimental Methods for the Investigation of Plant Nutrient Requirements

'Nevertheless, the results of our water-culture are scientifically of value; since they show that although the roots are compelled to take up the food materials under abnormal conditions, nevertheless with their help much vegetable substance is formed, which behaves normally so far that with its aid the whole process of development of a plant may be completed, including the formation of seeds capable of germination.'

Julius von Sachs, *translated by H. Marshall Ward*
Lectures on the Physiology of Plants, 1887

Some early developments in the experimental approach to plant-nutrient investigations have already been noted. The methods used by different laboratories for such studies are based on a few well-established principles but show an apparently wide range of modifications and innovations which may be confusing. Considerable effort has been devoted at Long Ashton to designing, testing and modifying techniques for growing plants in soil-less culture media, either in sand or in water. This work and that of many others is described in a more extensive monograph by Hewitt (1966). Some of the more important details requiring attention when plants are grown in culture media and the simplest methods for studying nutrient requirements are outlined here. A general view of a greenhouse used for nutrient investigations is shown in Plate 1.

General plant–culture technique

All plants should be grown with a balanced nutrient solution providing specified concentrations of all the elements known at present to be essential. Certain micronutrients should not therefore be omitted just because impurities in other salts or materials may provide sufficient. There are enough examples in the literature noted in the preceding chapter to show that sooner or later this approach will quite likely result in an accidental and unexpected deficiency condition. In any case, it is best to give what is known to be required in

Table 3.1 Complete nutrient solutions based on nitrate or ammonium nitrogen as used at Long Ashton

Solution type	Compound	g/l	mM	mEq/l				p.p.m.				Stock solution requirement g/l	Stock solution requirement ml/l
Macronutrients Nitrate-type solution	KNO$_3$	0·404	4	K$^+$	4	NO$_3^-$	4	K	156	N	57	50·6	8
	Ca(NO$_3$)$_2$ anhyd.	0·656	4	Ca^{2+}	8	NO$_3^-$	8	Ca	160	N	113	80·25	8
	MgSO$_4$·7H$_2$O	0·368	1·5	Mg^{2+}	3	SO$_4^{2-}$	3	Mg	36	S	48	46·0	8
	NaH$_2$PO$_4$·2H$_2$O	0·208	1·33	Na$^+$	1·33	PO$_4^{3-}$	4	Na	31	P	41	52·0	4
Macronutrients Ammonium-type or Ammonium nitrate-type solution (These compounds are used as alternatives)	K$_2$SO$_4$	0·348	2	K$^+$	4	SO$_4^{2-}$	4	K	156	S	64	21·75	16
	CaCl$_2$ anhyd.	0·444	4	Ca^{2+}	8	Cl$^-$	8	Ca	160	Cl	284	55·5	8
	MgSO$_4$·7H$_2$O	0·368	1·5	Mg^{2+}	3	SO$_4^{2-}$	3	Mg	36	S	48	46·0	8
	Na$_2$HPO$_4$·12H$_2$O	0·478	1·33	Na$^+$	2·67	PO$_4^{3-}$	4	Na	62	P	41	29·75	16
	(NH$_4$)$_2$SO$_4$*	0·528	4	NH$_4^+$	8	SO$_4^{2-}$	8	N	113	S	128	66·25	8
	NH$_4$NO$_3$*	0·402	5	NH$_4^+$	5	NO$_3^-$	5	N	141			50·25	8
Micronutrients common to both types	Fe citrate 5H$_2$O**	0·033 5	0·1	Fe^{3+}	0·3			Fe	5·6			6·70	5
	MnSO$_4$·4H$_2$O	0·002 23	0·01	Mn^{2+}	0·02			Mn	0·55			2·23	1
	ZnSO$_4$·7H$_2$O	0·000 29	0·001	Zn^{2+}	0·002			Zn	0·065			0·29	1
	CuSO$_4$·5H$_2$O	0·000 25	0·001	Cu^{2+}	0·002			Cu	0·064			0·25	1
	H$_3$BO$_3$	0·003 1	0·05	B as B III	0·15			B	0·54			3·10	1
	Na$_2$MoO$_4$·2H$_2$O	0·000 12	0·0005	Mo as Mo VI	0·003			Mo	0·048			0·12	1
	NaCl	0·005 8	0·1	Cl$^-$	0·1			Cl	3·5			5·85	1
	CoSO$_4$·7H$_2$O	0·000 056	0·0002	Co^{2+}	0·000 4			Co	0·012			0·053	1

* Smaller quantities may be preferable for young plants and certain species.

** Fe citrate can be replaced by Fe K EDTA (iron potassium sequestrene or versenate) at half the amount of iron.

Table 3.2 Macronutrient composition of some well known or useful nutrient solutions; nutrient concentration as g/l and molarity (slightly approximated)*

Compound	Knop (1865) g/l	mM	van der Crone (1902) g/l	mM	Hoagland and Snyder (1933) g/l	mM	Hoagland and Arnon (1938) g/l	mM	(Bond) g/l	mM	Nitrogen deficient (Long Ashton) g/l	mM
KNO_3	0·2	2	0·75	7·5	0·51	5	0·66	6	—	—	—	—
$Ca(NO_3)_2$	0·8	5	—	—	0·82	5	0·66	4	—	—	—	—
K_2SO_4	—	—	—	—	—	—	—	—	0·87	5	0·35	2
$NH_4H_2PO_4$	—	—	—	—	—	—	0·115	1	—	—	—	—
$NaH_2PO_4 \cdot 2H_2O$	—	—	—	—	—	—	—	—	—	—	0·21	1·33
$MgSO_4 \cdot 7H_2O$	0·2	0·8	0·5	2	0·49	2	0·49	2	0·5	2	0·37	1·5
KH_2PO_4	0·2	1·5	—	—	0·136	1	—	—	—	—	—	—
$Ca_3(PO_4)_2$*	—	—	0·25	0·8	—	—	—	—	0·25	0·8	—	—
$CaSO_4 \cdot 2H_2O$*	—	—	0·5	3	—	—	—	—	0·5	3	0·69	4
$Fe_3(PO_4)_2 \cdot 8H_2O$	—	—	0·25	0·5	—	—	—	—	0·25	0·5	—	—
$FePO_4$*	0·1	0·67	—	—	—	—	—	—	—	—	—	—

* Compounds marked thus are sparingly soluble and remain partly undissolved. The micronutrient supplement where given is not reproduced here, but the proportions shown in Table 3.1 are suitable.

optimal concentrations. A satisfactory general-purpose nutrient based on nitrate which will sustain healthy growth of a wide range of plant species is given in Table 3.1. Other equally good formulae used in a number of laboratories are shown in Table 3.2.

Nearly all plants grow well in these nutrient solutions: the best growth is usually obtained with nitrate as a nitrogen source. A few tolerate solutions containing only or a large proportion of ammonium nitrogen. An alternative solution based on ammonium nitrogen is therefore given in Table 3.1. This can be used in sand culture if between 0·1% and 0·5% by weight of calcium carbonate is intimately mixed into the top half of the sand in a pot. This helps to counteract the sharp fall in pH which occurs when ammonia-based nutrients are used, and may be additionally beneficial in countering the toxic effects of excess ammonia uptake. Because ammonia-based nutrients cause a drop in pH and nitrate-based ones the reverse effect, stability in pH values between 4·5 and 7·5 produced by suitable phosphate buffer mixtures can be largely maintained by certain ratios of nitrate to ammonia, e.g. 4 : 1, 5 : 1, 10 : 1, 20 : 1 though exact values will depend on species, age, season, etc. A second point regarding the use of ammonia-based nutrients is that substantial nitrification is likely to occur, especially when the experiments have been repeated once or twice and the environment has become enriched in nitrifying organisms.

When it is necessary to grow legumes or nodulated non-legumes without any fixed nitrogen, a nitrogen-free solution is used. Two are shown in Table 3.2; one found by Bond to be especially suited to water culture conditions and based on the original van der Crone solution, the other based on the Long Ashton formula which is ideal for sand cultures. In either medium inoculation by adding 1 ml/l of a suspension containing about 10^5 cells/ml of an appropriate strain of agar-culture or a ground nodule-bacterial suspension of *Rhizobium* is desirable, together with a starter treatment containing one-tenth the normal fixed nitrogen level for a week or until nodulation can be discerned, when the solution is changed to the minus nitrogen treatment. The cobalt supplement is normally only required and given when dependence on symbiotic nitrogen fixation is involved.

Where other macronutrient deficiencies are to be demonstrated the compounds providing them in the nitrate-type medium are substituted by others as follows. For phosphorus or magnesium deficiencies, sodium phosphate or magnesium sulphate are replaced by sodium sulphate at relevant concentrations. For potassium or calcium deficiencies, potassium or calcium nitrates are replaced by equivalent concentrations of sodium nitrate. For sulphur deficiency, magnesium sulphate is replaced by the chloride and the micronutrient sulphates are similarly replaced by the chlorides. Similar substitutions can be devised for the ammonium-type nutrient medium. Varying degrees of severity of a deficiency are induced by partial substitution or by transferring plants from complete nutrient to deficient nutrient after a few days or weeks growth.

The micronutrient supplement shown in Table 3.1 covers all known essential elements for higher plants. When used for water cultures iron deficiency may sometimes appear, especially if light enters the solution, because ferric citrate is photolabile and ferric phosphate is then precipitated. The ethylene-diaminetetra-acetic acid (EDTA) iron complex (Fig. 3.1) is preferable for water cultures unless extra iron is given frequently (often thrice weekly) although changing the remainder of the solution weekly is quite satisfactory. In the Crone's solution the ferrous phosphate supplies a constant but adequate level of iron by dissolving slowly and there is no excess of soluble phosphate.

Adequate aeration of plant roots is essential. Failure to ensure this, either by providing forced aeration in water culture or by free drainage of adequately

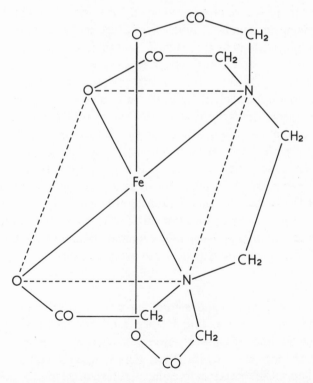

Figure 3.1 Coordinated complex of iron formed with the chelator ethylenediamine-tetra-acetic acid (EDTA). The iron complex shown is an anion, but it is normally used in nutrient solution as the monosodium salt. From Kroll (1956) in *Symposium on the Use of Metal Chelates in Plant Nutrition* (Ed. Wallace), p. 33.

deep sand cultures, causes failure to absorb nutrients, wilting because of impaired water uptake, death of the roots and even death of the plant in the most extreme situations. In sand cultures aeration by aspiration into the sand as the nutrient drains out is adequate. For water cultures a supply of filtered compressed air admitted through very thin orifices is usually necessary. Aeration need not be continuous, being provided for about one hour four times daily or perhaps for ten minutes in every hour. In warm weather, or if bacteria develop, or where root systems occupy a large proportion of the container volume, frequent aeration may be of utmost importance.

Different species vary in their requirements and some further points are discussed in the next chapter, and also below in relation to atmospheric contamination.

The remaining sections of this chapter are devoted chiefly to a more detailed consideration of the techniques employed in studying requirements for the micronutrients where special precautions against contamination are usually needed. A few other aspects of general technique are noted in passing.

Present techniques have progressed greatly in efficiency and in the exacting standards which are regularly achieved and are in fact required to obtain successful results with many elements. The problems of eliminating traces of mineral elements from a plant culture may be resolved into a number of components relating to the materials and environment, namely containers, water, solid rooting media (if present), nutrient reagents, seeds or other propagating organs, atmospheric contamination by dust or volatile substances of aerial parts, or of roots from aeration or simple exposure. Each of these may be a source of general or specific contamination and precautions can usually be taken to decrease their contribution. It may be pointed out here that for some elements, e.g. molybdenum or cobalt, extremely rigorous measures must be taken for the purpose of the investigation, whereas for some others, e.g. the macronutrients or manganese, iron and boron, there may be little point in taking extreme precautions to decrease contamination. The methods outlined below are based on those in regular use at Long Ashton.

Containers

Two materials, pyrex glass and natural *low-density* polythene, free from any pigments or fillers are outstanding for their value in micronutrient-deficiency investigations. For most purposes they may be regarded as equally satisfactory but some comments are offered. Pyrex glass is undoubtedly a potential or substantial source of boron in certain circumstances, more especially for water culture than for sand culture, and when pH values rise above neutrality as may result if rapid nitrate uptake occurs. Pyrex glass is said to be free from zinc but polythene may be appreciably superior in this respect. On the other hand, if the polythene vessel or materials have been extruded in manufacture, zinc stearate may be present and difficult to remove entirely. The use of sodium hydroxide during polymerisation of ethylene may introduce some sodium into the plastic and high-density (rigid) material should be avoided as cobalt and molybdenum compounds are used as catalysts in polymerisation.

Containers made of polystyrene, sold as food boxes with lids, and some types of small plastic flower-pots, e.g. black polythene or some PVC containers, are often suitable, cheap and easily modified for purposes of drainage, aeration and plant support. Covers for water cultures are easily made from black 3-mm thick polythene sheet, rigid PVC, or moulded from plaster of Paris with holes left for the plants. Split corks with a Terylene wool packing make good adjustable supports for the plants if these are first germinated and raised as seedlings in sand before transplanting suitable individuals. This can be done with care to avoid damage to the roots by lifting in a ball of sand and gently washing the surplus sand away by immersion in water.

Containers used for sand culture must be freely drained by a hole at the bottom. This is covered with glass wool and protected from the weight of the sand by a watch glass or strong plastic gauze. The depth of sand should not be less than 20 cm to prevent water-logging when a particle size of 0·2–1·0 mm is used. The finer the sand the deeper the pot should be.

Clay flower-pots painted with three coats of bitumen solution (Bituros paint) are quite satisfactory for holding sand cultures for study of macronutrients and for obtaining moderate deficiencies of iron and manganese, though if the paint film decays failure may occur in attempts to show severe calcium deficiency or boron deficiency.

Containers in plastic materials must be cleaned with abrasive detergents and hot 50% hydrochloric acid (below 80° for polythene) followed by washing in plenty of clean water when micronutrient deficiencies are to be studied.

Solid rooting media

If solid rooting media are used the choice is usually silica sand or pure crushed silica, but granulated polythene, polystyrene and crushed pyrex glass have also been used. The plastics tend to have low water retention capacities unless very small particle sizes (0·1–0·3 mm) are used and may tend to float when culture solution is added. Any solid medium could in theory, and probably also in practice, introduce an appreciable contamination. Some indication of the contamination in silica sand is provided in Table 3.3.

The extent to which these impurities are available to plants is not easily assessed. Different species differ in their ability to exploit sparingly soluble and adsorbed forms of the elements which are not readily dissolved by water alone. All plants seem to be able to absorb iron from the oxide and phosphate

Table 3.3   Contamination by nutrients and other elements in silica sands and water suppli
likely to be used for nutritional investigations. Figures in p.p.m.

Source of sand or water	N	P	S	Cl	Ca	Mg	K
Kuala Lumpur, Malaya, river sand acid-soluble		17			2·5	10	37
Leighton Buzzard, Bedfordshire, green sand inland deposits					40		
Rain water (various centres)	0·5 to 3·0		0·5 to 25	2·0 to 300	0·8 to 6·0	0·2 to 1·5	0·2 to 8·0
Rain water (Long Ashton):							
(a) from bitumen-painted tanks		0·01			2·7	0·6	3·0
(b) from greenhouse gutter		trace			0·07	0·05	0·5
Tap water (various centres)	0·1 to 2·0			2·0 to 20	8·0 to 21	1·0 to 110	0·2 to 14	0·4 to 3·0
Distilled water from metal stills					0·1 to 0·5		
Distilled water from pyrex glass or silica stills					0·01		
Ion-exchange resin-treated rain water							

forms and successful results for any micronutrient deficiency are rarely obtained when unpurified sand is used.

Sand can be purified efficiently in an apparatus of inert resin-bonded
asbestos called Keebush which uses steam to heat and circulate the sand
automatically. Between one and as many as eight day's treatment with 18%
hydrochloric acid containing 1% oxalic acid and also with sodium hydroxide
on other occasions are given at Long Ashton and such sand is practically
free from Fe, Mn, Cu, Zn, B and Mo. Deficiency of cobalt has also been
produced in this medium, but no results have been obtained for chlorine;
sulphuric acid might be used in preference for this purpose. When small-
scale experiments using purified sand are planned, the sand is heated in contact with 18% hydrochloric and 1% oxalic acids in large porcelain dishes in a
fume cupboard, or stirred in several changes of hot acid in large heavy pyrex
glass flasks or beakers. Considerable care is needed to avoid accidents in this
operation.

a	Fe	Mn	Cu	Zn	B	Mo	Co
	950	28	2·3	4·6			
	200	0·3	1·0	2·1	4·0	0·03	
5							
8							
3	0·4	0·025	0·06	2·9	0·04	0·001	
5	0·025	0·005	0·01	0·015	0·005	0·000 1	
6	0·01 to 0·6	0·001 to 0·02	0·007 to 0·04	<0·01 to 0·06	0·03 to 1·0	0·000 05 to 0·01	0·000 07
000 8	0·004 to 0·14	0·000 5 to 0·005	0·003 to 0·2	0·006 to 0·03	0·000 5 to 0·003	0·000 004 to 0·006	
000 2 / 006	0·000 02 to 0·004	0·000 08 to 0·001	0·001 to 0·004	0·000 04 to 0·006	0·01	0·000 001 to 0·000 01	0·000 002
	0·000 3 to 0·008	0·000 05 to 0·000 5	0·000 3 to 0·008	<0·000 1 to 0·005	0·002 to 0·006	0·000 001 to 0·000 07	0·000 005 to 0·000 015

When the acid digestion is complete the sand is leached with water several times to remove free acid, and then with a solution of calcium nitrate or di-sodium hydrogen phosphate of about 0·02 M concentration, suitably purified as described below where appropriate. Washing is continued until there is no further change in the pH of the solution after twenty-four hours in contact with the sand. This precaution is most important to ensure complete removal of adsorbed H^+ ions by a process of ion-exchange. Sand thus purified has been shown to contain less than 0·000 01 µg molybdenum per gram of sand, when tested with *Aspergillus niger* as described by Hewitt and Hallas (1951). For macronutrient-deficiency studies, sand may not need any treatment, but washing with cold 5% HCl for a few days followed by several volumes of water, leaching with a phosphate or nitrite solution as above, may also be advantageous if quantitative experiments are to be carried out. Seeds can be sown directly in the sand, about 5 mm deep for lettuce, tobacco and clover; 1 cm deep for tomato and *Brassica* species; 2 cm deep for cereals, and 5 cm deep for beans and peas. Seedlings are thinned out as required for uniformity and density shortly after maximum germination has occurred.

Water

Large volumes of water may be required over a period of several months and a pure supply is therefore important. Distillation from pyrex glass once or twice using a well-designed still may be expected to produce water of satisfactory quality. The use of a pyrex glass still and especially a pyrex condenser may however introduce more boron than was originally present and the distillate may contain sufficient boron to prevent the appearance of deficiency symptoms. A polythene condenser may however introduce sodium. The distillate from stills with tinned copper boiling pans is almost invariably heavily contaminated by copper and zinc, though iron and manganese levels may be relatively low and tolerable for deficiency experiments, and the chloride concentration may be quite satisfactory. Whatever materials are used in the construction of the still, it is desirable to include a spray-trap designed so that the steam is caused to pass through two sharp changes of angle of 180°, and to heat the surface of the still head with an electric heating tape to above 110°C so that creeping or continuity of a liquid film of water is prevented.

A simple and efficient alternative to the use of stills is provided by ion-exchange resins (Plate 1). At Long Ashton a series of eight large columns of resins is used to purify rain water and 50 000 litres are treated annually by this method. Single-stage resins removing either only cations or only anions are used first to remove most of the mineral impurities and three pairs of these resins are included. Final treatment is given by a mixed-bed resin Biodeminrolit F manufactured by the Permutit Company or a comparable mixture termed a mono-bed resin in the Amberlite group manufactured by the Resinour Products Corporation. These are highly efficient in removing the weakly dissociated salts by a salt splitting reaction. The effluent from the final mixed-bed resin has a specific conductance of 10^{-7} mhos or less. It is comparable with glass-distilled water and has been tested biologically for the production of deficiencies of Fe, Mn, Cu, Zn, Mo and B in several plants. Ion-exchange resin treatment of distilled water has been successfully used for experiments on cobalt deficiency in soybean by Evans and Ahmed and in the nodulate non-legume species of *Myrica*, *Casuarina* and *Alnus*. Water is conveniently stored in large acid-washed polythene bottles and can be delivered through polythene tubing to various points in the greenhouse. The general arrangements of the large-scale equipment at Long Ashton are shown in Plate 1. For small-scale investigations glass columns measuring 5 cm diameter by about 100 cm long are suitable. Two of these can be filled with Zeo-Karb 225 and De-Acidite FF respectively, and a third column is filled with an intimate mixture of these in the ratio of two parts De-Acidite FF to one part of Zeo-Karb 225. Operating and regenerating instructions are given in booklets published by the Permutit Co., Chiswick, London W.4.

The particular contamination present in water usually depends on the source, as already noted. Some examples are given in Table 3.3.

Nutrient reagents

The compounds used to supply the principal nutrient elements are often heavily contaminated with several trace elements including micronutrients. Analytical reagent grade salts may sometimes be less pure with respect to zinc or molybdenum or some other element than commercially less refined materials including fertiliser grades. It is sometimes difficult to detect chemically or spectrographically concentrations of such impurities which are nevertheless still sufficient to interfere with, or even altogether to prevent the production of nutrient-deficiency conditions. It is necessary therefore to assume the presence of impurities and to apply specific and efficient methods for their removal. Such methods must be reproducible, effective to the extent of removing 99·6 to 99·95% of the amount of the impurity even when this is equivalent to only a few micrograms per ml in stock solution *before* dilution and the reagents used for the purification must either be easily removed or must not introduce any toxic constituents which could harm the culture plants. It is also desirable, preferably by biological means, to be able to measure the actual efficiency of the process.

In general, different groups of elements demand different methods for their removal and the production of one batch of reagents simultaneously free from all known micronutrients is laborious and difficult and not worth attempting, unless for special reasons—for example, where interactions between elements of different groups are to be studied or where possible effects of yet unrecognised micronutrients are sought.

The known micronutrients may be divided into groups according to the methods convenient for their removal which are briefly listed here and summarised in Table 3.4. The methods given in the text are numbered in the order given in the Table.

(a) *Boron, chlorine, sodium, other halogens and alkali metals*

Repeated recrystallisation, up to six times, is probably the simplest effective method for removing the elements of this group (Method 1). The process is made less wasteful if pure ethanol is added during cooling of the solution, as this greatly improves the yield of salts obtained. Calcium chloride or nitrate are difficult to recrystallise. The preparation of calcium chloride or nitrate by mixing pure calcium carbonate and diluted pure hydrochloric or nitric

Table 3.4   Summary of some useful purification methods and their effectiveness

Method	Principal application
(1) Recrystallisation with ethanol	Boron, chlorine, sodium, calcium, about 90% efficiency
(2) Co-precipitation as carbonates or phosphates on autoclaving	Iron, manganese, 99% efficiency; copper, zinc, 90–95% efficiency
(3) Extraction with oxine in chloroform (*a*) at pH 3–5 (*b*) pH above 7	Iron, zinc, 99% efficiency Manganese, 99% efficiency
(4) Extraction with dithizone in chloroform at pH 6–7	Copper, zinc, 99% efficiency
(5) Co-precipitation by copper sulphate and hydrogen sulphide at pH 2–5	Molybdenum, 99·9% efficiency
(6) Precipitation of nitroso-R-salt in the presence of charcoal at pH 6·5	Cobalt, 99·9% efficiency
(7) Extraction with cupferron at pH 2 and use of charcoal	Vanadium, 99·9% efficiency
(8) Co-precipitation by copper and iron in the presence of calcium carbonate	Cobalt, vanadium, 99% efficiency
(9) Extraction of ferric chloride into ether in the presence of 7N hydrochloric acid	Copper, zinc, manganese, cobalt, vanadium

acid is simpler and quite satisfactory for elements of this group. Calcium carbonate suspended as a thin cream in water is slowly poured into the acid until there is an excess of calcium carbonate. The solution is filtered, made up to volume, and is then ready for use.

(b) *Iron and manganese*

These elements are easily removed by autoclaving for one hour at 110°C (20 lb per sq. in.) the stock solutions with 20 g/l calcium carbonate and 10 mM K_2HPO_4, 10 mM $NaHCO_3$ and 20 mM $CaCl_2$ or $Ca(NO_3)_2$ (Method 2). This procedure is practically identical to that introduced by Stout and Arnon (1939) as a modification of the earlier procedure of Steinberg, but the use of bicarbonate introduced by Hewitt causes the precipitation of highly

ther elements removed	*Remarks*
alogens, alkali metals, alkali earth metals, copper, zinc, manganese	Often unreliable because of mixed crystal formation
ɔbalt	Not always complete for copper and zinc, inadequate for cobalt, and ineffective for molybdenum
ɔpper, molybdenum, vanadium, gallium ɔpper, magnesium, cobalt	Residual traces of oxine may be toxic for excised cultured tissues
ʌany metals, e.g. lead, mercury, cadmium	Not suitable for cobalt or manganese under ordinary conditions. Convenient to use after Method 2 for copper and zinc
—	Outstandingly best method for molybdenum but may introduce appreciable residual copper
—	Simplest recommended method for cobalt. Correct pH important, especially with phosphates
ʌolybdenum, iron, gallium	Simplest recommended method for vanadium
—	Unreliable in the presence of phosphates
admium, gallium	Does not remove molybdenum which is best separated by application of Method 7 to ferrous salts

absorbent calcium carbonate from solution and increases the efficiency by a useful margin.

Extraction with 8-hydroxyquinoline (oxine) in chloroform at pH 3-5 (Method 3a) may be used for the removal of iron and also for zinc. At pH values above 7 this method is useful for the removal of manganese (Method 3b).

(c) *Copper and zinc*

Arnon and Stout considered that Method 2 was adequate for removal of copper and zinc but Piper (1942) preferred to use diphenylthiocarbazone (dithizone) dissolved in chloroform to extract the chelated metals (Method 4). At Long Ashton these two methods are combined and the residual heavy metals that are not completely removed by the calcium carbonate–phosphate adsorption technique react with dithizone to produce red or violet colours in the chloroform layer. When the residual levels are very low the dithizone solution remains bright green. The excess dithizone is removed by extraction with pure chloroform which is then itself removed by simmering until no longer detected by smell. By using a very small amount of purified dithizone in a few millilitres of chloroform the presence of minute traces of heavy metals in the stock nutrient solutions can be determined.

(d) *Molybdenum*

The first method that was specifically effective for the removal of molybdenum from nutrient reagents was that using co-precipitation of molybdenum with iron or aluminium and 8-hydroxyquinoline. This was introduced by Hewitt and Jones in 1947 and was based on methods developed by Mitchell and Scott for the concentration of trace elements in plant ash solutions prior to spectrographic analysis. In 1948 Stout and Meager suggested the use of co-precipitation of molybdenum with copper sulphide (Method 5). This procedure was investigated quantitatively by Hewitt and Hallas (1951) with the use of *Aspergillus niger* as a test organism and shown to be more efficient than the oxine method. Under favourable conditions using 50 p.p.m. copper as sulphate and vigorous gassing with hydrogen sulphide in a very well-ventilated fume cupboard the method would remove 99·95% of molybdenum present at an initial concentration of 1 μg/l (i.e. 0·001 p.p.m.). It should be noted here that a method which removes 99·95% of an impurity is ten times more efficient than one removing 99·5% because the residual amount, which is what matters, is ten times smaller in the first case than in the second; with molybdenum, this difference is of considerable importance. The process is normally carried out twice. The coagulated sulphide precipitate is stirred and then allowed to settle for several hours before filtering on acid-extracted analytical grade filter paper or a sintered glass filter disc, but the latter has to be cleaned each time with hot aqua regia. The dissolved hydrogen sulphide is removed by boiling and the stock solutions containing 0·1–1 M concentrations are then refiltered and made up to a convenient volume. Residual concentrations of molybdenum amount to less than 10^{-6} p.p.m. in the finally diluted nutrient solutions. The copper sulphide method is now widely used by most workers, and notably by Hewitt, Nicholas and Arnon and their associates for studies with higher plants, fungi, bacteria and green algae.

(e) *Cobalt*

The simplest effective method for removing cobalt depends on the adsorption on charcoal of the cobalt complex formed with nitroso-R-salt (1-nitroso-2-

hydroxynaphthalene 3, 6-disodium sulphonate) as originally proposed, together with an alternative procedure for nutrient culture experiments by Bolle-Jones and Mallikarjuneswara in 1958 and first exploited with great success by Ahmed and Evans in 1959–61 for their pioneering work on symbiotic nitrogen fixation by legumes (Plate 28). Several methods were compared for efficiency as determined by removal of radioactively labelled cobalt in experiments by Hewitt, James and Lloyd-Jones in 1965. From these studies the nitroso-R-salt procedure was recommended since it is reproducible and will remove 99·9% of trace amounts of cobalt from concentrated stock solutions of macronutrients. It is still the simplest and most effective of the methods known at present. The procedure consists in adjusting the pH to 6·5 in the presence of 0·8% sodium acetate adding 16 mg nitroso-R-salt (in aqueous solution) per litre of stock solution, followed by 8 g of acid- and water-extracted Darco G60 charcoal. The mixture is stirred and immediately filtered (Method 6). The precipitation and charcoal adsorption are repeated for best results.

(f) *Vanadium*

The vanadium requirement by *Scenedesmus* was discovered by Arnon and Wessel (1953) using major nutrient reagents purified by the copper sulphide co-precipitation technique at an acid pH as described above for molybdenum, and ferric chloride extracted with ether in the presence of 6N hydrochloric acid. Experiments by Hewitt, James and Lloyd-Jones at Long Ashton with radioactive vanadium shows that this method removes only about 60–80% of the vanadium. The removal of vanadium was also compared by several other methods, and the most efficient is achieved by extraction with cupferron in chloroform at pH 2 followed by adsorption of any residual cupferron and its vanadium complex on Darco G60 charcoal (Method 7). By this means, greater than 99·9% removal has been obtained when 100 $\mu g/l$ vanadium is added, and 92 to 99·8% removal is observed with a negligible weight of carrier-free vanadium as $VOCl_3$. This new method is slightly more efficient than the alkaline copper sulphide method of Arnon, Ichioka, Wessel, Fujiwara and Woolley described in 1955 (Method 8). Oxine with thionalid, and tannic acid with aluminium or iron is another very effective co-precipitation method for removing vanadium and was employed by Mitchell and Scott in 1947 for spectrographic work.

Purification of iron compounds

Iron compounds are notably contaminated by several elements and although relatively small amounts are normally given the impurities are often significant. Several elements including Mn, Cu, Zn, Co and V may be eliminated by

Table 3.5 Seed reserves of some micronutrient elements in terms of p.p.m. and μg per seed

Species		Fe	Mn	Cu	Zn	Mo	B	Na	Cl
Tomato *Lycopersicon esculentum*	p.p.m.	40–800	10–55	1·8–7	56–320	0·1–2·5	7–11	15–60	350
	μg/seed	0·13–2·6	0·003–0·16	0·006–0·02	0·2–1	0·003–0·008	0·02–0·03	0·05–0·2	1·1
Pea *Pisum sativum*	p.p.m.		4–12	4–9	7–24	0·6–8			
	μg/seed		1·2–3·6	1·2–2·6	2·3–6	0·16–1·8			
French beans *Phaseolus vulgaris*	p.p.m.		4–10	3–8	26–42	2–8			160
	μg/seed		2–5	1·8–4	13–20	1–5			83
Barley *Hordeum vulgare*	p.p.m.	14–350	75	6–41		0·25–1·25	0·3–2		870
Oat *Avena sativa*	μg/seed	0·25–12	3	0·15–1·5		0·01–0·05	0·014–0·07		35

extraction of ferric chloride into ether in the presence of 6–7N HCl (Method 9). The separation is very efficient and was investigated by Grahame and Seaborg (1938) and earlier by Hillebrand and Lundell and was first applied for nutritional work by Piper before 1942. The removal of vanadium is critically dependent on the use of peroxide-free ether, and exclusion of bright light. Molybdenum is carried into the ether phase with the iron and the method therefore cannot be used for this element. The method for removal of molybdenum developed at Long Ashton is to purify ferrous sulphate by the copper sulphide method. Chelating agents (EDTA, Versene, Sequestrene and some related complexing agents) can also be similarly purified separately as sodium salts, and then mixed with the ferrous sulphate and aerated to produce ferric versenate which is free from molybdenum.

Seeds

It is inevitable that any tissue used to propagate an organism must contain at least a small amount of all the elements essential for its growth. In many cases seed reserves may be neglected in connection with the production of mineral deficiencies, particularly if they tend to remain immobilised as appears likely for boron. However, the reserves of molybdenum and sometimes of copper, zinc and possibly chlorine, may be significant factors in the results obtained. In large-seeded species, especially e.g. beans and peas, there is enough molybdenum in the seeds for the continued growth of the whole plant for at least one generation under deficiency conditions, and effects of seed reserves may persist over two generations. Depletion of seed reserves may damage the embryo when manganese, copper or zinc deficiencies occur in beans and peas. In work on the unknown micronutrients preliminary depletion of seed reserves may well be necessary. This was done in work on cobalt and nickel and other elements by Hewitt and Bolle-Jones and by Woolley (1957) in work on sodium requirements of beet. The reserves in cuttings or other clonal organs may be greater than those in seeds. Some examples of seed reserves are shown in Table 3.5 and Plates 40 and 50.

Atmospheric and other sources of contamination

These sources of interference are difficult to assess, but some indication of their magnitude may be gained from discrepancies between amounts calculated to have been provided by water, nutrient reagents and seed and from containers and sand where used and amounts found by analysis to be present in the plants at the end of the experiment (Table 3.6). Woolley (1957) found that the sodium content in beet grown in water culture with polythene containers was 73 µg/plant. This compared quite well with a known contamination level equivalent to 63 µg of which 45 µg came from the

Table 3.6 Examples of relationships between calculated supply accounted for by all known sources and actual uptake (μg) of micronutrients or trace elements by plants grown in purified media. (Data of several independent studies)

Plant	Element	Conditions (water culture)	Amount given (μg)	Amount recovered (μg)
Phaseolus vulgaris	Chlorine	Untreated atmosphere	367	11 800
Lactuca sativa	Chlorine	Untreated atmosphere	285	2130
Fagopyrum esculentum	Chlorine	Untreated atmosphere	285	890
Lycopersicon esculentum	Sodium	Filtered atmosphere	63	73
Atriplex vesicaria	Sodium	Filtered atmosphere	140	140
Atriplex vesicaria	Sodium	Untreated atmosphere	2900	6800
Lycopersicon esculentum	Cobalt	Untreated atmosphere	1–2 600–1000*	11–23 257–1240
	Nickel	Untreated atmosphere	5–15 182–1690*	46–113 600–1000
	Chromium	Untreated atmosphere	3–4 600–1000*	70–220 60–135
	Vanadium	Untreated atmosphere	5–10 600–1000*	31–93 133–783
	Zinc	Untreated atmosphere	28 8 600* 6500* 1980*	37 5 70 2900 1700
	Copper	Untreated atmosphere	1950*	660–1130

polythene pots. For silica the amount recovered in the plant was 135 μg and the known contamination was estimated at only 14 μg. In the work of Brownell and Wood on *Atriplex vesicaria* there was an excess of 350 μg equivalents of sodium in the deficient plants over that known to have been present and this difference was ascribed to cyclic salt (atmospheric sodium chloride derived from sea spray) although plants were grown in a PVC cabinet with filtered air. Brownell in 1965 improved the aeration facilities by filtration through paper filters as well as liquid scrubbing, introduced more refined purification of nutrients, and grew the plants in a sealed greenhouse. In this way the ubiquitous sodium contamination was reduced from 6800 μg to 140 μg. The lower figure was completely accounted for by that present in seeds, reagents and water, whereas 3900 μg of that present in the other plants had been carried

Plant	Element	Conditions (sand culture)	Amount given (μg)	Amount recovered (μg)
Brassica spp.	Molybdenum	Untreated atmosphere	0·15–0·3	0·1–1
			1500*	290
Trifolium and *Medicago* spp.	Molybdenum	Untreated atmosphere	4800*	1000
L. esculentum	Molybdenum	Untreated atmosphere	1700*	370
Hevea braziliensis	Cobalt	Untreated atmosphere	2·3 approx.	9
Trifolium and			1	16·5
Medicago spp.	Cobalt	Untreated atmosphere	2000*	74
L. esculentum	Strontium	Untreated atmosphere	unknown (not added)	700–5000
L. esculentum	Silicon	(water culture) Filtered atmosphere	14	135

* Treatments in which known amounts of the element were *added* to nutrient solutions.

in by the aeration stream. Similar comparisons were made by Johnson *et al.* in their work on chlorine. Thus the 'intrinsic' contamination defined by them as that from all known sources of culture equipment was 7·5 μg atoms per culture together with another 2·7 μg atoms from seeds, making 10·2 μg atoms/culture (400 μg). The amount of chlorine actually recovered in beans, maize and squash (*Cucurbita pepo*) ranged from 200 to 330 μg atoms/culture—a very great discrepancy. Ulrich and Chki similarly reported figures of 50 and 400 μg atoms of chlorine respectively for calculated intrinsic contamination and that actually found in beet plants grown in refined water cultures. Sodium and chlorine are very abundant in the atmosphere in dust, or sea spray and are also abundant in nearly all reagents and materials. Although the requirements in plants for sodium and chlorine appear to be substantially greater than for molybdenum, the ubiquity and natural abundance of the former two elements makes the demonstration of their essential nature at least as difficult as for an element which is less abundant like molybdenum. The difficulty is increased by the fact that these elements are less efficiently eliminated by available procedures than molybdenum.

Elaborate air filtration to clean the air used to aerate roots in chlorine or sodium deficiency water cultures was adopted by Ozanne, Woolley and Broyer, by Woolley and by Brownell but not by Johnson, Stout, Woolley and Broyer whose results with chlorine were nevertheless highly successful. They estimated that air at Berkeley contained about 1 or 2 × 10^{-4} µg Cl/l and that during the experiments aeration might have introduced between 0·1 and 1·0 µg Cl per 3 l of culture solution per week. By contrast, the amount of chlorine found in precipitated residues amounted to 0·02 µg atoms (0·7 µg) per cm^2 per week. In an exposed culture or on leaves this would amount to more than 50 µg chlorine during the course of the experiments. Brownell was able to extract 30 µg sodium from the 100 000 l air used daily to maintain positive pressure in the sealed greenhouse, and even after filtration through paper, sodium would still be detected by its accumulation in water used for scrubbing.

Tentative calculations by Hewitt for the molybdenum contamination provided in sand culture suggest that practically the whole of the relatively small quantities, amounting to about 0·1 µg per plant found in deficient plants, can be accounted for by the estimated concentrations in the nutrient solution and sand. This agreement is of course consistent with the relatively low abundance of molybdenum as compared with sodium and chlorine, and as already pointed out helps to explain why molybdenum deficiency may be easier to induce than chlorine deficiency in spite of the relatively larger requirements for chlorine than for molybdenum. Chromium, strontium and barium have been found in plant material when none was given in the carefully conducted independent experiments of Liebig, Vanselow and Chapman and in the work of Hewitt, Abbott and Bolle-Jones. Unexpectedly large amounts of nickel, cobalt and vanadium were also found in the plants although it is clear from the work of Ahmed and Evans and Bond and Hewitt that cobalt is not necessarily always difficult to exclude. In the work of Hewitt on cobalt, vanadium, chromium and nickel between five and twenty times as much of these elements was found in the plants as was known to have been given as intrinsic contamination—that is, in the form of residual impurities in reagents and sand regardless of whether sand or water cultures were used. In the case of chromium there was very little difference in total chromium recovered in the plants irrespective of whether the element had been added at up to 0·02 p.p.m. or had been omitted from the nutrient solution. Furthermore, the uptake from the treatment where chromium had been added was only 10% of that provided.

It is important to realise that continual breakdown of greenhouse paint and corrosion of any metal parts can be serious sources of contamination by any of the elements mentioned. Transparent screens undoubtedly help to decrease contamination from this source and from general atmospheric dust. Analysis of dust collected on such screens has revealed the presence of over thirty elements. The rate of deposition of molybdenum corresponds to about 0·2 μg Mo per culture per season for exposed sand cultures. Not all the components of dust collected thus are derived from the greenhouse. Railway, boiler and soil dust are all significant sources of atmospheric contamination. From analyses made by Mitchell at the Macaulay Spectrographic Centre the principal constituents are found to be aluminium, silicon, sodium, potassium, calcium and magnesium which comprise up to 75% of the ashed dust. Important impurities present at 500–5000 p.p.m. in greenhouse dust include zinc, copper, manganese, nickel, vanadium, barium, lead, tin, strontium, titanium and zirconium. Cobalt and molybdenum may comprise only 20–30 and 8 p.p.m. respectively.

Unexpected contamination may be introduced from miscellaneous items of equipment. A notable example is that of zinc which cannot be removed from rubber bungs or tubing even by repeated boiling in 3N hydrochloric acid. Even when such sources as these are avoided, and all other likely precautions have been adopted, the production of zinc deficiency at Long Ashton has sometimes proved very difficult for reasons still not fully investigated.

Assessment of nutrient contamination

It was pointed out above that discrepancies are sometimes found between amounts of elements recovered in plants at the end of an experiment and the amounts calculated to have been provided by different factors in the environment. The methods used to determine the often very low concentrations of certain micronutrient elements in reagents, water, etc. are varied and cannot be described here in practical detail. Some elements may be determined spectrographically or by atomic absorption, and negative results may be an adequate criterion of purity for sodium, calcium and zinc. Chemical methods suitably modified and 'scaled down' are sometimes even more sensitive as for example for boron, zinc, copper, manganese and molybdenum but may still be insufficiently sensitive for some purposes. Biological tests based on the growth of *Rhizobium japonicum* as described by Lowe, Evans and Ahmed (1960), or based on the growth of *Aspergillus niger* for cobalt and molybdenum respectively as described by Hewitt and Hallas (1951) are preferable or even essential. In either case the yield of the organism is related to the supply of the element over a certain range which roughly corresponds to concentrations between 0·000 001 and 0·0001 p.p.m.

Further Reading

Bould, C. and Hewitt, E. J. (1963) Mineral nutrition in soils and in water culture media, Chap. 1, pp. 15–133, in Vol. III *Plant Physiology* (Ed. F. C. Steward). Academic Press: New York and London.

Hewitt, E. J. (1966) *Sand and Water Culture Methods used in the Study of Plant Nutrition.* 2nd edn. Commonwealth Agricultural Bureaux: Farnham Royal, England. 547 pp.

Plate 13 Potassium deficiency in apple leaves. Photo—Long Ashton Research Station, by courtesy of Dr C. Bould.

Plate 14 Effect of calcium deficiency on potato tubers. Photo—Long Ashton Research Station.

Plate 15 Calcium deficiency in sugar beet. Photo—Long Ashton Research Station.

Plate 16 Calcium deficiency in cauliflower. The younger leaves are hooked. Photo—Long Ashton Research Station.

Plate 17 Maize plants grown in water culture. Upper series with calcium supplied at 0, 0·15, 0·25, 0·5, 1·5 and 4·0 mEq/l (*from left to right*). Lower series—calcium deficiency overcome by addition of strontium. Calcium was supplied at 0, 0·15, 0·25, 0·5, 1·0, 2·0 and 4·0 mEq/l with strontium 4, 3·85, 3·75, 3·5, 3·0, 2·0, and 0 mEq/l respectively (*from left to right*). From P. G. Pinto da Silva (1962) *Agronomia Lusitana* **24**, 133–57.

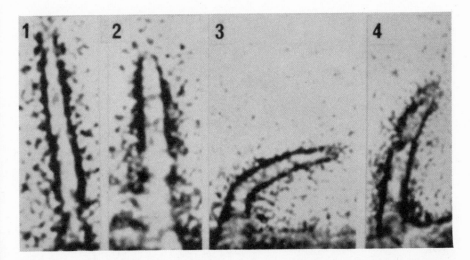

Plate 18 Radioautographs of young actively growing root hairs of white mustard (1, 2) and of tomato (3, 4) developed in moist air following seed treatment with $^{45}CaCl_2$. The hair in (1) has lost its contents while the other hairs are still intact but have been strongly plasmolysed. Radioactivity is absent or faint over the growing tip but is concentrated immediately behind this point. Hairs measure 50–100 μm in length. Magnification ×700. From Cormack, Lemay and Maclachlan (1963) *J. exp. Bot.* **14**, 311–15.

Plate 19 Magnesium deficiency in apple leaves. Photo—Long Ashton Research Station, by courtesy of Dr C. Bould.

Plate 20 Phosphorus deficient and normal barley plants. Photo—Long Ashton Research Station.

− NITROGEN   NORMAL

Plate 21   Nitrogen deficiency in barley. Photo—Long Ashton Research Station.
Plate 22   Nitrogen deficiency in flax. Photo—Long Ashton Research Station.

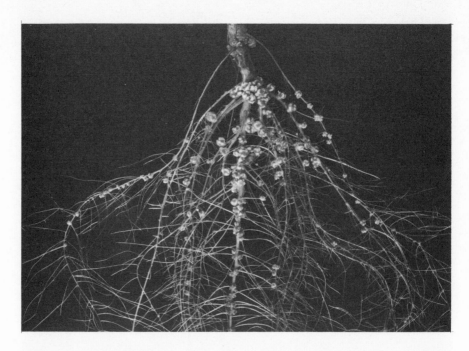

Plate 23 Typical nodules on the root of (*a*) soybean and (*b*) red clover, which have been grown in water culture. By courtesy of Professor G. Bond, F.R.S. Plate (*b*) reproduced from Ferguson and Bond (1954) *Ann. Bot.* **18**, 385–96.

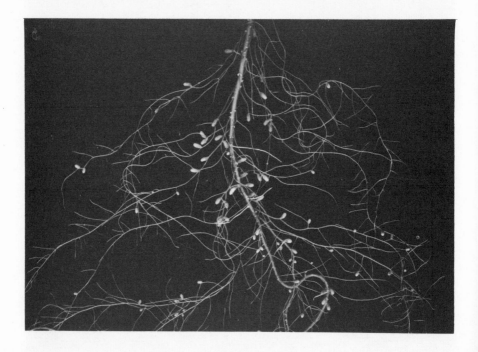

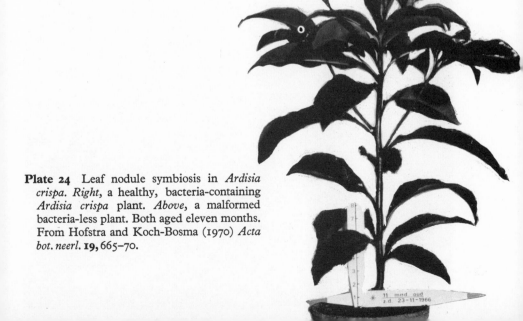

Plate 24 Leaf nodule symbiosis in *Ardisia crispa. Right*, a healthy, bacteria-containing *Ardisia crispa* plant. *Above*, a malformed bacteria-less plant. Both aged eleven months. From Hofstra and Koch-Bosma (1970) *Acta bot. neerl.* **19,** 665–70.

Plate 25   Nitrogen-fixing nodules on *Podocarpus rospigliosii*. Root system of eighteen-month-old plant grown in nitrogen-free nutrient solution. The root nodules are spaced more or less regularly in two opposite rows along the root. From Becking (1965) *Pl. Soil* **23**, 213–26.

Plate 26   Nitrogen-fixing root nodules of non-leguminous plants.
    (A) Coralloid root nodules of *Alnus glutinosa*. ×0·4.
    (B) Root nodules of *Alnus rubra* produced by an *Alnus glutinosa* inoculum. ×0·4.
    (C) Root nodule of *Casuarina equisetifolia* showing that the apex of each nodule
        lobe produces a negatively geotropic root. ×0·4.
    (D) Coralloid root nodules of *Alnus glutinosa*. Detached and divided root nodules
        showing dichotomous branching. ×0·7.
From Becking (1970) *Pl. Soil* **32**, 611–54.

Plate 27 Effect of cobalt deficiency on the growth of nodulated alders in a culture solution without combined nitrogen. The cobalt-deficient plant (*right*, 16 cm high) shows severe nitrogen deficiency. By courtesy of Professor G. Bond from work in association with E. J. Hewitt. From Hewitt (1966) in *Sand and Water Culture Methods*. Commonwealth Agricultural Bureaux.

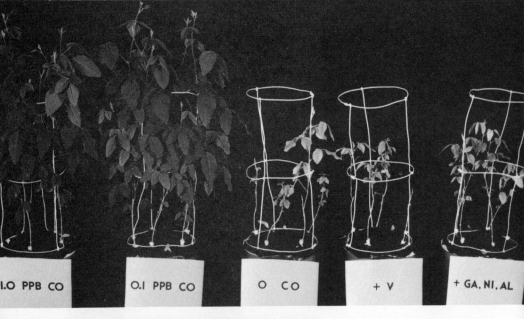

I.O PPB CO   O.I PPB CO   O CO   + V   + GA, NI, AL

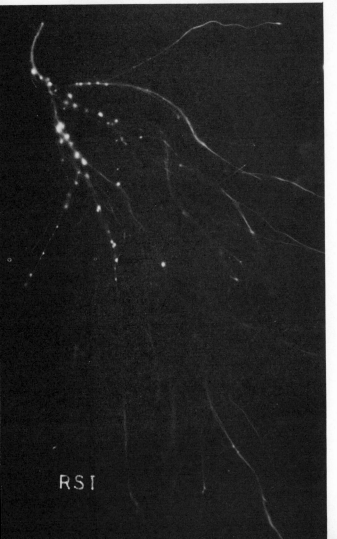

RSI

Plate 28 The second axillary growth of soybean cultures, showing the stimulatory effect of cobalt on growth. At the time of the photograph the plants had been growing for four weeks after the previous cutting. In the two cultures on the right of the photograph, vanadium at 1 p.p.b. and gallium, nickel and aluminium, each at 1 p.p.b., were added instead of cobalt. From Ahmed and Evans (1960) *Soil Sci.* **90**, 205–10. © 1960 The Williams & Wilkins Co, Baltimore, USA.

Plate 29 Distribution of ^{60}Co in the roots of clover (*Tri-folium subterraneum*) inoculated with an effective strain (R.S.I.) of *Rhizobium*. The ^{60}Co was introduced through the leaves. Cobalt is concentrated especially in the nodules containing the rhizobia. From Wilson and Hallsworth (1965) *Pl. Soil* **23**, 60–78.

Plate 30 Sulphur deficiency in cotton under field conditions. The plot in the background was treated with a sulphur-containing fertiliser. Photograph by Dr O. E. Anderson, University of Georgia, by courtesy of the Sulphur Institute.

Plate 31 Response of rape to sulphur fertilisation in Alberta, Canada. Photograph by Dr M. Nyborg, Canadian Dept. of Agriculture, Beaverlodge, Alberta. By courtesy of the Sulphur Institute (unpublished).

Plate 32   Iron deficiency in maize. Photo—Long Ashton Research Station.

Plate 33   Iron deficiency in mustard. Chlorosis appears in the first primary leaves, the cotyledons remaining green. Photo—Long Ashton Research Station.

Plate 34 Copper deficiency in tomato, comparing water from different sources. *From left to right:* complete nutrient; omission of copper—with water from metal still—with water from ion-exchange columns—with water from metal still, redistilled once, and twice, in pyrex glass stills. From Hewitt (1966) in *Sand and Water Culture Methods*. Commonwealth Agricultural Bureaux.

Plate 35 Copper deficiency in wheat under field conditions in South Australia. *Foreground,* no copper applied; *background,* copper applied as 75 kg copper sulphate per hectare. From Riceman, Donald and Evans (1940) *C.S.I.R. pamphlet* No. 96.

Plate 36 Copper deficiency in wheat. The spiral twisting in the leaves is characteristic of copper deficiency in this plant. Photo—Long Ashton Research Station.

Plate 37 Copper deficiency in oats. Photo—Long Ashton Research Station.

Plate 38 Copper deficiency in oats. Close spiral twisting of the leaf blades is characteristic of copper deficiency in this plant. Photo—Long Ashton Research Station.

Plate 39 Copper deficiency in red clover. The two lower leaves are from clover plants grown with full nutrients. Photo—Long Ashton Research Station.

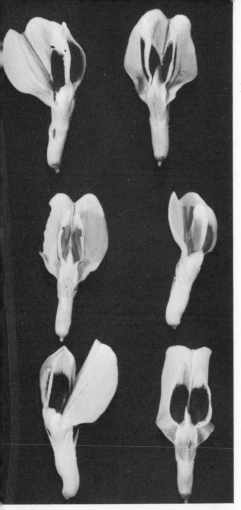

Plate 40 Copper deficiency in broad bean (*Vicia faba*) showing loss of chocolate brown pigment in 'keel' of flowers in centre pair, produced by plants grown from copper-deficient seed in the absence of copper. Upper pair of flowers produced by plants grown from normal seed in the absence of added copper. Lower flowers from plants grown from normal seed in full nutrient. From Hewitt (1963) in *Plant Physiology* (Ed. F. C. Steward), Academic Press, New York and London, **3**, 137–360.

Plate 41 Copper deficiency in pea showing seed abortion after pod development, and normal external appearance (*left*) of similar pods shown opened. Photo—Long Ashton Research Station.

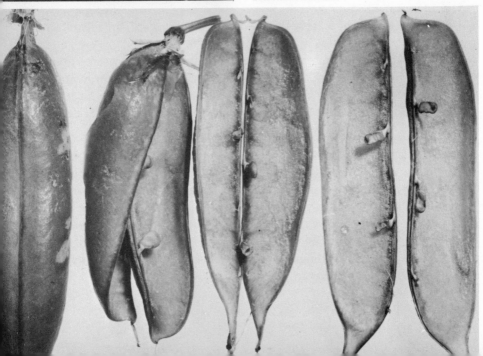

4
Mineral Absorption

'We don't see words in nature but always only the initial letters of words, and when we set out to spell we find that the so-called new words are in their turn merely the initial letters of others.'

Lichtenberg

Sites of uptake

Roots are naturally regarded as the primary absorbing organ for mineral uptake. Steward and Sutcliffe (1959) have summarised certain conclusions made on the basis of studies on roots carried out by several independent groups of investigators; these are:

(a) Salt absorption is usually most rapid in those root tissues where cell growth by expansion and vacuolation rather than cell division is the dominant feature.

(b) Root hairs may not be specifically or even more actively associated with salt uptake than any other cells exposed to the same medium.

(c) The site of most active absorption is often 1–2 mm behind the root apex, but the location of this region may vary considerably (sometimes with a periodic effect of time).

(d) Older regions of roots with non-dividing cells are still capable of active salt absorption.

(e) The compulsive pumping of accumulated solutes from roots to other parts of the plant is dependent on a relationship between living cells and does not occur in dead tissues. This point is dealt with in more detail in the context of translocation and distribution of mineral elements.

There are other views, observations and questions which merit consideration in relation to those put forward above. For instance, to what extent does the uptake by the root surface in cylinders of root immediately behind the growing apex account for the total salt content in terms of individual cations and anions in entire plants? Does the region of uptake for a particular ion vary at different stages of growth? An important feature with regard to the site of absorption is the integration of rate and area for all potential absorbing sites. A rate only one-tenth of that maximally observed may be of great importance to the plant if the available area is 200 times greater.

The nature of the ion or mineral being absorbed is also likely to be important. Many experiments have been carried out with ions of non-physiological elements, e.g. Rb^+ in place of K^+, or Br^- in place of Cl^-, since radioactive isotopes may be utilised for convenience in estimation. It is fair to note that many experiments with rubidium or caesium performed by Steward and his collaborators were checked against results obtained with potassium and did not indicate any invalidation of the principles deduced from the work. Nevertheless in general terms it is wise to remember that potassium is a macronutrient which has many functions, whereas rubidium and to an even lesser extent caesium only partly replace potassium, and they cannot support normal or continued growth. Chlorine is a micronutrient and uptake as chloride beyond quite low concentrations has no value to the plant. Bromide is much less efficient than chloride in the same role. It is a much larger ion and it usually causes toxic effects when absorbed by intact plants up to the luxury levels obtainable with chloride and which are likely to be produced by the external concentrations normally used to measure chloride uptake. Further complications may be expected when the absorption of complex molecules such as iron-EDTA and other chelates or complexes between metals and soil-chelating substances occurs, and conclusions reached with K^+ or Cl^- may not wholly or even in any way apply to the situation for Fe-EDTA, Cu-glycinate, metal-gluconates, etc. It is most important to include calcium ions in any medium used for investigating ion uptake by roots and experiments conducted in their absence may be meaningless due to the permeability changes which take place in the membranes of the cells.

The mechanisms of ion uptake from the rhizosphere by sterile roots may differ considerably from those operating in the presence of bacterial or mycorrhizal infections, as demonstrated by Barber and Frankenburg (1971). Bacteria are always present around the roots of normal plants. The contact between bacterial cell walls of potentially great absorptive capacity could be a significant factor influencing uptake rate by promotion or inhibition of salt absorption. The colonisation of a certain region of a root by bacteria could be more important in determining the uptake rate than the specific physiological capacity for salt absorption of that root surface. The rhizosphere almost certainly influences absorption of manganese because of the effects of certain bacteria on the oxidation states of this element. Phosphate is solubilised by bacteria, though phosphate uptake by the plant may be reduced, due to the high affinity of the bacteria for this element. The production and excretion of chelating compounds and of cell poisons by bacteria would also be expected to exert complex effects on the capacity of root surfaces to absorb mineral elements.

The presence of ectotrophic mycorrhiza (a symbiotic association between fungi and the roots of higher plants) seems quite definitely to influence salt absorption of the infected roots and to increase the total contents of nitrogen, potassium, magnesium and particularly phosphorus in the plants. This is especially so when the plants are growing in relatively impoverished soils. Mycorrhizal activity may be quite important in assisting colonisation of poorly developed soils by trees and appears to enhance their competitive efficiency against other species. The experiments of Harley, McCready and Brierly, and other associates, in progress since 1950 with beech mycorrhiza-root associations have shown beyond doubt that the mycorrhizal fungi absorb phosphate directly by processes dependent on respiratory metabolism and that they pass phosphate on to the host roots (Plate 5). Mycorrhizal fungi are associated with the roots of many forest trees and especially of conifer species (Plate 4). Infected roots of *Picea abies* are shown in Plate 3. Infection of apple tree roots by mycorrhiza was investigated by Mosse in 1957 and was found to lead to increased uptake of iron and copper and inhibition of the uptake of manganese. Although fungi commonly form mycorrhiza with tree roots, this association is also found in smaller herbaceous plants like onion, tobacco, tomato, maize, strawberry and many orchids (endotrophic mycorrhiza). However in these plants the association is not necessarily beneficial and may even be harmful.

The absorption of ions by excised barley roots was investigated in the classical work of Hoagland and Broyer in 1936–40 and the following points were established.

Roots of plants deprived of salts for some days (low salt) possessed a much greater capacity for salt uptake than did roots of plants provided with adequate nutrients up to the time of the experiment (high salt). When the roots were separated from the tops, uptake by high salt roots was very small (30%) compared with the uptake by entire plants. By contrast the uptake by low salt roots was not only considerably greater but was not greatly affected by removal of the aerial parts.

Aeration of the solution was essential for rapid uptake, the optimum oxygen tension being close to that produced by continuous flow of $20\% \ O_2$, $80\% \ N_2$ corresponding to the composition of the air. The reduction of absorbed nitrate was sometimes more rapid than the rate of uptake, showing how a specific metabolic transformation may be an important factor which could produce results different from those expected with, say, chloride or bromide. Uptake of cations in excess of anions resulted in synthesis of organic acids in the cell sap and differential uptake was balanced by excretion of HCO_3^- or H^+ ions.

Uptake by aerial parts of plants

Mineral uptake occurs through undamaged leaves and stems and through cut petioles and this fact is of practical importance in the use of sprays or injection techniques for diagnostic and curative measures in controlling plant nutrition. The application at intervals of a week or so of one or more sprays containing a leaf-wetting agent, e.g. 0·05% sodium lauryl sulphate together with 250–1000 p.p.m. of various micronutrients is an effective method of providing many plants with their requirements if soil conditions are such that root uptake is insufficient. Classical examples of curative or preventive treatments by these means include the work on zinc deficiency in fruit trees in the United States by Chandler, Hoagland and Hibbard in 1937, 'grey speck' (Plate 42) and 'marsh spot' (Plates 43 and 44) in manganese deficiency of oats and peas respectively in the United Kingdom by Wallace and his co-workers between 1939 and 1945, 'corky pit' or boron deficiency in apples by Atkinson in New Zealand in 1934, 'whiptail' or molybdenum deficiency in broccoli by Plant in 1955 (Plate 54), 'exanthema' or copper deficiency in pears by Oserkowsky and Thomas in 1938 and magnesium deficiency in greenhouse tomatoes by Wallace and others since 1939. The last requires the application of 1–2% solution of magnesium sulphate. Nitrogen as urea (if free from biuret) is commonly applied as a spray (1–4%) in orchards in the United States.

One of the most important applications of sprays is in the control of 'chlorosis' or iron deficiency in many plants (see Chapter 6). In this case, however, the use of an inorganic salt, e.g. $FeSO_4$ is often ineffective or injurious. The best results have been obtained by applying the iron as chelates of EDTA (Fig. 3.1) or related compounds when penetration and utilisation are both rapid and permanent without appreciable injury.

There is conflicting evidence regarding the relative importance of stomatal apertures and cuticular permeability as factors in absorption through leaves. Spraying is more effective during warm sunny periods than cold dull conditions, indicating an effect of stomatal opening. Uptake of some compounds is increased when stomata are known to be open and uptake from under surfaces of leaves is often more rapid than from upper surfaces, but upper and lower leaf cuticles also differ greatly in thickness and possibly in submicroscopic structure. Many cuticles appear to be impervious to uptake from an aqueous medium. The cuticle may have ion-exchange capacity and microscopic studies of leaf cuticles by Roberts, Southwick and Palnuter in 1948 indicates pectin-containing regions which may be in direct contact with the inner vascular elements of the leaves of apple trees. There is much scope for simple but ingenious investigation of this quite important subject. Some plants growing in submerged aquatic environments undoubtedly absorb considerable quantities of mineral elements through their leaves. This activity has been reviewed by Steward and Sutcliffe with regard especially to work on *Elodea*, *Vallisneria*, *Potamogeton* and *Myriophyllum*. Uptake of potassium is stimulated by light and inhibited by cell poisons such as cyanide and 2,4-dinitro-phenol (DNP). Uptake of bicarbonate to provide carbon dioxide for photosynthesis in these plants is accompanied and perhaps largely dependent on the simultaneous uptake of cations. It may be significant that carbonic anhydrase (see Chapter 8) which catalyses the reversible reaction between bicarbonate and water to give carbon dioxide is abundant in the leaves of many aquatic plants.

Mechanism of uptake

With the possible exception of mycorrhizal association, where penetration of root cells by hyphae is likely, the discussion of uptake to this point has been mainly concerned with the site of absorption on the outer surface of a plant and not how final penetration and accumulation of mineral elements against a concentration gradient can occur. No single mechanism can be responsible for all cases of salt uptake, and some theories to account for this process are summarised in Table 4.1.

In all instances where accumulation occurs against a concentration gradient this constitutes active transport and work must be done. There are two theoretical sources for the necessary energy: solar radiation as a physical factor in the evaporation of water from leaf surfaces, and oxidative, metabolic or chemical energy liberated by respiration. In excised roots, storage tissues, or in other conditions not involving transpiration, the source of energy for active transport must be metabolic whether the mechanism is manifested through such diverse reactions as exchange with H^+ ions, simultaneous movement with bicarbonate ions, maintenance of electric potential, hydrolysis of ATP or submicroscopic change in membrane structure analogous to muscular action.

Simple diffusion

When two fluids or gases, or a fluid and a gas, or a fluid and solute, or colloidal particles small enough to be subject to thermal movements rather than gravity are mixed in a heterogeneous manner, diffusion will take place in all directions until there is a uniform distribution of both materials or phases. At this time thermal movement continues but is randomly equivalent in all directions.

Table 4.1 Some theoretical mechanisms of ion uptake by biological systems

Mechanism	Ion accumulation	Ion selectivity	Principle	Probable distribution
Simple diffusion	No	No	Molecular movement	Universal
Facilitated diffusion	No	Yes	Polypeptide carrier	Micro-organisms
Mass flow	Yes	No	Transpiration	Universal in vascular land plants
Contact exchange	No	Yes?	Ion-exchange	Roots in contact with clay particles
Donnan equilibrium	Yes	Yes	Biopolymer synthesis	Universal
Redox pump	Yes	Yes	Electrophoretic transport	Yeast, animals
Chemi-osmosis	Yes	Yes	Charge separation	Mitochondria, chloroplasts
Anion respiration	Yes	Yes	Cytochrome dependent	Mitochondria?
Carrier complex	Yes	Yes	ATP-dependent protein movement	Tonoplast?

The process of diffusion in the absence of a membrane is described by Fick's law:

$$ds/dt = -D \cdot dc/dx$$

where ds/dt is the rate of diffusion per unit area, D is a diffusion coefficient or constant, and dc/dx is the concentration gradient. When a permeable but physically restrictive membrane is interposed between the two phases or solutes the law is modified thus:

$$ds/dt = P(C_1 - C_2)$$

where P is the permeability constant of the membrane and C_1 and C_2 are the external and internal concentrations (as mol/cm^3) of the diffusing solute. The term ds/dt is sometimes replaced by the flux as $mol/cm^2/s$ moving across the membrane.

Free space

The concept of 'free space' has been developed to account for the fact that the uptake of electrolytes into living plant tissues where the cells are not protected by relatively impermeable cuticles or endodermal structures, shows two phases. There is an initial rapid uptake which is not metabolically dependent, and a more prolonged, slower and ultimately greater uptake which is accumulative against concentration gradients and is metabolically dependent. The first phase of physical uptake is considered to be by diffusion into the 'free space', as contrasted with the osmotic volume which is not in equilibrium with the external solution. This free space is not easily measured and the term 'apparent free space' was introduced by Briggs and was given status in published papers by Hope and Stevens in 1952. The 'apparent free space' (AFS) was defined by Briggs and Robertson in 1957 as the amount of solute in the free space divided by the concentration of solute in the external medium at equilibrium. This is equal to the volume by which the tissue appears to dilute the external medium when initial non-metabolic uptake is complete. Ions in the AFS may be easily removed by washing roots in deionised water.

The Donnan free space (DFS) is the free space as defined above in which non-diffusible ions are located. The actual site of the AFS and DFS is a matter of some controversy (Jennings, 1963) but they may be in the cell wall and even extend beyond the plasmalemma into the cytoplasm (i.e. up to the tonoplast but not into the vacuole) while the AFS also comprises the intercellular spaces (Fig. 4.1). The magnitude of the DFS is about 2–3% of the tissue volume in red-beet root tissues according to the careful experiments of Briggs, Hope and Pitman in 1958. Ions in the DFS are easily exchanged for ions of the same charge in the outer medium.

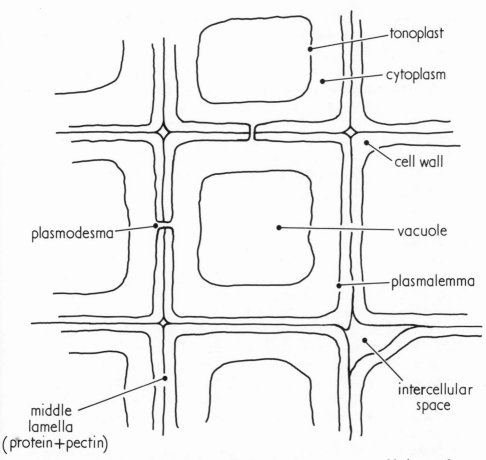

Figure 4.1 Diagram of typical plant cells showing the areas concerned in ion uptake and barriers to translocation (see text).

Mass flow

The transpiration stream in the xylem due to the evaporation of water from the aerial parts of the plant, notably the leaves, carries solutes derived from the soil water in contact with the roots. Although some accumulation may take place, this seems unimportant by comparison with that achieved by other mechanisms; moreover this process can only explain accumulation in intact land plants.

Contact ion–absorption mechanism

The majority of experiments on salt uptake by roots have been made with roots immersed in simple aqueous media in which the ions have been dissolved in a range of salt concentrations, and uptake has been measured often under aseptic conditions from the single aqueous phase. Leaving aside for the moment the practical and special aspects of rhizosphere organisms, there is another aspect of the problem of root absorption which must be noted. The idea was developed by Jenny and Overstreet in 1938 and subsequently by Jenny and his associates, that absorption of at least some elements takes place from the solid phase by direct exchange between root surfaces and soil or other mineral colloid particles having adsorptive and exchangeable-ion functions, without the intervention of the soil solution.

There are many observations and ideas connected with the contact-exchange concept which require careful consideration before rejection or unequivocal acceptance. Normally ion uptake occurs from extremely dilute solutions and continues until internal cell concentrations are several orders greater than external concentrations so that a considerable increase in free energy is involved and work must be done. This point is discussed later, but needs to be recognised at the outset. When a soil particle or mineral surface is saturated by adsorbed cations and is in contact with another surface, i.e. the exterior of a root cell, it is reasonable in theory for exchange or migration to take place with little change in free energy of the complex. However there is still an energy requirement for the delivery of the ions into the vacuole against a concentration gradient and contact exchange cannot account for ion accumulation, a subject which is considered later. Energy for accumulation cannot be provided from heat of adsorption by the external particles because the same energy would be involved in an opposite way when desorption from the cell surface occurred. If the heat of desorption were much less than that of adsorption on the external particles then exchange during contact would be negligible unless a high pressure of free ions in solution were present to maintain the flow. In its original form the contact-exchange hypothesis relied on the production of H^+ ions from respiratory activity in accordance with the basic equations for oxidative electron (i) or hydrogen transport (ii):

$$\text{(i)} \quad AH_2 \rightarrow A + 2H^+ + 2e^-$$

$$2Fe^{3+} + 2e^- \rightarrow 2Fe^{2+}$$

$$\text{(ii)} \quad AH_2 + NAD^+ \rightarrow A + NADH + H^+$$

where AH_2 is an oxidisable substrate; Fe^{3+}, Fe^{2+} represent the oxidised and reduced cytochromes respectively; and NAD is nicotine adenine dinucleotide.

The H^+ ions were balanced by respiratory carbon dioxide excreted as bicarbonate. The liberation and gaseous diffusion of carbon dioxide occurring at pH values around 5–6 at the root surface would result in a net increase in H^+ ions which would then provide the ion pressure for continued exchange to occur.

In order for exchange to continue the H^+ ions must either be balanced by the anions of the soil solution or must be adsorbed on particles in exchange for K^+, Ca^{2+} and Mg^{2+} ions. The net result of this system is an exchange of respiratory H^+ ions for soil cations. In theory the interposing of a contact complex becomes unnecessary since the migration of soil cations from particles outside the contact sphere to the contact complex may pass along aqueous layers surrounding soil particles.

However there is evidence for the existence of a contact complex. Jenny and Grossenbacher in 1963 obtained electron micrographs of roots showing the presence of a mucilaginous gel around the root surface in which clay particles and sub-microscopic particles of ferric oxide were thought to be held in an orientated structure. They visualised the gel as having thread-like molecules containing carboxyl groups which might bind the Al^{3+} or Fe^{3+} groups on the clay while H^+ ions liberated from the root were able to exchange with K^+ etc. adsorbed on the clay lattice. The reverse process of depletion of roots by clay particles has been demonstrated by Jenny and his co-workers and the movement of calcium from anorthite, a non-available form of phosphate, when a colloidal bentonite clay saturated by H^+ was added, was shown to occur by Graham in 1941. The uptake of iron by lucerne from an adsorbed state on sand in contact with the roots has been observed by Glauser and Jenny in 1960. When contact was prevented by semipermeable-dialysis membranes or by other means, iron uptake was prevented. The scope and potentialities of the contact-exchange mechanisms have been considered by Steward and Sutcliffe, and Lagerwerff in 1958 and 1960. The former pointed out that the molecular mechanism of contact exchange requires the overlapping of the movements of different ions which are oscillating about their respective sites of adsorption in order for exchange to occur in the adsorbed state. These oscillation volumes probably do not exceed 5×10^{-5} mm.

Although objections have been raised to this hypothesis, Sutcliffe (1962) does not consider it to be disproved. However Lagerwerff concludes that the contact-exchange mechanism is of benefit to a plant only when the ionic composition of the aqueous phase in contact with the external particles is more dilute than that required for thermodynamic equilibrium between the adsorbed and solution states. In other words, the complex is advantageous only when very sparingly soluble compounds are involved, but uptake from any dilute solution comparable to a dilute nutrient or soil solution will be just as rapid in the absence of any contact complex.

The Donnan equilibrium

This mechanism was formulated by F. G. Donnan in a series of papers in the period 1911–14. Donnan suggested that when a membrane is permeable to some ions but not to others, the movement of the diffusible ions can be contrary to concentration gradients. In a simple situation shown below

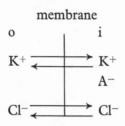

K^+ and Cl^- are freely diffusible ions o (outside) and i (inside) the membrane, while A^- is a non-diffusible anion. At equilibrium (writing activities equal to concentrations)

$$[K^+][Cl^-]o = [K^+][Cl^-]i \text{ but } [K^+]i = [Cl^-]i + [A^-]i \text{ and}$$

$$[K^+]o = [Cl^-]o.$$

When ions of different valencies are present, the charges must be taken into consideration for divalent and univalent cations M^{2+} and M^+, the relationship for the cation becomes:

$$\frac{[M^+]^2 i}{[M^+]^2 o} = \frac{[M^{2+}]i}{[M^{2+}]o}$$

and analogous relationships hold for anions and for homogeneous systems of ions of other valencies. The presence of the non-diffusible ion A^- means that at equilibrium there will be an excess of cations on the inside over those on the outside; and because of this inequality there will be an opposite inequality in anions. The inequality of the diffusible cations and anions on the two sides of the membrane also produces an electric potential difference usually between 10 and 150 mV negative with respect to the Donnan phase containing the non-diffusible anions. Because the Donnan phase contains the non-diffusible ions there is also a higher osmotic pressure within the membrane containing the Donnan phase. Measurements made by Briggs and Robertson in 1957 and Briggs, Hope and Pitman in 1958 on discs of carrot or red-beet storage roots respectively and by Dainty and Hope in 1959 with giant cells of the alga *Chara australis* indicate that the concentration of the non-diffusible ion is between 400 and 600 mEq/l in all three cases in the actual *free space* occupied by the Donnan phase. Osmotic pressures produced within the Donnan phase are about 10^6 Nm^{-2} (11 atm).

It is clear that accumulation in a Donnan system will occur if a non-diffusible ion is steadily synthesised. Protein or polyribonucleotides would fulfil such requirements. The production of these in sufficient quantities seems doubtful unless they are effectively highly multivalent so that one non-diffusible molecule could be associated with a large number of free ions.

The redox pump hypothesis

This hypothesis was suggested by Conway in 1951 and elaborated later in 1953, 1954 and 1955. The proposed mechanism is dependent on the co-ordinated interaction of two spatially segregated redox systems.

System A is a metal-protein system capable of reversible electron transport but independent of pH

$$\bar{M} \rightarrow M + e^-$$

Where $\bar{M}$ and M are reduced and oxidised states respectively; e^- is the electron. System B can be represented by a typical dehydrogenase system:

$$AH_2 \rightleftharpoons A + 2H^+ + 2e^-$$

or
$$AH_2 + NAD^+(P) \rightleftharpoons A + NADH(P) + H^+$$

This is pH dependent. AH_2 and A are reduced and oxidised substrates; $NAD^+(P)$ and $NADH(P)$ are oxidised and reduced co-enzymes I or II respectively.

Conway used equations relating changes in free energy to electrode potentials of the pH dependent and independent systems to show that the work done by an electron in moving through a potential difference equal to that existing between the two redox systems A and B at the same pH when the ratios of oxidised to reduced substrates were unity in both systems, is:

$$\Delta G^0 = -nF\Delta E_0'$$

where ΔG_0 is the standard free-energy change, n is the number of electrons, F is the Faraday and $\Delta E_0'$ the difference in standard electrode potentials under physiological conditions (e.g. pH 7). This electron energy is theoretically equal to the osmotic energy required to transport that amount of cations which is equivalent to the change in H^+ ion concentration needed to make the potential of system B equal to that of system A. The total transport is therefore a function of the relative redox potential. H^+ ions are secreted and cations are accumulated in corresponding amounts.

If the difference in redox potential can be maintained by metabolic activity, i.e. respiratory energy, then an ion pump is established. This can operate for anions or cations depending on the sign of the potential difference across the membrane. This mechanism may operate in yeast cells and in gastric mucosa.

Membrane structure and facilitated diffusion

There are good reasons for believing that the movement of solutes across biological membranes is not strictly in accordance with physical principles of simple diffusion. It is convenient to postulate some properties of such membranes and to relate to the model some of the more important views and facts regarding uptake of solutes, especially of inorganic ions.

The penetration of a biological membrane by a solute was first analysed by Davson and Danielli in 1943 in terms of the thermodynamic steps likely to be concerned. They suggested that three sites are involved in the process and each will be subject to potential energy barriers. These sites are (*a*) the external membrane-water interface; (*b*) the interior of the membrane (one site, if of uniform or regular structure across this part); (*c*) the interior membrane-cell cytoplasm interface. In order to overcome each of these barriers the solute must either acquire an equivalent amount of kinetic energy or its movement must be aided by reversible formation and decomposition of intermediate compounds of increased membrane solubility. This is called 'facilitated diffusion'; a term introduced by Danielli in 1954.

The cyclic antibiotic valinomycin, extracted from *Streptococcus fulvissimus* forms a specific complex with potassium ions. On incorporation into an artificial membrane composed of lipid bilayers, it accelerates the diffusion of potassium ions selectively across the membrane. The ability of valinomycin to uncouple oxidative and photophosphorylation at 10^{-7} M is probably related to its ability to facilitate diffusion of the potassium ion. A series of cyclic polyethers ('crown' compounds) capable of complexing with the alkali metals has been synthesized by Professor Mary Truter of University College, London. Compounds like these may be the natural ion carriers in cell membranes.

Membranes of animal cells, and probably of cells in general, have a low surface tension at their exterior surfaces, a high electrical specific resistance, amphoteric charge properties in relation to pH, a thickness of about 7·5 to 10 nm and differential permeability to water, inorganic-charged solutes, sugars and lipid-soluble compounds.

The basic structure consistent with these properties was proposed by Danielli and Davson in 1952 and Danielli in 1954 and has been modified from time to time as more sophisticated ideas and increased knowledge became available (Fig. 4.2).

The basic structure is that of a lipo-protein double layer made up of micelles of lipid molecules coated with protein molecules along the surfaces and the aqueous pores. The protein would be bound to the lipids either by electrostatic bonds and salt bridges if the lipids were arranged with their polar groups outwards. This is predicted if the lipids are synthesised else-

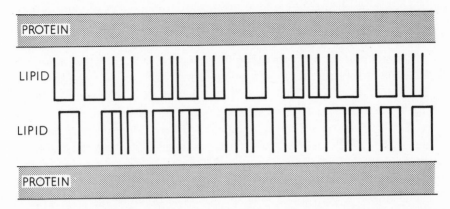

Figure 4.2 Diagram showing a transverse section of a typical membrane according to the theory of Danielli (1954).

where in the cell and discharged into an aqueous phase before being aligned in the membrane. Alternatively if the lipids are formed *in situ* as the membrane is organised it is suggested that they will be orientated with their non-polar groups outwards in a highly stable arrangement as shown in Fig. 4.2. The protein layer would then be bound to the lipid by non-polar bonds. This seems more acceptable as it would then leave the polar groups of the proteins exposed in the pores to react with charged solutes by electrostatic forces or for uncharged solutes by hydrogen bonding which would permit facilitated diffusion for which the experimental evidence is strong. Nevertheless lipids such as phosphatidic acid have ionised carboxyl groups capable of performing this function. The presence of exposed protein polar groups is supported by the value for the isoelectric pH, about 3–4.

The pores in the membrane are envisaged as having probable diameters of the order of ionic radii in most cases, so that movement of larger molecules would be relatively restricted and related to their solubility in lipid complexes. The movement of inorganic and small organic ions would be related to their charge, ionic radius and hydration, e.g. the sodium ion is large, compared with the potassium ion, because of the hydration shell of water around it. The behaviour of membrane pores with ions of opposite sign is not yet clear from this model.

The Danielli–Davson membrane hypothesis was originally formulated on the basis of electron micrographs like those shown in Plates 85 and 86 in which the membranes are clearly two layered, but there is little chemical evidence to substantiate it. A more recent model for mitochondrial membranes proposed by Green and his co-workers (1967) introduces a sub-unit concept. It is suggested that the membrane is made of cuboidal sub-units which adhere at their edges. The sub-units are composed of proteins *between* two phospholipid layers and it is the latter which form the membrane surface, the adhesion being provided by the protein layer. Although this model may be important in structures other than mitochondria, it is likely that more than one membrane system occurs in a single cell.

The retention of some ions by cells is not complete. The work of Briggs in 1957, continued in 1958 with Hope and Pitman, showed that K^+ ions moved out (efflux) as well as into (influx) red-beet storage tissues and bean roots. Although the net uptake (influx minus efflux) is normally large, in some cases the net uptake was quite small compared with the actual rates of influx and efflux. Na^+ ions impede K^+ influx and accelerate K^+ efflux but K^+ ions appear to have much smaller effects on Na^+ fluxes.

In many of the experiments on ion uptake, especially of K^+, Rb^+, etc., an *empirical* relationship exists between external concentration and velocity of uptake over a limited range:

$$v = \frac{V_{\max} c}{c + k}$$

where v is the observed rate of uptake at external ion concentration c, $V_{\max}$ is the asymptotic maximum value of v, and k is the value of c producing a value of $\frac{1}{2} V_{\max}$. This relationship has been inferred from the fit of the data to the expression, and the analogy between the idea of a carrier A and an ion M^+ reacting thus:

$$A + M^+ \underset{k_1}{\overset{k_2}{\rightleftharpoons}} AM \xrightarrow{k_3} A' + M$$

where A is the active site or carrier, A' a modified form and M^+ and M are ionic and other forms of the element.

$$\text{then } v = \frac{V_{\max} c}{c + \dfrac{k_2 + k_3}{k_1}} \quad \text{and} \quad \frac{k_2 + k_3}{k_1} = k \text{ or } K_m$$

(cf. the similar expression used for enzyme kinetics). When $1/v$ is plotted against $1/c$ a straight line should be obtained and experimentally this often appears to be verified, as it is in much of the work on K^+ and Rb^+ uptake studied by Epstein and his associates. When $1/v = 0$ the negative intercept value of $1/c$ equals $-1/k$. From these studies values of k of 10^{-5} to 10^{-2} M have been obtained by different investigators for various cations with different species and the idea of an active site is assumed to be verified. However Briggs (1963) pointed out that very accurate data and additional information are needed to confirm the hypothesis. The passive uptake of cations to balance the operation of an ion pump as defined above operating for anions can equally well explain the data at present available. Briggs suggested that by adjusting the parameters, either an anion pump or an active site hypothesis would explain the observed data of cation uptake, and it is not yet justifiable to choose between the possibilities on the basis of available and insufficiently precise data. It seems that as the uptake of micronutrients Cu, Mn, Zn, etc. from extremely dilute solutions ($0.1-1$ μmol/l) is not appreciably antagonised or profoundly influenced by quite large changes of much higher concentrations of other cations (K^+, Ca^{2+}, etc. at 2–20 ml concentrations) there must be separate sites for their uptake. As the anions Cl^-, SO_4^{2-}, NO_3^- are more limited in variety and often available at high concentrations, the uptake of a wide range of cations with widely differing optimal concentrations cannot be adequately explained on the basis of anion pumps. The matter is nevertheless an open subject for speculation and further study.

Anion respiration hypothesis

This concept, introduced as the result of experiments by Lundegårdh and Burström in 1933, was formulated by Lundegårdh in 1940 and has been progressively modified up to 1955. The basic observation was that the respiration of wheat seedling roots is directly stimulated above a ground level by transfer from distilled water to a dilute salt solution. Lundegårdh decided that the uptake of anions was directly proportional to the increased respiration and that cation uptake was a passive concomitant process. The hypothesis initially rested on the assumption that salt uptake was linked to cyanide- and carbon-monoxide-sensitive respiration, indicative of a cytochrome oxidase dependent system. The anions were thought to be combined with, or electrically associated with the iron in the 'cytochrome' which is reversibly either trivalent Fe^{3+} or divalent Fe^{2+}. The 'cytochrome' was thought to be held in association with the outer cell membrane in such a way that the cytochrome is in the oxidised state at the external surface of the membrane and in the reduced state at the internal surface as implied in Fig. 4.3. The oxidation of ferrocytochrome yields H^+ ions which then exchange for cations, e.g. K^+, while the decrease in charge from Fe^{3+} to Fe^{2+} liberates an associated anion. As one molecule of O_2 yields 4 H^+ ions and absorbs four electrons the anion uptake to oxygen consumption ratio should approach four.

There are several difficulties regarding this hypothesis.

(*a*) Uptake of cations may be as effective as that of anions in stimulating respiration as shown by Epstein in 1954 for uptake of cations from an insoluble cation resin in the absence of anions. There should be non-specific competition between anions for the available carrier, but this is not observed.

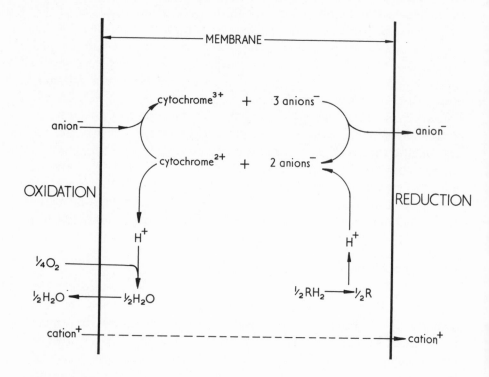

Figure 4.3 The Lundegårdh hypothesis of ion transport across mitochondrial membranes.

While similar ions, e.g. halides, or sulphate and selenate show marked mutual competition, halides, divalent anions or phosphate or nitrate do not compete with ions of a different group in this list. In contrast to this negative situation, cations show highly specific competitive effects, e.g. K^+ and Na^+ at one K^+ concentration range (or site?) but not at another.

(*b*) If the system is operative, the mitochondria, which contain the cytochrome oxidase and other cytochromes of b and c groups, and not the cell-wall membrane must be the site of accumulation, as pointed out by Robertson, Wilkins, Hope and Nestel in 1955 and Robertson in 1956. This was conceded by Lundegårdh in 1955.

(*c*) The uncoupler of oxidative phosphorylation, DNP, was shown by Wilkins and Weeks in 1951 to severely inhibit KCl accumulation by carrot discs in a progressive manner over the whole concentration range tested in spite of the characteristic *increase* in oxygen uptake observed at low and intermediate concentrations. Therefore as noted previously respiration as such is

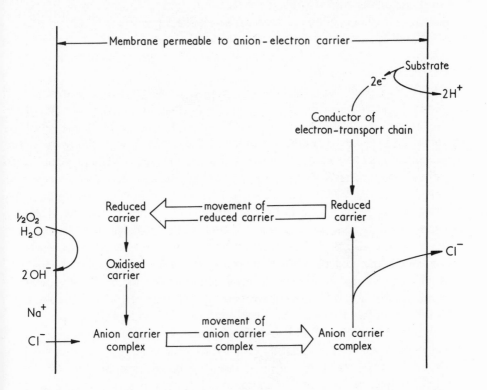

Figure 4.4 Anion (salt) respiration according to the hypothesis of Robertson. From Robertson (1960) *Biol. Rev.* **35**, 231–64.

not directly involved in salt accumulation but ATP formation probably is.

(*d*) The indirectness of effects of respiration and the fact that in the work of Sutcliffe and Hackett in 1957, and later work of Sutcliffe, ratios for anion uptake to oxygen consumption have on occasion substantially exceeded 4:1, indicate that reserve compounds synthesised at some other time can influence or promote ion uptake, and that mechanisms other than those of ion-exchange and direct electron-coupled transport must exist. Sutcliffe found that the highest Na^+ uptake/O_2 consumption ratio by red-beet discs was obtained when sodium bicarbonate was used; values of about 14–15 were observed for short uptake periods (one hour) with 0·01 to 0·04 M bicarbonate decreasing to a ratio of about 6:1 after six hours. With sodium chloride the initial ratio was 6·5 and this fell to 3·3–4·0 over a corresponding period. Two points may be considered in regard to this work. Firstly sodium bicarbonate is a potential inhibitor of cytochrome oxidase. It competes with cytochrome c and also inhibits other iron protein oxidases. The greater Na^+/O_2 ratio obtained with bicarbonate than with chloride is possibly indicative of suppressed O_2 uptake and the operation of alternative mechanisms of energy utilisation. The second point is that the ratio fell sharply after one to two hours indicating that reserve energy mechanisms not demanding immediate oxygen consumption were being exhausted with time.

It is most probable that in plant cells the respiratory activity which is coupled to salt uptake, is located in the mitochondrial particles. These are also the site of oxidative phosphorylation which is strongly inhibited by DNP. Robertson has pointed out that the mitochondria are likely to be centres of ion accumulation. They have a double membrane of about 15 nm width and an unusually low permeability to ions, i.e. a diffusion constant of 10^{-13} cm^2/s compared to 10^{-5} for water. The separation of electrons from protons (H^+ ions) can readily occur in lipid membranes of $7 \cdot 5$ nm or more, so that a respiratory movement of electrons through a matrix of enzymes in structural association across a membrane would provide a pump for the active transport of anions and would simultaneously transport cations as a passive response in exchange for H^+ ions. The electrons would produce OH^- ions at the outer membrane surface. This is the basic principle of anion respiration as viewed by Robertson (see Fig. 4.4) and differs from that of Lundegårdh in involving both the participation of ATP and of the separation of electrons and protons, and in not specifically depending on a cytochrome system. Robertson cited his own work in which in only two cases out of 263 was the ratio of ion uptake to oxygen consumption appreciably in excess of four and concluded that anion respiration was the controlling mechanism in washed carrot tissue. The extra respiration induced by exposure to salts was totally inhibited by carbon monoxide in the dark, by cyanide and by DNP. Azide also inhibits this process, and the carbon monoxide inhibition is reversed by light.

Role of high-energy phosphate and protein synthesis

When one molecule of glucose is oxidised, the heat energy is equal to about 673 000 calories (2820 kJ), and six molecules of oxygen are required. This is equivalent to between seventy-seven and ninety molecules of ATP (depending on the accepted value for heat of hydrolysis of ATP to ADP). The ratio of the number of atoms of acid-labile phosphorus fixed in ATP to the number of atoms of oxygen used in respiration (the P/O ratio) is over six. In fact a P/O ratio of four is more realistic and even this value is possibly high in many tissues, but values approaching six might occur in highly organised sites, e.g. mitochondria or membranes of intact cells, and have been reported very recently.

The basic equation for phosphate esterification into ATP may be written:

$$
\underset{\substack{\| \quad \| \\ O \quad O}}{\underset{| \quad \quad |}{\text{Adenosine}-\text{P}-\text{O}-\text{P}-\text{OH}}} \quad + \quad \underset{\substack{\| \\ O}}{\underset{|}{\text{HO}-\text{P}-\text{OH}}}
$$

$$
\underset{\substack{\| \quad \| \quad \| \\ O \quad O \quad O}}{\underset{| \quad \quad | \quad \quad |}{\text{Adenosine}-\text{P}-\text{O}-\text{P}-\text{O}-\text{P}-\text{OH}}} + H_2O
$$

The uptake of extracellular $H_2PO_4^-$ therefore leads to a net increase of one negative charge and this can be balanced by the uptake of one cation. Since the ATP will probably be bound to protein or some other macromolecule, possibly ribonucleic acid, the Donnan ion will increase in charge and the Donnan equilibrium will change, with complex effects on anion and cation balance.

If the inorganic phosphate is already within the cell (and usually 50–90% of the total phosphate is inorganic phosphate in cells), ATP formation will involve no net change in charge. There will still be a change in the Donnan ion-charge concentration and a change in Donnan equilibrium can occur, but the effect on final equilibrium will be different from that where initially external phosphate is esterified. The magnitude of possible ion uptake associated with direct effects of phosphate esterification is at present unknown.

A situation involving inorganic phosphate esterification other than in ATP can also be envisaged. This could arise from the hydrolysis of reserve carbohydrate such as starch. In the presence of phosphorylase and inorganic phosphate (P_i) the reversible formation of glucose-1-phosphate occurs.

$$
\text{Starch} + P_i \underset{\text{(phosphorylase)}}{\rightleftarrows} \text{Glucose-1-phosphate}
$$

Glucose-1-phosphate is an energy-rich phosphate-bond ester (about 21 kJ/mol) compared with ATP (ADP) (about 29 kJ/mol). However, in a review in 1961 on phosphorylation in plants, Marré regarded this reaction as only a minor source of phosphate energy. It could nevertheless be a 'sink' for removal of inorganic phosphate after absorption because the dissociation of ester phosphate is less than that of inorganic phosphate. Marré emphasised the generally accepted view that in air, ATP is generated almost entirely by oxidative phosphorylation in storage tissues, while in photosynthetic cells ATP is generated by photolysis of water. Marré considered that active or metabolic salt accumulation most probably depends on utilisation of ATP.

Another hypothesis which is now only of historical interest was devised by Steward and Miller in 1954 to explain how ATP and protein synthesis might be related in the process of salt absorption. The essence of the idea was that γ-glutamyl peptides whose synthesis requires ATP could bind ions as carriers, and that when these carriers became attached to RNA, probably in the tonoplast of the vacuole, a rearrangement to produce α-peptide (i.e. protein) linkage occurred. When the protein dissociated from the RNA the bound ions were released into the vacuole. This hypothesis has two limitations. First, it requires that a continual supply of glutamic acid is maintained and presupposes continual protein synthesis; second the process of α-peptide bond formation then visualised is not compatible with current and undoubtedly correct views on protein synthesis.

There is much evidence to link protein synthesis with salt absorption. Apart from the classical work of Steward and his collaborators which showed the usually close relationship between these processes in storage tissues, the experiments of Sutcliffe in 1960 and later in association with Jacoby showed that chloramphenicol, a fairly specific inhibitor of protein synthesis, sharply inhibited salt uptake by red-beet discs. A likely interpretation adopted by Sutcliffe is that protein turnover, i.e. steady synthesis and breakdown at the plasmalemma or outer membrane and probably also at the tonoplast or vacuolar membrane is responsible for reversible ion binding and discharge. This process is nevertheless distinct from the contractile protein hypothesis of Danielli discussed later. Bennett (1956) visualised the actual vesiculation of membrane protein into sacs containing ions as a mechanism of transport but observational evidence for this idea is still lacking. Protein turnover would require a high turnover of ATP for amino-acid activation and for turnover of the various RNA fractions in the cell which are involved in protein synthesis. It is likely that the relationship between protein synthesis and salt uptake is indirect, particularly as Steward (1954) showed that non-growing carrot tissue has a greater ability for ion accumulation than growing carrot cells. Although Steward and Lyndon (1965) do not discount the role of protein turnover in the membranes as a possible mechanism, they prefer to regard the *potential capacity* of the cell to achieve protein synthesis as the important factor in providing another mechanism.

The ions approaching and penetrating the plasmalemma could be bound by randomly circulating carrier molecules consisting of perhaps soluble RNA. These molecules are identified with processes of protein synthesis as amino-acid carriers but might be additionally specialised in nature. Specialised properties of the tonoplast may favour the release of the bound ions into the vacuole. In fact the synthesis of protein in the tonoplast as the vacuole grows could be linked to this process, each amino-acid residue to be incorporated being matched by the discharge of an ion and the simultaneous transport of an ion of opposite sign. The carrier soluble-RNA would then be free to transport another ion and another amino acid.

The conclusions and problems concerning the identity of carriers were discussed by Laties (1959). Carriers for phosphate may be produced at a concentration of about 7×10^{-4} M and for potassium the carrier concentration might be 8×10^{-3} M. The work of Hagen and Hopkins in 1955, noted again later, indicated two carrier sites for phosphate, one specific for $H_2PO_4^-$, and one for HPO_4^{2-}, each with greatly differing affinities. Laties, also in 1959, attempted to show that carriers are continually synthesised and broken down in living cells. By transferring washed chicory root discs to potassium chloride solutions at $0°C$ after being held at room temperature there is a temporary high rate of uptake and if the discs are then transferred to water at $30°C$ and back to potassium chloride at $0°$ there is again a temporary high rate of salt uptake. It was concluded that the rate of synthesis of carrier exceeded breakdown and that the synthetic process is accelerated at higher temperatures.

One other hypothesis concerning the role of ATP in ion transport was proposed by Bennet-Clark in 1956. It was suggested that lecithin, which contains an ionised phosphate group to bind cations, and a quaternary (positively charged) nitrogen atom to bind anions, could be simultaneously a carrier for both anions and cations. Hydrolysis of the lecithin to phosphatidic acid and choline was thought to occur, liberating both bound ions. The choline, with ATP and choline acetylase, could form acetylcholine and this could be sufficiently reactive to regenerate lecithin by a choline-transfer reaction to phosphatidic acid. Rhodamine, which inhibits lecithinase also inhibits salt uptake.

It is conceivable that the cell membrane, in addition to being naturally elastic, may have specific elastic properties at the pores. Goldacre in 1952 supported a mechanism based on the analogy with animal muscular contraction, and the operation of contractile protein in plants is also probable. In this mechanism the reversible combination of a protein resembling myosin with an energy-rich phosphate compound, e.g. ATP, would lead to contraction on hydrolysis of the ATP to ADP, and relaxation when the ADP is rephosphorylated by contact with a supply of metabolically produced ATP or an energy-rich phosphate compound, analogous to the phosphocreatine found in muscle. A contractile protein depending on metabolic energy and ATP could facilitate ion or uncharged solute movement in two quite different ways. One way would be that of a physical carrier, the 'propelled shuttle', as suggested by Danielli in 1954. The carrier protein which is fixed to one side of the membrane extends through the membrane to the other surface. The solute is attached to the free end of the protein and the protein then contracts, moving the solute across the barrier.

Another mechanism depends on the probability that when a conformational change occurs in protein shape its binding affinity for ions by charged sites or for uncharged solutes, e.g. glucose, by hydrogen bonds can change considerably. Hydrolysis of ATP to yield ADP liberates energy which may result in protein contraction. In this form the protein might bind K^+ ions more tightly. This metal-combined state might then promote re-phosphorylation of the ADP group with release of contraction and weakening of the protein-K^+ bond. The K^+ ions might then be released. Hydrolysis of the ATP groups would then recur to repeat the cycle. Protein bound chelating structures (see page 84) might provide a transporting system of this type.

Metabolic requirements and responses

In any of the mechanisms mentioned in the previous section a constant source of energy-rich phosphate derived from metabolic activity would be needed. Energy-rich phosphate is produced, particularly as ATP, by the uptake of inorganic phosphate in several ways, including: (*a*) oxidative phosphorylation in mitochondrial particles where oxidation of intermediate electron carriers is coupled to esterification of phosphate into ATP; (*b*) glycolytic reactions where oxidation of soluble glyceraldehyde-3-phosphate by NAD^+ is linked to uptake of inorganic phosphate eventually producing ATP; (*c*) in photosynthetic phosphorylation by chloroplasts to yield ATP. Each of these ways could be linked to cation uptake in the appropriate sites, e.g. roots, storage tissues, mitochondria or chloroplasts.

Good evidence for the close relationship between production of ATP and uptake of salts is provided by the work of Robertson, Wilkins and Weeks (1951) who showed that KCl uptake by carrot tissues is almost totally inhibited by concentrations of 2, 4-dinitrophenol (DNP) which uncouple oxidative phosphorylation without inhibiting oxygen uptake. Steward and Lyndon found that Gramicidin-S, which is thought to inhibit phosphorylation, also somewhat inhibited absorption of caesium by carrot tissues. The effects of DNP have been widely observed in many salt-accumulating tissues.

Salt respiration, originally called anion respiration, which was first observed by Lundegårdh and Burström in 1955 is the increase of oxygen uptake produced when a tissue is exposed to a salt solution from which uptake can occur, in comparison with the rate of respiration in distilled water.

It is widely believed that the rate of respiration (oxygen uptake) is controlled in many tissues by the *availability* of phosphate acceptors. In effect this is the concentration of ADP or the ADP/ATP ratio. If it is postulated that the uptake of ions or even their approach to the site of uptake promotes the conversion of ATP to ADP then respiration will be stimulated in the manner of salt respiration. The evidence for phosphate-coupled respiration as the enzyme source for ion uptake seems undeniably strong. Experiments by MacRobbie and Dainty in 1959 on the uptake of KCl by *Nitellopsis obtusa* which is a member of the Characeae with giant cells, found in brackish habitats, indicated that the chloride pump is sited in the vacuolar membrane while the sodium-excluding pump is sited in the outer cytoplasmic membrane. Robertson considers that mitochondria carried by protoplasmic streaming could act as carriers between the outer and inner cell membranes.

Robertson has pointed out that the specificity of salt-accumulation mechanisms may differ greatly in different species and organs. Widely differing ratios of Na^+/K^+ uptake, effects of Ca^{2+} but not Mg^{2+} on K^+ uptake, nonspecificity for uptake of Cl^-, Br^- or I^- by barley or carrot, but specific accumulation of I^- by marine algae, and the importance of reduction of NO_3^- to NH_4^+ within the plant all indicate a different emphasis to be found in different circumstances. The discovery that the movement of K^+ ions into and out of chloroplasts is photochemically controlled, provides an additional potential mechanism for ion accumulation in leaves stimulated by light.

The chemi-osmotic hypothesis of Mitchell

In 1961 Mitchell proposed a mechanism for ion accumulation in mitochondria and chloroplasts which is compatible with many of the properties of the system known to operate in these organelles. The principle of this hypothesis is that ATP is split and resynthesised on a single-oriented enzyme which is situated in the organelle membrane and in this process a charge separation occurs across the membrane. Due to the orientation of the electron carriers (cytochromes, flavins, etc.) the oxidation-reduction step responsible for ATP regeneration and the step of ATP hydrolysis both generate hydrogen ions on the same side of the membrane. Since the ATP-ase is reversible, hydrogen ions formed during the process of respiration or photosynthesis would cause ATP synthesis. The hydrogen ions formed on the opposite side of the membrane during the process of ATP regeneration are neutralised by the hydroxyl ions formed by the simultaneous electron transfer process (oxidative or photosynthetic phosphorylation) on the same side of the membrane (Fig. 4.5). The accumulation of the hydrogen ions on one side of the membrane and the corresponding hydrogen-ion depletion (hydroxyl-ion accumulation) on the opposite side of the membrane causes a considerable imbalance in pH across the membrane. The system therefore operates as a hydrogen-ion

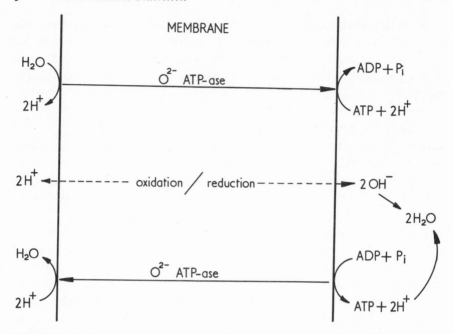

Figure 4.5 The chemi-osmotic hypothesis of Mitchell (1961). From Robertson (1968) in *Protons, Electrons, Phosphorylation, and Active Transport.* Cambridge University Press.

pump, and since the process is reversible the establishment of a pH gradient across the membrane would result in the synthesis of ATP. Ion transport would occur if a cation exchanges for a hydrogen ion or if an anion exchanges for a hydroxyl ion. Specificity of accumulation would result if the membrane has properties of differential permeability to the ions. Charge separation can also account for the light-induced swelling of chloroplasts. The experimentally determined stoicheiometry for electron transfer, H^+ transport and ATP formation in chloroplasts suggest that these processes are sequentially linked, and gives added support to the chemi-osmotic hypothesis. Effects of uncouplers are explained by their properties of rendering membranes permeable to H^+ ions, resulting in the suppression of phosphorylation. Circulation of mitochondria in the cytoplasm could explain the transport of ions through cells and tissues.

ATP-ases which are stimulated by potassium ions have been demonstrated in the mitochondrial, microsomal, and cell-wall membranes of oat leaves by Fisher and Hedges (1969). These enzymes, which are also magnesium dependent, may form a part of the mechanism involved in ion uptake.

The importance of the chemi-osmotic hypothesis lies in the fact that both chloroplasts and mitochondria are known to be major sites of ion accumulation in plant cells. However, although this theory undoubtedly has wide implications for ion accumulation in plants it is at present difficult to account for vacuolar accumulation by this process and it seems certain that no single hypothesis can account for all aspects of ion accumulation in plant cells.

Specific ion-absorption effects

The uptake of particular ions has been studied by many different investigators. Some specific points are summarised here.

Epstein, Hagen and their associates, Fried and Noggle, and Bange and Tanada, have made intensive studies on the uptake of monovalent cations and interactions of them with calcium in barley and maize roots. On the assumption that the ion reacts with a carrier or an uptake site by a dissociable combination which is determined by ion concentration and affinity for the site, just as an enzyme is considered to combine with a substrate, they applied the methods of enzyme kinetics to the study of monovalent ion uptake. One of the parameters determined in such studies is the concentration producing half maximal rate of uptake or reaction velocity (K_m in molar units) and the other parameter is the maximum velocity (V_{max}). These values are determined by plotting the reciprocal of concentration (horizontally) against the reciprocal of observed velocity (vertically) from which the K_m is found as the reciprocal of the horizontal intercept (negative) and V_{max} as the reciprocal of the vertical intercept. If C/V is plotted against C, the K_m (negative) is equal to the horizontal intercept. A small value for the K_m indicates a high affinity between the reactants. From such analyses Epstein's group find that there are two separate K_m values for uptake of K^+ by barley roots indicating either two sites, mechanisms or conditions of the receptor, termed here condition I and condition II. The K_m values are about 2×10^{-5} M for condition I, and 2 or 3×10^{-4} M for condition II in barley, and $1 \cdot 5 \times 10^{-6}$ M for I and $2 \cdot 6 \times 10^{-4}$ M for II in maize.

Tanada's work showed that the presence of calcium in the medium increased potassium and rubidium uptake up to eight times. The affinity of the monovalent ion for the binding site was increased by calcium (5×10^{-4} to 10^{-3} M). It was suggested that RNA and $-SH$ groups on proteins were the binding sites involved in potassium uptake. In further studies with maize using rubidium and caesium as radioactively labelled ions Bange and Meyer have questioned the idea originally presented by Epstein and Hagen that there are two sites of different affinities for monovalent ions. They consider the possibility, again by analogy with current ideas on enzyme structure, that there is only one site, but that its affinity for an ion is a function of the ionic concentration.

When the affinity of an enzyme for its substrate increases with substrate concentration this is known as substrate co-operation. Reaction velocity under these conditions increases in a sigmoidal rather than a hyperbolic relationship with increasing concentration of substrate. This phenomenon occurs as a result of structural changes in the protein induced by the substrate, as substrate concentration increases. A single uptake site may therefore show kinetics which vary with the ionic concentration.

Sutcliffe in 1957 similarly questioned the interpretation of Epstein's group and suggested that his own data with red-beet tissue were adequately explained by the existence of only one site or mechanism for all monovalent cation uptake. Sutcliffe, like Briggs, has pointed out that more extensive data are essential before a distinction can be made between these different ideas, namely mechanisms dependent on specific sites, co-operative sites or ion pumps.

The uptake of inorganic phosphorus as phosphate ions has been studied by Hagen and his associates since 1955, by Loughman and Scott Russell between 1953 and 1957, and by Jackson, Hendricks and Vasta in 1962. Hagen's group concluded that the ions $H_2PO_4^-$ and HPO_4^{2-} were absorbed at separate sites. This was deduced from the effects of pH on uptake in relation to the relative proportions of the two ions present at different pH values. HPO_4^{2-} is the ion most readily absorbed by barley roots for which the affinity of the site is 10^5 times greater than for $H_2PO_4^-$. Jackson, Hendricks and Vasta compared the effects of inhibitors and other factors on uptake of phosphate by barley roots and phosphorylation by mitochondria and decided that the comparisons were so close that the mitochondria are the site of the phosphate uptake, and that the rate of phosphorylation is the rate-limiting factor in uptake. This conclusion may be related to the discussion on the role of ATP formation in phosphate uptake outlined above. These results are in fact in accordance with the earlier work of Loughman and Scott Russell who found that inorganic phosphate is esterified in a nucleotide within one minute of coming into contact with the roots of barley, and that at very low concentrations (0·001 p.p.m.), phosphate uptake is independent of DNP-sensitive respiration but probably combines with a previous product of respiration (i.e. a phosphate-acceptor) which is linked metabolically with a nucleotide phosphate.

The work of Harley and his associates on the uptake of phosphate by mycorrhiza of beech roots (page 74) has shown beyond doubt that respiratory activity is essential for continuous uptake, and it seems unnecessary at this stage to draw a distinction between direct respiratory dependence and the activity of a product of respiration as a carrier.

The absorption of nitrogen occurs readily as nitrate anions or as ammonium cations. The former will be reduced in the cytoplasm (or possibly in microbodies—see Chapter 7) before yielding ammonia. This, whether produced *in situ*, or absorbed as such will be further metabolised to amino acids and proteins and removed from the system. Lycklama in 1963 found that ammonium nitrogen inhibited nitrate uptake by rye-grass roots between 15°C and 35°C but had no effect between 5°C and 15°C. He interpreted this as a complex response, depending on the uptake process and the reduction of nitrate in the cell by nitrate reductase. It was suggested that the inhibition of nitrate reductase by ammonium was not operative on the absorption process until the rate of nitrate reductase activity in the absence of ammonium was sufficiently rapid at the higher temperatures to influence the rate of uptake.

The uptake of nitrate and ammonium at high concentrations (5–10 mM) tends to be affected in opposite ways by pH, that of nitrate being favoured at pH values of 4–6, that of ammonium being most rapid between 6 and 7·5 in many plants. H^+ ions or other cations may exchange for NH_4^+ ions but may be absorbed simultaneously with NO_3^- ions. Experiments of Van der Honert and Hoogmans in 1955, and Wallace and Mueller in 1957 together suggest that at low concentrations (below 2 mM) the affinity of sites for nitrate uptake is scarcely affected by pH but that the number of functional sites decreases with increasing pH from 5 to 8. Becking in 1956 found that the affinity of maize roots for NH_4^+ ions was very high (K_m $1·3 \times 10^{-5}$ M) but that pH over the range 4·6–7·0 had little effect on apparent K_m. This indicates that uptake at very low concentrations occurs as NH_4^+ rather than as NH_4OH. At higher concentrations, it is likely from the work of Lycklama in 1963 with rye grass, that uptake occurs mainly in the form of NH_4OH above pH 6·3. Moreover, the effects of pH in the solution relate both to the concentration of NH_4OH in the external medium and to the corresponding cellular pH and cellular NH_4OH concentration. Experimental results of Clark and Shine and Arrington and Shine obtained in 1934 and 1936 relating pH to uptake by tomatoes of ammonium nitrogen at high concentrations are adequately explained in terms of the relationship of Warren:

$$\frac{[NH_4OH] \; intra \; \text{cellular}}{[NH_4OH] \; extra \; \text{cellular}} = \frac{1 + 10 \, (pK_a - \text{pH intra})}{1 + 10 \, (pK_a - \text{pH extra})}$$

where $pK_a = 9·3$ for NH_4OH.

Becking found that the exchange of H^+ ions for NH_4^+ ions observed at low concentrations in young roots of maize was replaced by exchange of K^+ ions at higher concentrations or by older roots. The experiments of Kylin in 1953 have similarly shown that assimilation of sulphate into organic forms occurs rapidly after absorption by wheat roots.

Translocation

Inside the root tissues the ions diffuse (or are pumped) towards the endodermis which is characterised by a suberised layer, the Casparian strip, within the cellulose of the radial cell walls, and the ions are therefore compelled to move within the protoplasts of the endodermis. The cells of the endodermis are therefore capable of regulating the access of ions to the stele. Stelar tissue appears to be active in pumping ions into the xylem vessels and tracheids. The ions are moved from the roots in the xylem with the transpiration stream, or in water delivered by root pressure, to the aerial parts of the plant. Root pressure is an osmotic phenomenon resulting from the pumping of ions into the xylem.

Gunning and Pate (1969) have described specialised cells in many different species of plants which have a very large surface to volume ratio. These cells are undoubtedly concerned with the movement of solutes within the plant and have for this reason been called 'transfer cells' (Plate 2). They may be seen in the cuticle of the submerged leaves of aquatic plants (e.g. *Elodea*, *Vallisneria* and *Ranunculus fluitans*). They are also associated with the xylem and phloem in many terrestrial vascular plants.

Mineral content of tissues

Plants tend to absorb all elements present in nutrient media but show some selectivity and species variation. The mineral content of the leaves of a typical normal plant is shown in Table 4.2. The last column shows the concentrations

Table 4.2   Typical concentrations of mineral elements in foliage of normal plants

Element	p.p.m. in dry matter	mM in cell sap*	Nutrient solution† (mM)
N	15 000–35 000	150–350	15
P	1500–3000	7–14	1
S	1000–3000	4·5–140	1·5
Ca	10 000–50 000	35–175	5
Mg	2500–10 000	15–60	1·5
K	15 000–50 000	55–180	5
Na	200–2000	1–12	1
Fe	50–300	0·15–0·75	0·1
Mn	25–250	0·06–0·6	0·01
Cu	5–15	0·01–0·03	0·001
Zn	15–75	0·03–0·15	0·002
Co	0·2–29	0·005–0·05	0·0002
B	15–100	0·2–1·3	0·05
Mo	0·5–5	0·004–0·075	0·0005
Cl	100–1000	0·4–4	0·1

* This value merely indicates in round numbers the total aqueous concentration possible without regard to insoluble, lipid, or other structural fractions.
† Typical nutrient solution concentrations.

provided in a normal nutrient solution which would be expected to yield values similar to those shown in the preceding column.

The location of mineral elements may be heterogeneous. Roots tend to retain metals such as lead, cobalt, nickel, copper, zinc, iron, manganese, chromium and vanadium; chloroplasts are rich in copper, iron and magnesium compared with the total leaf cytoplasm, and calcium may be accumulated in mitochondria whereas these organelles are relatively lacking in boron.

Some species appear to be confined to certain soils which are volcanic or mineralised and often accumulate unusually high concentrations of particular elements in certain parts. Some plants appear to extract unusually large amounts of certain elements from the soil. These types of plants are referred to as biogeochemical indicators and accumulator species and examples are given in Table 4.3. Plants of these species and genera are often associated with

Table 4.3 Examples of some accumulator plants and biogeochemical indicators

Element	Species	Remarks
Gold	*Equisetum palustre*	60 p.p.m. Au in ash (?). Volcanic soils of Slovakia
	Typha latifolia	Brazil
Mercury	*Holosteum umbellatum*	Deposited as elemental Hg in sterile seed capsules. Volcanic soils of Bohemia
	Arenaria setacea	Spain
Lead	*Tussilago farfara*	Germany
Selenium	*Astragalus racemosus* A. *pattersonii*, A. *bisulcatus* A. *pectinatus*, *Stanleya pinnata* *Oonopsis* spp.	Primary Se indicators restricted to seleniferous soils. Contain up to 15 000 p.p.m. Se in dry matter
	Machaeranthera ramosa *Aster* spp. *Atriplex canescens*	Secondary indicators accumulate Se from seleniferous soils but are not confined thereto
Aluminium	*Camellia sinensis* (Tea)	May require Al in addition to being an accumulator
	Hydrangea macrophylla	Accumulates Al, and this also determines blue flower colour as in several other species
	Faramea spp. *Rudgea* sp. *Symplocos tinctoria*	N. and S. America. Up to 50% Al_2O_3 in dry matter
Fluorine	*Dichapetalum cymosum* D. *toxicarium*	60–235 p.p.m. F in dry matter. S. African soils
Barium	*Bertholletia excelsa* (Brazil nut)	40 000 p.p.m. in nut
Zinc	*Thlaspi calaminare* *Viola tricolor*	20% Zn in ash The calamine flora, often restricted to Zn-rich soils of Germany and Austria

Element	Species	Remarks
Copper	*Caryophyllaceae* gen. *Lychnis* spp. *Silene* spp. *Bechium homblei*	
Manganese	*Digitalis purpurea*	Germany and Switzerland
Nickel	*Betula alba* *Alyssum bertolonii* *Hybanthus floribundus*	Serpentine soils. Ni 2% in ash Serpentine soils. Ni 10% in ash Ni 23% in ash
Cobalt	*Alyssum bertoloni*	Serpentine soils endemic flora up to 15 000 p.p.m. Co in dry matter
Lithium	*Thalictrum* spp. *Lycium* spp. and others of Ranunculaceae and Solanaceae	Characteristic of Lithium flora
Rare Earth group	*Carya illinoensis* (Pecan) *Carya* sp. (Hickory)	Up to 2000 p.p.m. in dry matter. Parts of USA
Silver	*Eriogonum ovalifolium*	Indicator plant
Arsenic	*Pseudotsuga menziesii*	Up to 2000–5000 p.p.m. in ash
Boron	*Chenopodiaceae, Plumbaginaceae* gen.	Indicator plants
Bromine	*Cucurbitaceae* gen.	More than 15 p.p.m. Br in some spp.
Radium	*Bertholletia excelsa* (Brazil nut)	2–2·3 pCi/g
Iodine	*Laminaria* Kelp (seaweed)	First discovery of iodine
Uranium	*Sarcobatus* sp.	7400 p.p.m. of ash in roots

particular soil conditions, e.g. the seleniferous soils; the serpentine flora on soils rich in variable amounts of chromium, nickel and cobalt; the calamine flora on soils rich in zinc; the volcanic aged soils often of very complex composition, and the active volcanic areas or solfatara 'regions' often high in aluminium, sulphur and boron. The plants are often highly adapted to these soils. There is evidence from the work of Bradshaw in 1952 and Jowett in 1958 and 1959 that the operation of the selective process of adaptation can be observed in recent history in relation to the colonisation of mine dumps and similar outcrops by ecotypes of common species confined to or found in such habitats (page 109).

In addition to the problems arising from the generally acknowledged toxicity of heavy metals for animals, accumulation of lead, zinc and cadmium in food plants may be a factor in determining the development of human cancer.

The supposed ability of *Equisetum* to accumulate gold has recently been questioned by Cannon *et al.* (1968) who found that this plant and many others tested contain no more than 1 p.p.m. of gold. Further study by Cannon of the analytical procedures used in demonstrating the high levels of gold in previous work suggest that other metals beside gold were included in the analysis. Although it may seem surprising that gold can be sufficiently soluble to be taken up by plants even to 1 p.p.m., it appears from the work of Shacklette *et al.* (1970) that plants possessing cyanogenic glycosides might have the ability to accumulate this element by dissolving the gold as the cyanide complex.

Further Reading

Andersen, W. P. (Ed.) (1973) *Ion Transport in Plants*. Academic Press: London and New York. 630 pp.

Bowen, H. J. M. (1966) *Trace Elements in Biochemistry*. Academic Press: London and New York. 241 pp.

Briggs, G. E., Hope, A. B. and Robertson, R. N. (1961) *Electrolytes and Plant Cells*. Blackwell Scientific Publications: Oxford. 217 pp.

Dainty, J. (1962) Ion transport and electrical potential in plant cells. *A. Rev. Pl. Physiol.* **13**, 379–402.

Epstein, E. (1972) *Mineral Nutrition of Plants*. Chapters 5 to 9. John Wiley: New York, London, Sydney and Toronto.

Harley, J. L. (1969) *The Biology of Mycorrhiza*. 2nd edn. Leonard Hill: London. 334 pp.

Humphries, E. C. (1958) Entry of nutrients into the plant and their movement within it. *Fertilizer Society Proceedings* No. 48.

Jennings, D. H. (1963) *The Absorption of Solutes by Plant Cells*. Oliver and Boyd: Edinburgh and London. 204 pp.

Lamb, C. A., Bentley, O. G. and Beattie, J. M. (1958) *Trace Elements*. Academic Press: New York and London. 416 pp.

Mitchell, P. (1966) Chemiosmotic coupling in oxidative and photosynthetic phosphorylation. *Biol. Rev.* **41**, 445–502.

Packer, L., Murakami, S. and Mehard, C. W. (1970) Ion transport in chloroplasts and plant mitochondria. *A. Rev. Pl. Physiol.* **21**, 271–304.

Peterson, P. J. (1971) Unusual accumulations of elements by plants and animals. *Sci. Prog. Oxf.* **59**, 505–26.

Richardson, M. (1968) *Translocation in Plants*. Studies in Biology No. 10. Edward Arnold (Sponsored by the Institute of Biology). 60 pp.

Robertson, R. N. (1960) Ion transport and respiration. *Biol. Rev.* **35**, 231–64.

Schütte, K. H. (1964) *The Biology of the Trace Elements*. Crosby Lockwood: London. 228 pp.

Society of Experimental Biology Symposium No. 8 (1954) *Active Transport and Secretion*. Cambridge University Press. 516 pp.

Steward, F. C. and Sutcliffe, J. F. (1959) Plants in relation to inorganic salts. Chapter 4, pp. 253–478 in Vol. II *Plant Physiology* (Ed. F. C. Steward). Academic Press: New York and London.

Sutcliffe, J. F. (1962) *Mineral Salts Absorption in Plants*. Pergamon Press: New York, Oxford, London and Paris. 194 pp.

Sutcliffe, J. F. and Baker, D. (in press) *Plants and Mineral Salts*. Studies in Biology. Edward Arnold (Sponsored by the Institute of Biology).

5
Soil Problems and Diagnostic Aspects of Mineral Nutrition

'For a scientist should be prompted by the desire to relate science to things other than science, to the world in which science is used, to the values of a civilised society.'

Sir Edward Appleton

This chapter presents some examples of nutrient disorders which are associated with particular soils or soil conditions and discusses methods and problems of diagnosis of mineral disorders. Symbols are used for most of the elements for purposes of brevity, preceded by $-$(deficiency) or $+$(excess).

Many disorders in field conditions are associated with the soil pH or H^+ ion concentration when this is markedly below or above neutrality (pH 7·0) (Fig. 5.1).

Soil acidity and mineral toxicity

When pH values lie below about 6·5 many crop plants are unable to grow satisfactorily. However, the tolerance of plants to soil acidity varies greatly and the causes of poor fertility or injury are complex. The subject has been investigated using sand culture to separate the possible factors and reproduce the characteristic symptoms and relative sensitivity associated with different crop species.

The factors which may be important in determining behaviour in acid soils have been summarised as follows:

1. Direct injurious effects of H^+ ions.
2. Indirect effects of H^+ ions.
    (a) Impaired absorption of several elements, especially Ca, Mg, K, P, as a physiological effect.
    (b) Increased soil availability of Mn, Al, sometimes Fe, and possibly heavy metals including Cu and Ni, leading to uptake of toxic quantities.
    (c) Reduced availability of P when fixed by Al or Fe before or after absorption.
    (d) Reduced availability of Mo.

(e) Low actual concentration of Ca, Mg, K, B, and sometimes Cu or other micronutrients as a result of prolonged leaching of the soil profile at low pH.

(f) Unfavourable biotic conditions, e.g.
   (i) impaired N fixation;
   (ii) poor mycorrhizal activity resulting in reduced absorption of P and K;
   (iii) increased infection by some soil pathogens, especially clubroot of brassicas (*Plasmodiophora brassicae*).

(g) Accumulation of organic acids and failure of micro-organisms to decompose toxic residues and production of unfavourable redox balance resulting in reducing conditions.

Some examples of the complexity of plant response to soil acidity may be noted. Brassicas and French beans are especially sensitive to excess Mn, swedes and cauliflowers being more sensitive, and some kale varieties and rape being less sensitive in this group. Leaf-cupping and chlorotic leaf margins with blue-black necrotic areas in marginal veins and midribs are typical symptoms of Mn toxicity (Plate 69). Brassicas are, however, relatively tolerant to excess Al. Brassicas such as swedes or cauliflowers cannot tolerate acid soils because of the Mn factor and also because they are liable to suffer from Ca or Mo deficiencies. Any of these conditions or a complex of them can occur under field conditions and their relative importance may change year by year until lime is applied.

Sugar beet and celery are particularly sensitive to excess Al which causes severe root injury, but tolerate high concentrations of Mn. The Al factor is the cause of failure of beet to grow in even slightly acid soils. Potatoes are generally considered to tolerate soil acidity and are not particularly sensitive to concentrations of Al or Mn which are toxic to beet or cauliflowers respectively. However, in some soils the Ca supply is insufficient for normal tuber formation and the multiple diminutive and deformed tubers described in Chapter 6 are produced (Plate 14). Light applications of lime are effective in curing this condition which can occur before leaf symptoms of Ca deficiency are produced.

Barley is injured by both Al and Mn excess, though its sensitivity to either may be slightly less than that of beet or swedes to their respective injurious factors. Oats and rye on the other hand are relatively tolerant to both Al and Mn excess and have low Ca requirements so that they do well in fairly acid soils where barley will fail. Many plants fail at the flowering stage when deficient in Ca. Clovers, linseed and tulips are examples of crops which suffer in this way as a result of soil acidity. Lack of Mg and low pH inhibit nodulation

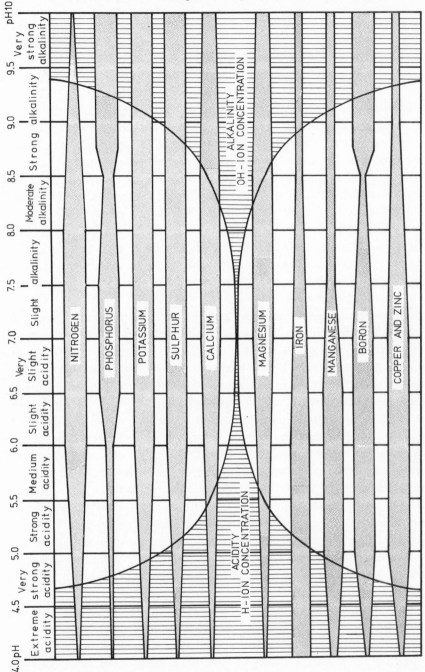

Figure 5.1 Chart showing the general trend of the relation between soil pH and the availability of plant nutrients. From Truog (1951) in *Mineral Nutrition of Plants*. University of Wisconsin Press.

of legumes and nitrogen deficiency results because of inability to fix nitrogen. Lack of Mo also has this effect and is controlled usually either by liming to raise the pH or by application of small amounts of Mo to the soil.

The relative tolerance of a wide range of plants to soil acidity as a whole was classified in 1926 by Arrhenius, the Swedish agriculturalist. When the various separate factors studied by sand culture are combined, the relative behaviour of experimental crops closely reproduces the classification derived for field conditions, thus showing the validity of the approach and the integrated effect of the numerous factors in producing the overall response. In some cases in the same area of acid soil, cauliflower may show Mo deficiency, marrowstem kale Mn toxicity, beet and barley Al toxicity, oats Mg deficiency and potatoes Ca deficiency in the tubers. The leaching factor may be revealed when lime is applied. In some cases liming a formerly acid soil results in Bo deficiency when magnesian (dolomitic) limestone is used and magnesium deficiency when plain lime ($CaCO_3$) is applied to a sugar-beet crop. Calcium ions antagonise Mn uptake and protect against Mn excess but do not influence Al toxicity in the same way.

Manganese excess sometimes induces Fe deficiency under field conditions. The classical example is the chlorosis of pineapples growing in the manganiferous soils of Hawaii. Beans also show Fe deficiency in Puerto Rico in acid-manganiferous soils. The problems of manganese and other types of metal-induced iron deficiency will be discussed in Chapter 6. Extensive analytical studies have all shown beyond doubt that wide variations in Mn/Fe ratio and in total Mn content have little or no relationship with iron deficiency. There are however notable differences in the ratio for different species.

Aluminium excess immobilises P in many soils, but some crops, e.g. swedes, can obtain phosphorus from aluminium phosphate without injury. Some plants, e.g. barley, show P deficiency symptoms when Al is present at only 2–5 p.p.m. in the rooting medium. Roots fail to elongate and become gelatinous. Of two varieties of dwarf bean, one—'The Prince'—is severely injured by Al at 3–9 p.p.m. even when P is in excess in chemically equivalent concentrations, but another variety—'Masterpiece'—tolerates Al at concentrations up to 27 p.p.m. (1 mM) when P is present in equivalent concentrations.

The complexity of the soil acidity problem is illustrated by an experiment summarised in Table 5.1. Here are recorded the appearance of visible symptoms of deficiencies of Ca, Mg, K, P and N, and excess of Mn as they occurred in potatoes grown in a multiplot lime-fertiliser trial on acid heathland. Magnesium deficiency was general except for P only, NK unlimed and NP limed. Giving P induced deficiency of K, and K induced deficiency of P.

Table 5.1   Summary of visible symptom diagnosis on potatoes growing in a field trial on newly ploughed acid heathland soil. (From work of Wallace, Morley Davies, Nicholas and Hewitt, 1946)

Treatments	Nil	+P	+K	+NK	+NP	+PK	+NPK
No lime	−Ca	−Ca	−Ca	−Ca	−Ca	−Ca	−Ca
	−Mg		−Mg		−Mg	−Mg	−Mg
	−K	−K	−P	−P	−K	−N	
	+Mn	+Mn	+Mn	+Mn	+Mn	+Mn	+Mn
Lime (1–3 tonnes/hectare)	−Mg		−Mg	−Mg		−Mg	−Mg
		−N	−P	−P		−N	
	−K	−K	−K		−K		
		(+Mn)	−N				+Mn

Edaphic ecotypes and toxic soils

Studies by Bradshaw, Jowett and their collaborators have shown that *Festuca ovina* has evolved into edaphic ecotypes with considerable differences in Ca requirements. Ecotypes from upland acid soils produced optimal growth with 20 p.p.m. Ca in culture solutions and were depressed by 100 p.p.m. Ecotypes from calcareous soils showed progressive increase in yield up to 100 p.p.m. Ca. By contrast, *Agrostis tenuis* did not show ecotype evolution of this nature. All strains tested showed negligible response to Ca supply at pH 4–5·5 but showed a positive response to Ca at higher pH values, as did also *Cynosurus cristatus*. *Nardus stricta* grew well at low Ca levels, 20 p.p.m. being optimal at pH 4·0; at pH 5·5, 5 p.p.m. Ca was adequate, and at pH 6·5 the calcium requirement was extremely low.

Knowledge of the tolerance of plants to excesses of certain elements is important in the reclamation of toxic mine wastes.

Evolution of strains tolerant to heavy metals including Pb, Cu, Ni and Zn has been studied in *Agrostis tenuis*, *Festuca ovina* and other Gramineae by Bradshaw (see Plate 64). In some strains the excess soil concentrations of Cu, Pb or Zn appear marginally beneficial. There is therefore evidence for a great degree of selection in a short period of time because many of these examples come from mine areas of very recent geological history. The evolution is also quite specific in the nature of tolerance. A strain which has become tolerant to Cu is not tolerant to Pb or Zn; tolerance to Ni does not carry tolerance to Cu or Zn. Bradshaw has shown that tolerant plants of *Agrostis* do not exclude the heavy metals, and Turner (1970) suggests that the cell walls of the root bind the toxic metals in the tolerant strains of this grass. Wilkins has found that tolerance to Pb in strains of *Festuca ovina* is gene-controlled and dominant in selected parents. Some Pb-adapted strains grew better in the mine dump soils than in normal garden soils. The species *Streptanthus glandulosus* is practically confined to serpentine soils which have excesses of Cr and Ni as well as Mg. On some volcanic soils in parts of Czechoslovakia, an *Equisetum* was said to accumulate gold in sufficient quantity to allow its isolation as the pure metal (see page 102), and elemental mercury was found to occur in the fruits of *Holosteum umbellatum* growing in these soils. In Japanese volcanic soils some species accumulate and appear to benefit from aluminium. Serpentine soils are rich in magnesium and this factor has been found to cause calcium deficiency in lettuce and tomatoes.

Plants growing under galvanised fencing become tolerant to the zinc which is eluted into the soil, and evolutionary adaptation can arise very rapidly in these circumstances. The physiological mechanism of heavy metal tolerance is not clear, and in some cases it may be due to ionic exclusion while in other cases the explanation is due almost certainly to metabolic adaptation.

Soils derived from overlying igneous or volcanic rocks, serpentine formations and shales frequently contain relatively high concentrations of toxic elements including Ni, Cr, Cu, Zn, V and Se. Oats show symptoms of Ni toxicity in areas of north-east Scotland. Mitchell found over 5000 p.p.m. Ni in soils derived from ultrabasic or serpentine rocks. The symptoms of the toxicity may be reproduced by growing oats in sand culture with 25 p.p.m. Ni. Leaves show irregular diagonally-banded chlorotic (white) striations. Excess especially of Zn but also of Cu (Plate 65) and Cr (Plate 70) usually causes the appearance of yellow/green interveinal chlorosis closely resembling Fe deficiency as described in Chapter 6. Ni toxicity (Plate 71) may also induce Fe deficiency and possibly symptoms most nearly resembling Mn deficiency in potatoes, and Zn may induce Mn deficiency in beet. Other examples of heavy metal toxicity are given in Plates 66 to 68.

The analysis of appropriate parts of certain species is sometimes a valuable and even specific indication of mineral deposits some distance beneath the surface. The technique of bio-geochemical prospecting which has been developed to a finely specialised subject by Professor Webb at Imperial College, London, based on this type of specific relationship is economically important in revealing potential mineral ore concentrations and in delineating areas of potential toxity to animals.

Boron attains toxic levels in some irrigated soils or where sodium borate occurs in the soil surface, as in maritime or arid soils.

The chlorosis of pineapples in Hawaii and Puerto Rico is a classical example of iron deficiency induced in manganiferous soils containing up to 10% MnO_2. Industrial sewage deposits distributed on arable soils can cause complex and characteristic symptoms in potatoes, cereals, beet and kale, but it is difficult to elucidate which metal is the cause of the disorders. Such crops often contain 100 to 5000 p.p.m. of Zn, Mn, Cr, Co, Ni, V, etc. and the distinction between affected and relatively healthy plants in the same area is often not obvious from analysis of the leaves.

Calcareous and alkaline soils

Soil pH may be considerably above neutrality when sodium bicarbonate, magnesium carbonate or limestone or excess calcium carbonate is present. The pH range is above 9 for bicarbonate to just above 8 for magnesium carbonate and about 7·7 for calcium carbonate.

One of the most widely known conditions, which is especially important with woody deciduous fruit plants is that of lime-induced chlorosis, or Fe deficiency. The appearance of symptoms of true Fe deficiency, chlorosis in the young leaves, is associated with a higher K/Ca ratio than that found in normal leaves which was first observed by the late Professor T. Wallace. Chlorotic tissues of dicotyledons also tend to accumulate citric acid, but this is not true of monocotyledons. The total Fe content is often poorly correlated with the symptoms. Cereals, brassicas, spinach and beet more rarely show symptoms of the same disorder. The particle size of the calcareous mineral is a factor, and finely divided forms are the most active. Bicarbonate also induces iron deficiency and a high K/Ca ratio. There is therefore a relationship between bicarbonate and lime-induced chlorosis which may perhaps be due to bicarbonate rather than to Ca or Mg ions, and the mechanism may involve a competitive inhibition of Fe uptake, or even inhibition of cytochrome oxidase activity in roots. Boron deficiency is readily induced by excess calcium carbonate in formerly acid, sandy, organic or clay soils.

Organic soils

Soils with high organic carbon are prone to some characteristic deficiency conditions. The most important are copper deficiency, often known as 'reclamation disease' in cereals, legumes, carrots and some other plants, and manganese deficiency known by several names, e.g. 'grey speck' in oats (Plate 42), 'speckled yellows' in sugar beet, 'marsh spot' in peas (Plate 43). Potatoes are also relatively susceptible.

The occurrence of manganese deficiency is quite widespread in Fenland soils, and occurs locally when high rates of lime and organic manuring have been applied for several years, or where moorland soils are limed heavily to cure the initial problems of acidity.

Manganese deficiency is probably most usually caused by an oxidation process elucidated by Mann and Quastel according to the following scheme:

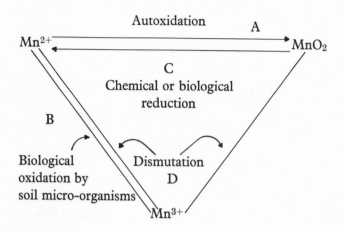

The reaction A is favoured by high pH and aerobic conditions. With a low pH MnO_2 availability may yield toxic concentrations of Mn. Reaction B is favoured by pH values between 7 and 8·5, optimal for the activity of the manganese-oxidising soil micro-organisms, and is dependent on a carbon source provided by the high organic carbon level of the soil. Reaction C is favoured by the same pH range for biological action and again depends on organic carbon supplies but the chemical reduction by phenolics, thiols, ferrous salts and other compounds including thiosulphate is favoured by low pH values below 7. The Mn^{3+} state is stabilised by some chelating agents, e.g. EDTA and pyrophosphate. However, the important dismutation reaction D : $2Mn^{3+} \rightarrow Mn^{2+} + Mn^{4+}$ which is favoured by pH values between 6 and 7 is not normally reversible. The net effect of the operation of the cycle in the pH range 6–8 is therefore that of accumulation of Mn^{4+} as MnO_2. This is not available under alkaline conditions and manganese deficiency is the usual result. A fluctuating water table tends to accelerate the immobilisation by the cycle of oxidation and dismutation.

Quastel has also pointed out that manganese as MnO_2 serves as an important buffer against the toxic effects of sulphides and thiols which accumulate in soils under anaerobic conditions. This reaction probably protects rice against toxic effects of sulphides in flooded paddy fields. Under acid conditions MnO_2 is rapidly reduced and manganese excess is the result.

Copper deficiency is the other nutritional condition most usually associated with highly organic soils. It is widespread in western Europe, in Holland and Denmark, and in milder forms in the Fenland soils of East Anglia. In severe cases these soils are able to immobilise copper very rapidly when it is applied as copper sulphate. Sparingly soluble compounds such as cuprous oxide, copper oxychloride and even glazed vitreous frits yield continuous supplies at low but adequate concentrations for one or more seasons. The immobilising substances in organic soils may be chelating compounds analogous to EDTA, polypeptides or phenanthrolines, with very high stability constants. On passing soil solutions through a cation exchange column, metals which are not retained, i.e. non-ionic, are probably chelated in this way.

Saline alkaline and coastal soils

Saline soils may occur in desert conditions where excessive evaporation causes salt accumulation and in low-lying coastal regions where salt marshes occur. In the former alkaline salt areas the species are often xerophytic and include *Suaeda fruticosa, Salicornia herbacea, Salsola soda* and *Petrisimonia* spp. *Tamarix articulata* accumulates potassium in soils where this element is also high. Bicarbonate, sulphate and chloride concentrations are high and calcium, sodium and magnesium are abundant. Borate may also become toxic. The conditions are therefore different in the existence of higher pH (up to 8) and higher soluble Mg^{2+}, K^+, Ca^{2+} and SO_4^{2-} concentration than in salt marsh and dune land, where $NaCl$ and $CaCO_3$ from sea salt and shell sand are the dominant features.

Conductivities may be high, of the order of 4 mmhos/cm. The high sodium level in the soluble and exchangeable fraction may induce calcium deficiency in lucerne, tobacco and celery. Barley, rye, beet and onion are however generally relatively tolerant of high salt conditions.

In the salt marshes and salt dunes characteristic species include *Atriplex hastata, A. glabriuscula, Salicornia europaeus, Suaeda maritima, Beta maritima, Triglochin maritima, Limonium vulgare, Aster tripolium, Apium graveolens, Psamma arenaria, Hippophae rhamnoides* (with nitrogen-fixing root nodules) and *Halogeton glomeratus.*

The species *Atriplex vesicaria* which occurs in Australian saline soils requires sodium, but only in amounts associated with micronutrients. No role for this sodium is known at present. R. Ahmed of the University of Karachi has observed an interesting effect of salinity in *Suaeda fruticosa* growing in saline habitats in W. Pakistan. The leaf cells develop organic particles rich in silica (3%) and copper (0·8%) which produces a grey-green colour. These mineral-rich particles appear to be an adaptation to the saline conditions and may provide a mechanism for segregation in the cell of alkali cations. *S. fruticosa* was substantially improved in fresh and dry weight yield and general vigour in sand cultures when given a high concentration of sodium (1%) above the normal concentration for other plants of 0·002% (23 p.p.m.). High copper (10 p.p.m.) was toxic at the low sodium but was beneficial at the 1% sodium level. Ability to accumulate salt ions is correlated with salt tolerance as shown by Hayward and Wadleigh in 1949.

As coastal sandy soils and dunes become leached of salt they may become acid or remain calcareous if derived from shell sand. In these soils deficiencies of Cu and Zn may be acute, as in the sandy Ninety-Mile coastal belt of South Australia, from which the term 'coastal disease' was derived. The seleniferous soils of Western China were first noted to be poisonous by Marco Polo in 1295 and poisonous soils of Columbia were reported in 1566 by a local priest. Seleniferous soils may originate by concentration of volcanic selenium in sediments, by erosion or by calcareous precipitation, and alkali disease caused by Fe excess occurs in Mexico, Arizona, Wyoming, South Dakota, and also in parts of Ireland, Queensland, South Africa, Alberta, Saskatchewan, Manitoba and Israel.

The importance of phosphate in growth limitation

In nature phosphate is commonly in short supply due to the insolubility of its salts and may be present in growth-limiting amounts in soils, rivers and lakes. It is for this reason that phosphatic fertilisers or phosphate-containing detergents can cause the proliferation of algae on draining into lakes, a process which may disturb the natural stability of the habitat and which results in silting. Under these circumstances nitrate may eventually become the limiting factor. Treatment is possible by addition of sodium aluminate or aluminium sulphate to precipitate the insoluble aluminium phosphate. In the soil, phosphate tends to be immobilised as the insoluble calcium or iron salts. Any that is washed into the sea remains there, since there is no natural cycle for the return of this element to the land as may be found for the elements nitrogen and sulphur in which volatile compounds are formed by major biological processes.

Diagnosis of mineral disorders in plants

It will be evident from Chapters 2 and 6 that many nutrient-deficiency conditions result in the production of specific symptoms which are easily recognised. These symptoms are most valuable in the diagnosis of the disorders causing them. The visual method of diagnosis was developed into a powerful technique by the late Professor T. Wallace.

It is also true that in many cases visible symptoms are not specific, or are vague or even if apparently clearly recognisable, e.g. as of iron deficiency, the causes may be manifold. It is therefore necessary to employ other methods of diagnosis. Finally it is good practice to use two or more independent procedures in order to obtain satisfactory confirmation of the diagnosis and to elucidate complex problems where the disorder may be the result of two or even more deficiency or excess effects.

Visual diagnostic methods

The simple approach to diagnosis by recognition of specific visible symptoms has already been mentioned. Examples of practically fool-proof diagnostic symptoms to experienced eyes include marsh spot of peas and some beans due to manganese deficiency (—Mn) (Plates 43 and 44), speckled yellows of sugar beet and analogous conditions in globe table beet (—Mn), grey speck of oats (—Mn) (Plate 42), crown rot of sugar beet, canker of table beet, water core of swede and turnip (Plate 61), die-back of sunflower, stem crack of celery, internal cork, malformation and drought spot in apples (Plate 62), alfalfa yellows (all —B), white bud of maize (—Zn), little leaf of Citrus (—Zn) (Plate 49), sickle leaf of cocoa (—Zn), exanthema of Citrus (—Cu), reclamation disease (white tip disease) of wheat and oats (—Cu), whiptail of cauliflower (—Mo) (Plates 55 and 56), symptoms in certain apple varieties (Plate 19), sweet cherry, cauliflowers, tomatoes, potato, clovers (—Mg), potato and red clover (—K), swede (—P), tuber malformations in potato (Plate 14), and 'topple' in tulips (—Ca).

However, bitter pit of apples (—Ca with low N) and corky pit, also drought spot and corky core of apples (—B) might be confused. Excess and deficiency of Mn produce similar symptoms in barley. Even white tip effects of reclamation disease in cereals caused by —Ca would be confused with similar effects caused by —B or —Cu, although there are some subtle but fairly specific differences. Typical chlorosis caused by —Fe is often easily recognised, but the cause of the —Fe condition may be simple —Fe, excess Cu, Mn, Zn, Cr, Cd, Co, Ni, etc. (Plates 65 and 70), excess $CaCO_3$ in certain soils, bicarbonate in irrigation water or even —K. —N and —P effects may be similar; —Ca and —B effects may be confused; —Zn, —Mn and —Fe symptoms may also be difficult to distinguish in some plants. Nitrogen deficiency in herbage legumes may be due to Mo or S deficiencies which prevent nitrogen fixation. Environmental effects can be large. Shaded trees and branches away from the direct sun may be free of Zn deficiency; high light intensities and long days lead to accumulation of boron into older leaves. Toxicity can occur in these, while deficiency is found in younger leaves of the same plants. Short days may mask Zn deficiency and Mn excess is accentuated by high light intensity which increases Mn uptake.

The plants for which diagnostic symptoms are considered almost infallible are called 'Indicator' plants. When consistent conclusions are based on two or more different indicators, the diagnosis of an unknown condition in another plant is quite likely to be correct. However, it must be noted that different plants can suffer from different disorders in adjacent areas or even on growing together. Thus, on a calcareous clay-loam, potatoes might show —K, maize and sugar beet —Fe, and peas —Mn. On a calcareous organic (fen or peat) soil potatoes, peas and beet may show —Mn, wheat —Cu and oats —Cu or —Mn. On an acid soil with a high clay content, cauliflower may show —Mo, Mn excess or —Ca or —Mg. Potatoes —Ca, —Mg or —K; beet, excess Al. On an acid peaty soil after liming, beet may show —Mn or —B, swede —B, potatoes —K, —Mg or —Mn. Therefore it is obvious that different indicators can indicate simultaneously the existence of several potential disorders. Conclusions regarding the unknown symptoms are then less certain and other methods outlined below must be applied.

Nutrient–application methods

It would be expected that response to a deficient nutrient resulting from its application would be a specific diagnostic criterion. Giving nitrogen or molybdenum or boron generally results in rapid recovery of plants deficient in one of these elements. However, there are many circumstances where giving an element in expected appropriate amounts to the soil may not be of diagnostic use. Thus, in some soils the addition of manganese, copper, iron or potassium may produce little effect or the response may be delayed for a season because of severe immobilisation of the element before significant amounts reach the roots. Some disorders are caused by excess of an element and giving other elements to the soil is rarely beneficial. In cases of heavy metal-induced iron deficiency the application of iron may cure the chlorosis. In a few cases multiple deficiencies may occur together so that adding any one element alone has little effect and only giving all the deficient elements together is effective. A technique devised by Dr R. A. Webb for these conditions comprises transferring soil to inert containers (e.g. polythene) and supplying the plants grown in them with highly purified nutrient solutions each deficient in only one element (see Chapter 3), and also a complete nutrient solution is given to separate pots. Under these conditions the existence of multiple deficiencies in one soil is revealed and each is identified by the poor growth obtained in the respective deficiency treatment. Specific visible symptoms are often revealed for each deficiency.

The direct application of an element to leaves or shoots by dilute sprays, painting on to a leaf, injection of a shoot by dipping a cut leaf stalk or shoot tip into the solution, or boring a hole in a tree trunk and inserting a powdered form of the element have all been employed. The results are often rapid and dramatic. These methods are useful where soil availability problems impede rapid root uptake and sprays are often used with Mn, Fe, Cu, Zn and Mg; the first four usually as 0.2% solutions of their sulphates and $MgSO_4.7H_2O$ as a 2% solution with a leaf-wetting agent. A spray containing 0.1% Na_2MoO_4 is a good treatment for cauliflower or lettuce seedlings before planting out into molybdenum-deficient soils. Iron salts are sometimes injurious and better results are obtained by applying a solution of a chelated-iron compound, e.g. Fe EDTA to the soil. The chelated iron is not immobilised and remains available in a physiologically active form for several weeks after absorption by the plant.

Soil analysis

One of the oldest approaches to diagnosis is chemical analysis of the soil in which the affected plants are growing. In some circumstances the measurement of soil pH is an excellent guide to the problem if this is simple acidity or acute alkalinity. A pH value of 5·5 may be found in soils where the problems can be deficiency of Mo, excess of Mn or Al, deficiency of Ca or Mg, excess of some heavy metals, and deficiency of Cu or Zn. Addition of lime may cure Mo deficiency or excess Mn or Al, but could also induce deficiency of B, Cu, Zn, Mn, Mg or K. Analyses for Mn, Ca, K and Mg may be instructive but many of the effects of liming are hard to predict accurately. A pH value of 7·5–8·5 may be associated with unavailability and deficiency of Mn, B, Cu, Zn or Fe, the presence of bicarbonate or sodium chloride. Soil analysis will indicate the last two possibilities and specialised methods may reveal non-availability of Mn, Cu, B or Zn although total amounts appear adequate. In some cases an available fraction of the element can be extracted from the soil by a salt solution such as 0·1 M ammonium acetate to determine exchangeable Mg, Ca or K; by EDTA solution to determine Cu or Zn; by hydroquinone to determine Mn.

A specialised analytical method is the use of a fungus, *Aspergillus niger*, to indicate available fractions of some elements in soils. The technique was developed by Mulder in Holland and extended by Nicholas in England. The principle is based on the idea that the fungus can grow on the fraction of the element which is readily available in the soil rather than on the total amount present. The method has been used particularly for Mg, Mo, Cu and Zn. The nutrient solutions are especially purified to remove the respective elements and a weighed amount (0·1 –2·0 g) of soil is added to the sterilised medium which is inoculated with a spore suspension. The growth of the mycelium (as dry weight) at 25 –35°C for 5–7 days is compared with a standard growth series prepared with graded additions of the element.

Plant analysis

The analysis of dried plant material should provide a reliable indication of the nutrient status of a plant. Assuming the analysis is accurate and for iron this may be far from certain unless very many precautions including leaf washing are adopted, the results indicate the total content of the element in the organ or tissue sampled. Older or younger parts may show widely different values and considerable experience is needed to evaluate results in relation to age, season, morphological region and species or even variety, and interaction effects caused by high or low levels of other elements. The actual amount determined may be in excess, e.g. 500 p.p.m. Mn gives toxicity in a brassica, but 500–1000 p.p.m. Mn may be normal in tea. Concentrations of 20–40 p.p.m. Zn may occur equally in healthy and deficient plants. The technique of plant analysis is based ideally on three sets of determinations. The morphologically most indicative region is sampled, often on 'mid-stem' leaves and samples are taken from healthy and affected plants in the same region, and from healthy plants in a well-separated region. These three results often provide clear evidence of the deficiency conditions. A classical review of the nutrient content of plants was published by Goodall and Gregory in 1947. This examines the differences between different plants in normal conditions as well as the effects of deficiency or excess conditions on nutrient uptake. Study of this work reveals the complexity of the difficulties and the value of nutrient analysis as a diagnostic method.

Another approach, useful in field conditions, but less accurate, is to extract fresh tissue with a dilute acid or a buffered salt solution, e.g. 0·5 M sodium acetate at pH 4, and to determine the concentrations of K, Mg, Ca, NO_3 and PO_4 in the extract using simple colorimetric tests, and comparing the densities of the test solutions in the Lovibond Comparator with accurately standardised coloured glass discs.

The question of which organs to sample is illustrated by the following points. Old leaves accumulate boron and old leaves may contain adequate boron when young leaves are markedly deficient. Old leaves also accumulate Ca in the same way. On the other hand, N, K, Mg and Mn tend to migrate from old leaves to young ones in most plants, but Mn may be retained in old leaves of tomatoes and some other plants. The mobility of Cu, Zn and Mo is variable, depending on species, age when deficiency occurs, season and perhaps other factors. Old leaves retain Fe but differences between young leaves showing chlorosis and those which are green may be small or even the opposite of that to be expected from their appearance when the chlorosis is induced by excess of a heavy metal, and surface dust provides more iron than is present inside the leaf. Roots accumulate Mn, Cu, Zn, Cr, Co, V and several other elements sometimes to ten or twenty times the concentrations found in leaves. Seasonal effects are often important. Figure 5.2 shows results of Bould, Bradfield and Clarke for nitrogen and calcium in blackcurrant leaves. Nitrogen is highest in apical and lowest in basal leaves, while calcium shows the opposite trend. Moreover, the nitrogen content falls whereas that of calcium rises as the season progresses.

Analysis of plants which are severely deficient in some elements, e.g. Cu or Mn, may indicate higher concentrations of the element than is found in slightly less deficient plants. This effect was first pointed out by Steenbjerg in connection with deficiencies of cereals on Danish peat soils. Examples of

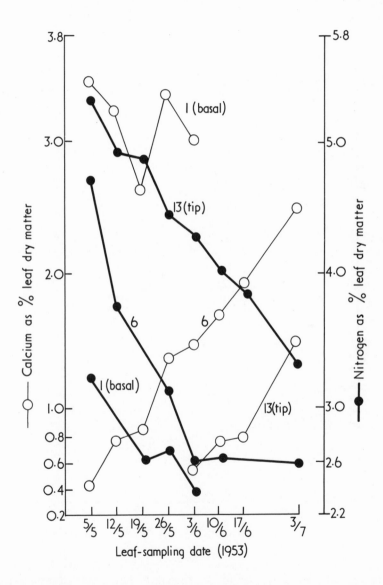

Figure 5.2 Effect of position and time of sampling on the calcium and nitrogen status of blackcurrant leaves. From Bould, Bradfield and Clarke (1960) *J. Sci. Food Agric.* **11**, 229–42.

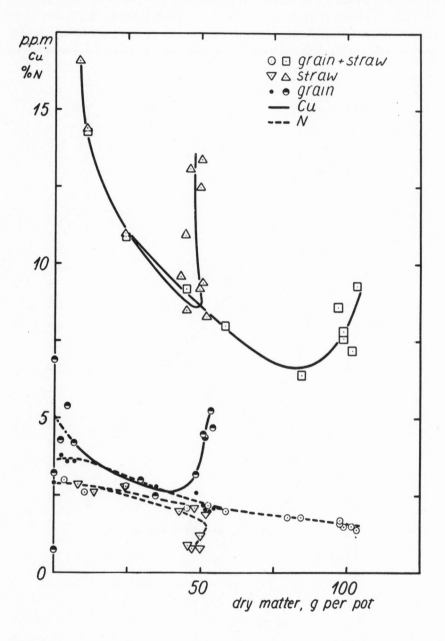

Figure 5.3 Dry matter and the relative content of copper and nitrogen in barley plants. From Steenbjerg (1951) *Pl. Soil* **3**, 97–109.

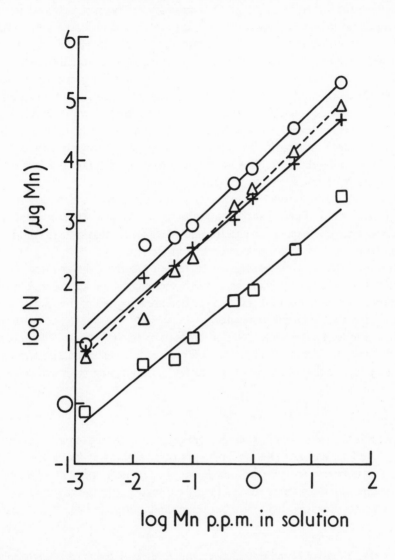

Figure 5.4 Relationships between Log N and manganese supply in tomato.
Squares: Log N = Log C (tops) + Log Y (plants) (age 5 weeks)
Crosses: Log N = Log C (lower stems) + Log Y (plants) (age 18 weeks)
Circles: Log N = Log C (lower leaves) + Log Y (plants) (age 18 weeks)
Triangles: Log N = Log C (leaves and stems) + Log Y (leaves and stems)
  (age 18 weeks)
Where N is the nutrient (Mn) concentration, C is the concentration in the dry
matter and Y is the total yield. From Hewitt (1956) in *Plant Analysis and Fertilizer
Problems*. Institut de recherches pour les huiles et oléagineux, Paris, pp. 104–18.

this effect are shown in Fig. 5.3. This anomaly has been reproduced in sand culture experiments by Hewitt for Mo and Mn in cauliflower and tomato, and by Piper in water culture experiments for Cu in oats. However, when the data are transformed in the way illustrated in Fig. 5.4, in which the log of the total content of the metal in leaves or plants is plotted against log available concentration or supply of the element, a linear relationship is observed. This holds over a wide range from the Steenbjerg anomaly level to excess levels where yield is depressed. This technique can be used to evaluate the threshold levels of supply in a purified culture medium and is probably applicable to measuring availability in a soil when all other elements than the one in question are also provided in adequate amounts.

There are several ways of expressing the relationship between uptake, supply and yield. These have been deduced by classical experimental work of Liebig and of Mitscherlich and from later work on sugar cane in Mauritius, on oil palm in the Congo, and on cereals in Denmark.

In most cases a specific sample unit, leaf of a certain age or node, or at a definite time of year, is taken as a fixed reference. This approach contrasts with the healthy *v.* diseased and good *v.* bad area method of the Long Ashton school of Wallace and his associates.

An example of a fairly successful attempt to relate yield to available nutrient supply was provided by the Resistance Formula of Maskell and illustrated by Gregory for yield experiments with barley. The formula is shown below:

$$\frac{1}{Y} = \frac{KA}{A_1 + A_0} + \frac{KB}{B_1 + B_0} + K$$

where Y is the yield, and K_A and K_B are constants specific to particular nutrients A and B, e.g. nitrogen and phosphorus, supplied at levels A_1 and B_1. When no nutrients are given A_0 and B_0 are the quantities present, presumably including available plant reserves, if large compared with the rooting medium. Table 5.2 for an experiment with barley in sand culture (where Y_1, Y_2 are the

Table 5.2 Levels of N and P (mg) given and yields Y of dry wt (g) of barley plants and values of $1/Y_1-1/Y_2$ used to demonstrate the Resistance Formula of Maskell (data of Gregory, 1951)

	P_1 5 mg	P_2 405 mg	$1/Y_1-1/Y_2$ (N)
N_1	$Y_{1,1}$	$Y_{1,2}$	
15 mg	3·06	3·60	0·048
N_2	$Y_{2,1}$	$Y_{2,2}$	
1215 mg	15·0	86·4	0·055
$1/Y_1-1/Y_2$ (P)	0·259	0·266	

yields at nutrient levels of A_1 and A_2, B_1 and B_2) shows the validity of the relationship, illustrated by the constant value for $1/Y_1$ and $1/Y_2$ for a given nutrient when another nutrient level is varied. An exposition of the more elaborate theory of Homes is given by Hewitt (1966).

Biochemical diagnosis

This technique has been introduced recently by Bar-Akiva for citrus and has useful applications. The principle involved is that certain enzymes are particularly responsive to the presence of adequate concentrations of the metal on which both the formation and activity of the enzyme depends. The enzymes which come in this category are shown in Table 5.3 with the metals involved and effects of mineral deficiencies on their activity. The defective activity in deficient plants and the response to the specific metal when introduced by infiltration or spray and incubated for a few hours before extraction are in theory specific criteria of the requirement for the element. It is necessary however to ensure that traces of the deficient element are excluded from the solutions of all but that of the element used for the infiltration, as shown by Afridi and Hewitt in studies on the induction of nitrate reductase. As little as 10^{-7} M Mo will produce a substantial response in terms of the enzyme activity induced in molybdenum-deficient cauliflower leaves in a few hours. Another limitation is the inherent capacity of the tissue to respond. Thus leaf discs or excised leaves from Mo deficient cauliflower or radish respond readily to Mo but leaves of spinach are unable to do so if detached from the plant. Only intact spinach plants with their root systems are able to respond and the time required for a marked increase in enzyme activity is longer, 24–48 hours compared with about six hours for cauliflower. In the case of nitrate reductase the absence of nitrate or nitrogen deficiency also causes low enzyme activities and infiltration by Mo may have no effect, but nitrate will induce the enzyme if the Mo status is adequate. There are nevertheless correlations between yield and response to Mo in terms of nitrate reductase in grapefruit.

Two other possible approaches to biochemical diagnosis may be noted. The studies of the late F. J. Richards led to the discovery that the diamine putrescine is accumulated to fifty times the normal concentration in potassium-deficient leaves of several plants (see page 152). The biosynthesis of putrescine from arginine involves three enzymes. Arginine is first decarboxylated to agmatine, which is converted to N-carbamylputrescine and finally to putrescine. The agmatine may be increased tenfold in potassium-deficient barley leaves. Deficiencies of other elements particularly magnesium also cause putrescine accumulation, though the highest putrescine levels are usually

Table 5.3 Effects of mineral status in citrus plants on some enzymes containing a specific metal: enzyme activities relative to full nutrient plants as 100

Mineral status	*Enzyme and associated specific metal:*						
	Nitrate reductase (Mo) (%)	*Response to Mo (%)**	*Peroxidase (Fe)*	*Response to Fe (%)**	*Carbonic anhydrase (Zn)*	*Ascorbic acid oxidase (Cu)*	*Response to Cu (%)**
Complete	100		100	−7	100	100	
−Fe	63		36	+110	110	102	
−Mn	100		165	0	86	120	
−Zn	51		100	+9	20–30	106	
−Cu	88		110	−3	96	57	+450
−Mo	9	1200	108	+15	83	126	
−N	20		75	0			

* From results of Bar-Akiva (1964–9). The response to the metal is the increase or decrease in activity after infiltration of leaf discs with the metal for a few hours before extraction and assay of enzyme.

found with potassium deficiency. The practical value of putrescine and agmatine estimation in assessing mineral deficiencies in relation to symptoms and yields has been studied by Murty, Smith and Bould (1971), Nowakowski (1971) and Smith (1974). It is possible that putrescine estimation will be useful in assessing potassium deficiency in certain legumes, since this amine is accumulated by the leaves before visual deficiency symptoms occur.

The other possible relationship is the spectacular effect of copper supply on photosynthesis (CO_2 uptake and O_2 evolution) first noted by Drosdoff and Sell in 1937. This can now be explained in terms of the effects of copper supply on the formation of plastocyanin (Chapter 8, Table 8.5), the copper containing protein of chloroplasts which is an essential link in the electron transport system between the two photosystems I and II in chloroplasts. The work of Hewitt and Scawen has shown that copper deficiency drastically decreases plastocyanin content. The extraction of the protein by a new standardised procedure from normal and suspected copper-deficient leaves may have a diagnostic value as an independent criterion or even an initial indicator of impending copper deficiency.

Further Reading

Chapman, H. D. (1966) *Diagnostic Criteria for Plants and Soils*. University of California, Riverside.

Cooke, G. W. (1967) *The Control of Soil Fertility*. Crosby Lockwood: London. 526 pp.

Hewitt, E. J. (1952) A biological approach to the problems of soil acidity. *Internat. Soc. Soil Sci. Comm. II & IV. Congress* 1952. Transactions Vol. 1, p. 105.

Kilmer, V. J., Younts, S. E. and Brady, N. C. (Eds.) (1968) *The Role of Potassium in Agriculture*, American Society of Agronomy. Crop Science Society of America, and Soil Science Society of America. Madison, Wisconsin, USA.

Rorison, I. H. (1969) *Ecological Aspects of the Mineral Nutrition of Plants*. Blackwell: Oxford. 484 pp.

Russell, E. J. Revised by Russell, E. W. (1961) *Soil Conditions and Plant Growth*. 9th edn. Longmans Green: London. 688 pp.

Webber, J. (Ed.) (1971) *Proceedings of the N.A.A.S. Open Conference on Trace Elements in Soils and Crops* (1966) Tech. Bull. No. 21 H.M. Stationery Office.

Whatley, J. M. (1971) Ultrastructural changes in chloroplasts of *Phaseolus vulgaris* during development under conditions of nutrient deficiency. *New Phytol.* **70**, 725–42.

Plate 42 Manganese deficiency in oats (grey speck). Photo—Long Ashton Research Station.

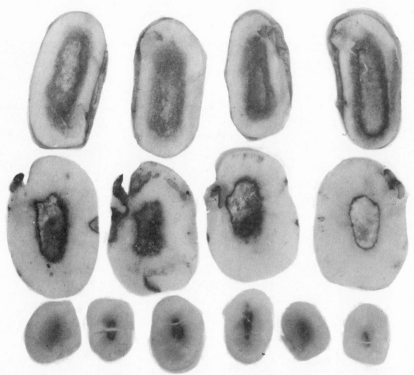

Plate 43 Typical marsh spot symptoms in runner bean (*above*), broad bean (*middle*) and peas (*below*) due to manganese deficiency. From Hewitt (1945) *Nature, Lond.* **155**, 22–3.

Plate 44 Manganese deficiency in haricot beans (*Phaseolus vulgaris*). Necrosis may occur in the plumule only (*upper line*), in the cotyledons only (*lower line*) or in both areas (*centre*). Photo—Long Ashton Research Station.

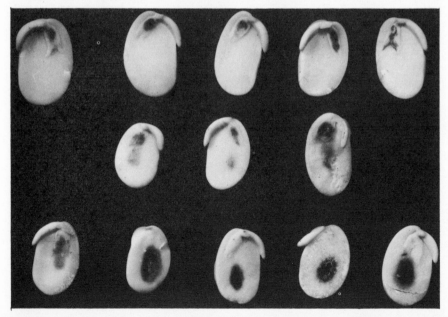

Plate 45 Zinc (*left*) and copper (*right*) deficiency in tomato. The central plant is the control. Photo—Long Ashton Research Station.

Plate 46 Leaves from red-clover plants grown in a zinc-deficient medium (*left*) and in a full nutrient medium (*right*). Photo—Long Ashton Research Station.

Plate 47 Apple shoots showing zinc-deficiency symptoms. *Left*—normal growth of terminal shoot and 'little leaves' from lateral buds. *Right*—rosette formation from the apical bud and 'little leaves' from the lateral ones. From Démétriadès, Holevas and Gavolas (1963) *Ann. Inst. Phytopath Benaki* 5, 149–54.

Plate 48 Orange twigs showing patterns and effects of zinc deficiency: moderate (*left*): acute (*right*). By courtesy of Professor H. D. Chapman (unpublished).

Plate 49 Terminal twigs of lemon which are acutely deficient in zinc (*right*) and showing striking recovery (*left*) when 0·5 p.p.m. zinc was added to previously zinc-deficient nutrient solution. It is not uncommon to see growth behaviour such as this in the field, in which there is a succession of zinc-deficient and healthy growth cycles on the same branch. By courtesy of Professor H. D. Chapman (unpublished).

Plate 50 Effect of molybdenum status on growth of peas in sand culture. *Left container:* without molybdenum; left-hand plants produced from seed saved from molybdenum-deficient plants; right-hand plants produced from normal seed. *Right container:* plants grown from similar seed in presence of molybdenum. From Hewitt (1963) in *Plant Physiology* (Ed. F. C. Steward), Academic Press, New York and London, 3, 137–360.

Plate 51 Symptoms of molybdenum deficiency in orange leaves. By courtesy of Professor Ivan Stewart, University of Florida (unpublished).

Plate 52 Molybdenum deficiency in tomato (aged sixty days). The tips of the shoots remain green while the other leaves are withered and yellow. From Hewitt and Bolle-Jones (1952) *J. hort. Sci.* **27**, 257–65.

Plate 53 Molybdenum deficiency in radish, showing leaf-cupping, mottling and scorching of leaves in seedlings with normal cotyledons. From Hewitt (1956) *Soil Sci.* **81**, 159–71. © 1956 The Williams & Wilkins Co, Baltimore, USA.

Plate 54   Whiptail in broccoli in field conditions due to molybdenum deficiency
From Plant (1951) *Agriculture, Lond.* **57**, 130–4.

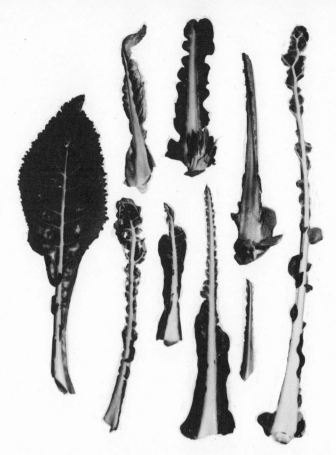

Plate 55 Whiptail leaves in molybdenum-deficient cauliflower given ammonium sulphate. Note chlorotic breakdown in leaf at left. From Hewitt (1956) *Soil Sci.* **81,** 159–71. © 1956 The Williams & Wilkins Co, Baltimore, USA.

Plate 56 Whiptail in molybdenum-deficient cauliflower grown with ammonium sulphate as nitrogen source under non-sterile conditions. From Agarwala and Hewitt (1955) *J. hort. Sci.* **30,** 163–80.

Plate 57 Boron deficiency in sugar beet. Severe deficiency can cause complete crop failure which often occurs in patches as shown here, especially on land which has been heavily limed. Photo—Kali-Chemie, A.G. Hanover, Germany, by courtesy of Borax Consolidated Ltd.

Plate 58 Boron deficiency in pine (*Pinus radiata*). *Left*—normal needles. *Right*—distorted, thick and misshapen leaves from boron-deficient plants. Photograph by Dr Marcos de Lanuza, Forestry Institute, Ministry of Agriculture, Madrid, Spain, by courtesy of Borax Consolidated Ltd.

Plate 59 Boron deficiency in carnations. Healthy flowering shoots on left and deficient shoots on right with curled leaves and abortive flower development. Photograph by Dr G. W. Winsor, Glasshouse Crops Research Institute, Littlehampton, UK, by courtesy of Borax Consolidated Ltd.

Plate 60 Boron deficiency in broad bean. Photo—Long Ashton Research Station.

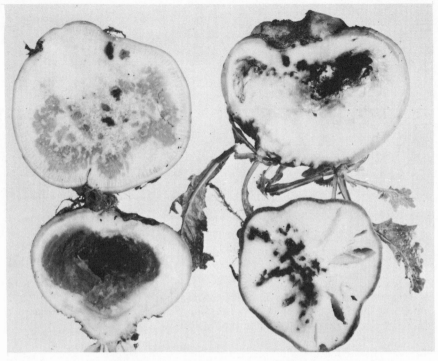

Plate 61   Boron deficiency in turnip. Photo—Long Ashton Research Station.

Plate 62   Boron deficiency in apples. Photo—Long Ashton Research Station.

Plate 63 Cabbage plants grown with deficient (*left*) and adequate (*right*) chlorine supply. By courtesy of Professor C. M. Johnson, University of California Experiment Station.

Plate 64 Large-scale trial of tolerant grasses growing on previously uncolonised mine waste. The far block is of *Festuca rubra*; the near block *Agrostis stolonifera*. Both are tolerant to the lead and zinc which occur at 1% and 3·6% respectively in the waste. Some general fertiliser has been added to correct nutrient deficiencies. By courtesy of Professor A. Bradshaw (unpublished).

Plate 65 Heavy metal toxicity in sugar beet. Copper-induced iron deficiency. Photo—Long Ashton Research Station.

Plate 66 Cobalt toxicity in tomato; leaflets reduced to peg-like rudiments, severe interveinal chlorosis, abnormal or abortive flower trusses. From Hewitt (1953) *J. exp. Bot.* **4**, 59–64.

Plate 67 Cobalt toxicity in oats causing symptoms of iron deficiency. Photo—Long Ashton Research Station.

Plate 68 Manganese toxicity in potato grown in sand culture. Photo—Long Ashton Research Station.

Plate 69 Manganese excess in marrowstem kale. Symptoms include leaf marginal cupping, necrotic spotting and interveinal mottling. Photo—Long Ashton Research Station.

Plate 70 Chromium toxicity induced by 0·5 mEq. Cr^{3+} per litre resulting in chlorosis due to iron deficiency. From Hewitt (1953) *J. exp. Bot.* **4,** 59–64.

Plate 71 Nickel toxicity in oats. Oblique dark banding alternating with chlorotic areas. From Hewitt (1953) *J. exp. Bot.* **4,** 59–64.

6
Effects of Mineral Nutrients on Growth and Composition

. . . to comprehend the continuing mystery that distinguishes the animate from the inanimate and the seeming miracle of higher plants that have so evolved that majestically they may grow and persist in an otherwise inorganic world.

F. C. Steward.

Nitrogen

Effects of nitrogen supply on growth and morphology

Nitrogen deficiency usually has overriding control of growth and dominates the effects of other elements. Plants deprived of nitrogen show decreased cell division and expansion, prolonged dormancy and therefore delayed swelling of buds. All morphological parts are reduced in size, and leaves and fruits are especially sensitive. Premature senescence is also a common feature. Apical meristems associated with secondary axes or tillers are repressed and plants such as cereals may be reduced to single stems. Lateral axillary buds are also repressed and this results in the growth of single unbranched stems. Differentiation of xylem may be accentuated but phloem and other protein-rich tissues is decreased. Leaf abscission is often premature (Plates 21 and 22).

Chlorophyll production is decreased by nitrogen deficiency and this is associated in some species with the increased formation of anthocyanin and the appearance of yellow pigments. Pigmentation characteristics may vary in different species. Red, orange and purple tints appear in brassica species first in adaxial mesophyll cells. In tomato, first the abaxial vascular tissues, and later the adaxial and interveinal tissues particularly parenchyma, show purple pigments. In apple, the fruits are often intensely red and in cereals the lower stems and leaf bases are especially concerned. Potato leaves turn yellow, a sign of proteolysis, but do not pigment. Decreased light intensity tends to repress pigment formation. The changes in leaf cells of cauliflower during the onset of nitrogen deficiency have been studied by Hewitt and Hucklesby in unpublished work. Chloroplasts initially enlarged and became densely packed with greatly enlarged starch grains, while lipo-protein staining in chloroplasts decreased and was reduced to a membranous region around the periphery of the enlarged starch grain. Histochemical staining reactions for ribonucleic acid (RNA) also decreased. As deficiency progressed the chloroplasts disintegrated. Lipo-protein material collected into intensely yellow globules which adhered to the starch grains or formed chains of globules along starch grain interfaces. Later they became detached and fused into fewer and larger globules. The starch grains then shrank and anthocyanin pigments appeared in cell vacuoles of epidermal and of the first sub-epidermal layer. When lysis of the starch grains was complete the anthocyanin pigments also disappeared and the cytoplasm of mesophyll cells contained just the nucleus and one or two large lipo-protein residues from chloroplasts and numerous much smaller and colourless liquid globules. Bosemark in 1954 found that roots of wheat (*Triticum vulgare*) plants grown in a controlled environment underwent 30% increased elongation when the nitrogen supply was decreased from 10^{-3} M to 10^{-4} M sodium nitrate. The change in root length was associated with an increase in average cell length of about 60%. There must therefore have been a decrease in total cell numbers and in meristematic cell division and the relative increase in cell expansion exceeded increased total elongation. Total and insoluble nitrogen contents were decreased to about one-third. These experiments were carried out in a rather unusual nutrient medium which contained only 10^{-4} M Ca^{2+}, and 10^{-3} M Mg^{2+} and PO_4^{3-} and no specified supply of potassium. When 'high' nitrogen treatments were given (10^{-2} M) the sodium/calcium ratio was raised to 100 : 1. The observations would be advantageously repeated in the presence of a more normal mineral environment. Excessive expansion of undifferentiated cells of excised carrot (*Daucus carota*) tissue in conditions of nitrogen deficiency was observed by Toren in 1955.

Lutman in 1934 found that nitrogen deficiency led to the appearance of abnormally small nuclei in root tissues of Japanese millet (*Setaria italica*) but actual cells of the undifferentiated tissues were normal in size. It would be interesting to know whether the deoxyribonucleic acid (DNA) content was affected. In buckwheat (*Fagopyrum esculentum*) cell size was reduced and in rape (*Brassica napus*) premature vacuolation which is a manifestation of early differentiation or accelerated senescence, occurred. Leaf epidermal cell size was decreased in millet and buckwheat, but not in rape. In millet the outer cell walls and cuticle were decreased in thickness by lack of nitrogen. Chloroplasts were smaller and fewer in millet but in potato, chloroplasts were enlarged with abundant starch.

Njoku in 1957 observed that leaf cells of *Ipomoea caerulea* as contrasted with root cells of wheat studied by Bosemark were decreased in size (30%) as well as in number (25%) by low nitrogen supply and the leaf areas of deficient plants were therefore about half the normal values. In younger leaves, produced after the nitrogen supply had been given or withheld for a longer period, the cell numbers of deficient leaves were only 40% of the normal. Morton and Watson in 1948 found that in *Beta vulgaris* leaf cell numbers were about half the normal number when nitrogen was deficient and the production of new leaf primordia was decreased by 20%. In the 20th leaf, cell volumes in deficient leaves were about half those in normal leaves and the combined effect of decreased cell numbers and sizes resulted in a leaf area ratio of 5·4:1 for normal and nitrogen-deficient leaves at this stage of growth.

Cytological effects of nitrogen deficiency

The limitation of cell division and expansion under conditions of nitrogen deficiency are the result of decreased protein and RNA synthesis, and this is the most direct effect. An indirect consequence is the accumulation of carbohydrate, often as starch in the chloroplasts until chloroplast disintegration occurs. Effects of nitrogen deficiency on cellular ultrastructure were described by Thomson and Weier (1962) and Whatley (1971) for bean leaves, Marinos in 1963 for barley stem apex, and by Vesk, Possingham and Mercer (1966) for tomato and spinach leaves.

Plastids of bean leaves (Plate 77) remained oval and regular in outline. The lamellar system was often aggregated around a core. Surrounding the core a few membranes occur, separated by wide spaces which may be excessively swollen locules. Starch grains were abundant. The appearance of barley stem apex cells was similar for nitrogen and magnesium deficiencies and is described in connection with the latter. In tomato leaves the chloroplasts contained small starch grains. The stroma was greatly increased and the grana were joined by short frets and there were unattached long parallel lamellae. Mitochondria were large and the cristae were elongated. As in beans the chloroplasts showed some resemblance to those in senescent leaves. In spinach the chloroplasts were small and often grouped around the nucleus. Grana thickness was reduced and the compartments were swollen. Mitochondria were abundant.

Relation of nitrogen supply to respiration and assimilation

The effect of nitrogen supply on respiration and photosynthesis as measured in terms of carbon assimilation have been studied in considerable detail in relation to the effects of potassium and phosphorus supplies to barley in the important work of Gregory and Richards and their collaborators, Templeman, Baptiste and Sen between 1929 and 1938.

Nitrogen deficiency tended to decrease respiration rate expressed as mg CO_2/hour, but on a protein basis the respiration rate (mg CO_2/mg protein) was high. When normal detached leaves were held in darkness there was a fairly rapid and progressive fall in respiration rate (mg CO_2/hour/g dry wt) for up to thirty-six hours. This change did not occur in detached nitrogen-deficient leaves in which a steady low rate of respiration in the dark was a characteristic feature. Net assimilation rate in g dry wt/cm^2/day was practically unaffected at low light intensity but was depressed at high light intensity relative to normal nitrogen nutrition, and Muller (1932) obtained similar results with mustard (*Sinapis alba*). Nitrogen deficiency, as expected, caused an increase in total leaf sugar concentration but effects on free reducing sugars were inconsistent. The high concentration of total sugars in nitrogen-deficient plants was associated with a high rate of translocation from leaf to root thus producing a relatively high root/shoot ratio in these plants.

Phosphorus

Effects of phosphorus supply on morphology, growth and composition

Phosphorus deficiency causes prolonged dormancy of buds and suppresses lateral bud development or tillering, and growth habit is often thin and erect. Purple tints are particularly characteristic but are not always produced. In tomato stems the cell walls of the pericycle and xylem may be thin and the phloem is poorly differentiated. Intercellular spaces in the pith are extensive and the walls of the pith parenchyma become necrotic (Plate 20).

Phosphorus deficiency generally causes changes in composition, including an accumulation of sucrose and reducing sugars, and sometimes of starch, but in older plants the opposite effects may occur and effects on starch are not consistent. Protein and nucleic acids are generally decreased, but amides, although requiring ATP for synthesis are increased indicating their origin from protein breakdown, and amino acids also accumulate. Phosphate esters tend to be decreased but the ratio of organic to inorganic phosphorus is often increased because the reserves of inorganic phosphorus are the first to fall. Acid phosphatase activity in tomato leaves was found by Hewitt and Tatham to be increased ten times or more by phosphorus deficiency (see Table 6.1).

Table 6.1 Effects of macronutrient deficiencies on acid phosphatase activity in tomato leaf tissue. (From Hewitt and Tatham (1960) *J. exp. Bot.* **11**, 367–76)

	Control	−Mg	−K	−P
μmol phenolphthalein phosphate hydrolysed/100 mg tissue in 20 min	8·8	8·4	13·3	61·3
μmol phenolphthalein phosphate hydrolysed/mg protein/min	0·23	0·29	0·45	2·18

Cytological effects of phosphorus supply

Phosphorus is a component of ribonucleic acid (RNA) and deoxyribonucleic acid (DNA). It might be expected therefore that phosphorus supply would have important effects on the nucleus or on genetic characteristics since the synthesis of DNA which occurs prior to chromosome doubling and cell division may depend on the availability of deoxyribonucleotides and therefore on that of the nucleotide pyrophosphates. Such effects do in fact occur though their explanation is not wholly understood. Experiments by Durrant and Tyson in 1960 on the effects of phosphorus and other fertilisers on the growth of flax indicated that a genetically heritable and permanent size characteristic had been induced by the supply of phosphorus to parent plants. The control of size in plants may reflect the effects of endogenous auxins and gibberellins on control of cell expansion or cell numbers. Increased or decreased numbers of multiple or allelomorphic genes could increase or decrease the production of such compounds. Genes are molecules of DNA and their numbers might be susceptible to the availability of phosphorus. This type of explanation is different from ideas based on mutation where either a change or a deletion in DNA of a specific gene locus occurs. Either type of explanation could be correct and both mechanisms would produce permanent and inheritable changes.

Thomson, Weier and Drever; Marinos; and Vesk, Possingham and Mercer investigated the effects of phosphorus deficiency on the ultrastructure of leaf and stem apex cells of beans, barley, tomato and spinach (Plates 82 and 86). Bean chloroplasts were at first regular in outline and contained starch but the intergrana frets were transformed into electron-dense single membrane structures surrounding rounded electron-transparent areas. In more severely deficient leaves the plastids were irregular, with collapsed electron-dense marginal areas, and the frets were transformed into very elongated parallel lamellae. Enlarged osmiophilic (lipid?) globules appeared and the grana were completely disorganised and replaced by a regular system of elongated parallel lamellae comprising pairs of electron-dense regions 6·5 nm wide, separated by an electron-transparent area 4·5 nm wide. The lamellae were about 24 nm apart. This excessive development of the frets was also observed in tomato plants. In spinach, however, the grana and frets were reduced, and stroma was extensive. The grana compartments were swollen, often extremely so. The frets were also swollen with vesicles. Effects in barley stem apex were similar to those produced by nitrogen and magnesium deficiencies except for the presence of starch in the plastids which was absent in the other two treatments.

Sulphur

Morphological effects of deficiency

Many effects of sulphur deficiency resemble those of nitrogen. This similarity arises from the presence of essential sulphur-containing amino acids, cysteine and methionine in practically all proteins. Plants are usually pale green with red and purple tints, but often the young leaves are more chlorotic than older ones, unlike nitrogen deficiency. A classical case of economic sulphur deficiency was the condition known as 'tea yellows' identified by Storey and Leach in 1933. Plants became acutely chlorotic, leaves were drastically decreased in size, margins became necrotic and the stem apex was killed. Lateral buds developed and died back, and stem internodes were shortened, producing a stunted bushy habit. In other plants, e.g. citrus, the lateral buds remain dormant or the internodes may be elongated, e.g. tomato (Plates 30 and 31).

Stem diameters are often much decreased. Phloem tissues and cambial layers are especially deficient. Cell sizes are smaller and cell walls may be thinner or thicker than normal, according to species and location.

Cytological effects

Sulphur deficiency causes abnormal cell division. Steffensen found that *Tradescantia paludosa* cells failed to form bivalent chromosomes at the first anaphase of meiosis and formed micronuclei. These sometimes contained only a single pair of bivalent chromosomes. Tripolar spindles also occurred. When less acutely deficient, chromosome separation was delayed or unequal. Micronuclei also appeared in root tips of sulphur-deficient plants. The studies on chloroplasts by various workers reported for other nutrient deficiencies indicated relatively little effect of sulphur deficiency on chloroplast structure. Plate 78 illustrates the effect of sulphur deficiency on bean (*Phaseolus*) chloroplasts.

Effects of sulphur supply on composition

Sulphur deficiency decreases insoluble and protein nitrogen and causes accumulation of amino, amide and ammonia nitrogen with little change in total nitrogen. Changes in sugars are less consistent but concentrations of reducing sugars are higher in the presence of sulphur and that of starch is lower.

Potassium

Effects of potassium on growth, morphology and composition

One of the commonest effects of potassium deficiency is that of leaf scorch of the older leaves and pronounced telescoping of the stem internodes causing a rosette or condensed habit. In cereals, citrus, flax and some other plants there is a marked loss of apical dominance and abnormally numerous lateral tillers or shoots extend (Plate 13).

In some plants, e.g. sugar cane, maize, potato, oats and some grasses, potassium deficiency is associated with chlorosis caused by iron deficiency. The experiments of Bolle-Jones and Hewitt, showed that this response could be explained in terms of the phosphorus status of the plants. Potassium deficiency resulted in a substantial increase in the ratio of inorganic to organic phosphorus from 0·9 to 3·8 so that the tendency for iron to be immobilised by phosphate was greatly increased. In the cereals and other Gramineae iron and phosphorus are deposited in the stem nodes. In potassium-deficient potato plants given a low iron supply the symptoms of potassium deficiency occurred in old leaves and those of iron deficiency were acute in the young leaves but plants continued to grow from the apex. When the iron level was raised to high values potassium deficiency was delayed in appearance and then occurred in the young leaves in a different manner and the stem apices were killed. When plants lacking iron and potassium were grown with a low phosphorus level the whole plant was generally chlorotic and potassium deficiency was scarcely evident. Plants deficient in phosphorus and potassium showed mild potassium deficiency when given a low iron level but showed phosphorus deficiency with a high iron level.

The effects of potassium supply on the immobilisation of iron by phosphate results from three separate effects, namely the increase in inorganic/organic phosphorus ratio, increase in uptake of phosphate and localisation of iron in the roots. The change in the ratio of the inorganic to organic phosphorus is most probably caused by a decline of the potassium-activated phosphokinase systems, e.g. pyruvic kinase which produces ATP from phosphoenol pyruvate and ADP. The ATP in turn is essential for the incorporation of phosphate into many different compounds such as the sugar phosphate esters (via glucose and hexokinase) and the synthesis of the nucleic acids via the nucleotide phosphates, so that decreased ATP production will impede the assimilation of inorganic into organic phosphate at practically any point.

Another effect of potassium deficiency observed in many species of higher plants is the accumulation of putrescine. This was first reported by Coleman and Richards for barley in which the amine may attain a concentration of 1% of the dry weight of the leaves. The grey lesions characteristic of potassium deficiency in barley leaves were reproduced by feeding with putrescine. The replacement of potassium by rubidium or sodium prevented the accumulation of putrescine.

The putrescine was originally thought to arise by the decarboxylation of ornithine, since when ^{14}C-labelled ornithine was fed to excised barley leaves of potassium-deficient plants, labelled putrescine was formed, though only in small amounts. The demonstration of agmatine by Smith and Richards at high levels in potassium-deficient barley plants indicated the operation of an alternative pathway. The agmatine was shown to be formed by the decarboxylation of arginine to yield agmatine which is hydrolysed in two steps to the diamine putrescine.

$$
\begin{array}{c}
NH \\
\parallel \\
NH_2-C-NH(CH_2)_3\ CH-NH_2 \qquad \text{arginine} \\
\mid \\
COOH
\end{array}
$$

arginine decarboxylase $\quad\Big\downarrow -CO_2$

$$
\begin{array}{c}
NH \\
\parallel \\
NH_2-C-NH(CH_2)_4NH_2 \qquad\qquad \text{agmatine}
\end{array}
$$

agmatine iminohydrolase $\quad\Big\downarrow -NH_3$

$$
\begin{array}{c}
O \\
\parallel \\
NH_2-C-NH(CH_2)_4NH_2 \qquad\qquad \textit{N}\text{-carbamylputrescine}
\end{array}
$$

N-carbamylputrescine $\quad\Big\downarrow \begin{array}{l}-CO_2 \\ -NH_3\end{array}$
amidohydrolase

$$NH_2(CH_2)_4NH_2 \qquad\qquad\qquad \text{putrescine}$$

The activities of the enzymes arginine decarboxylase and N-carbamyl-putrescine amidohydrolase found in extracts of barley leaves were increased two to four times in the potassium-deficient plants and these enhanced activities would account for the increase levels of agmatine and putrescine. Although agmatine iminohydrolase activity could not be detected in extracts of barley plants, this enzyme must have been present in the intact plants since on feeding agmatine to barley seedlings, *N*-carbamylputrescine was formed. Feeding dilute acid (0·025N HCl) to barley seedlings through the roots induced the formation of arginine decarboxylase and *N*-carbamylputrescine amidohydrolase. It was therefore suggested that the putrescine may be accumulated in response to a drop in pH associated with potassium deficiency. The basic nature of the diamine would tend to restore the pH and act as a homeostatic mechanism in the control of cellular pH.

Potassium deficiency causes changes in the pattern of amino acids as well as in the production of putrescine. The example in Table 6.2 shows the relative changes induced in banana leaves. The amides asparagine and glutamine were increased to exceptionally high concentrations whereas proline decreased to 5% of that in normal leaves and similar changes have been observed in tobacco. In potatoes tyrosine was increased about threefold but opposite effects have been found in banana. Allantoin attained high concentrations in banana leaves apparently at the expense of allantoic acid. In barley lysine and the amides increased with potassium deficiency while aspartic and glutamic acids decreased.

Effects of potassium on ultrastructure

These were studied by Thomson and Weier in 1962 and by Vesk, Possingham and Mercer in 1966 in bean and tomato chloroplasts (Plate 83).

Bean chloroplasts attained full size and development before showing abnormality. Grana first lost their normal compartmented structure and became diffuse, electron-dense bodies. The intergrana fretwork, at first long and parallel, was later absent and was replaced by elongated lamellae often not connected to the collapsed electron dense grana residues, and the plastids were irregular in outline. Tomato chloroplasts were lacking in starch grains. Grana numbers were reduced and intergrana connections were very elongated double-membraned lamellae which were sometimes branched, but normal plastids in *older* leaves also showed these features. Dense small structures termed star bodies were relatively very numerous.

Calcium

Morphological effects of deficiency

Rapidly expanding leaves often show chlorosis and impaired growth in marginal areas just behind the leaf apex. This results in a typical 'hook' shape when the leaf margins fold backwards and the leaf apex curls in the opposite direction. The cells of these marginal regions may either have the highest calcium requirements or they may be the first to be deprived of the element as deficiency progresses. As younger leaves emerge the marginal growth becomes more restricted until no lamina expansion at all occurs and only necrotic, rudimentary leaves with central midrib are produced. The growing point of the shoot axis is killed but lateral buds do not usually start to develop even though apical dominance is no longer effective (Plates 14 to 17).

The abnormal effects in stem tissues appear in other different ways. In potatoes the tubers remain diminutive and become severely malformed. They also proliferate excessively and are sometimes joined by short lengths of stolon, sometimes appearing as successive or multiple outgrowths from an earlier diminutive tuber. There is often necrosis of cells in the surface regions of these tubers and in the inner vascular tissues. These symptoms occur quite

Table 6.2 Effects of some nutrient deficiencies on relative amino-acid concentrations in plants: figures as ratios to normal nutrient condition

Deficiency	Plant	Alanine	Aspartic acid	Asparagine	Arginine	γ-Amino butyric acid
Potassium	Banana leaf 5	1·5	1·8	4·0	1·7	1·4
Magnesium	Banana leaf 5	0·6	8·7	—	—	0·5
Phosphorus	Lucerne	1·5	2·1	7·4	19	—
	Banana leaf 5	0·7	7·2	0·4	6·7	0·4
Sulphur	Lucerne	0·5	3·3	—	1·1	—
	Mentha piperita	0·8	1·8	—	—	12
Chlorine	Cauliflower	1·9	1·1	2·1	40	1·2
Iron	Tomato	—	2·3	15	2·5	3·0
	Tobacco	0·1	>6	>40	>15	0·2
Manganese	Tomato	—	3·2	1·6	1·8	1·2
	Tobacco	0·2	>8	>40	>20	0·5
Copper	Tomato	—	3·6	2·0	2·0	0·7
	Tobacco	0·2	>5	>50	>15	0·3
Zinc	Tomato	—	2·9	48	5·8	1·2
	Tobacco	0·1	>7	>10	>20	0·2
Boron	Tobacco	0·2	>3	>9	>6	0·5
Molybdenum	Tobacco	0·1	>3	<0·5	>4	0·4
With Nitrate N	Cauliflower	—	<0·1	—	0·3	—
With Ammonium N	Cauliflower	—	3·0	—	2·7	—
With Nitrate N	Tomato	—	0·2	0·3	2·2	5·0

Values shown as > or < are estimates based on ratios of 'trace' to observed values in the original papers and indicate relatively low actual concentrations in many cases.
From experiments of Freney, Delwiche and Johnson, Gleiter and Parker, Mertz, Singleton and Garey, Freiberg and Steward, Hewitt, Agarwala and Williams, Possingham and Steinberg.

extensively at levels of calcium which have relatively little effect on the aerial parts of the stem and leaves. In many plants the onset of flowering appears to accentuate the need for calcium by stem tissues. Flower stalks and stems of plants about to flower often wilt and collapse suddenly, presumably because of necrosis of the vascular tissues. A characteristic disorder of tulips called 'topple' is caused in this way.

Root growth is particularly sensitive to lack of calcium. Apical extension ceases, tissues become translucent and lateral roots which emerge soon die. The apex may become bulbous, the root cap cells may be absent, as in *Pinus taeda*. Root hairs are probably deficient in calcium pectate, and root hairs of calcium-deficient plants expand apically to produce abnormal bulbous shapes.

?lutamic cid	Glutamine	Histidine	Lysine	Proline	Serine	Threonine	Valine
·1	4·3	—	2·1	0·05	4·0	2·5	1·7
·3	1·0	—	—	0·7	0·6	0·7	0·6
·7	4	2·9	1·8	1·0	1·1	—	1·3
·4	12·1	—	—	1·8	0·8	2·5	0·1
·4	—	0·7	0·6	0·6	0·7	0·5	0·6
·0	1·8	—	—	—	5·5	—	2·0
·1	3·4	—	—	7·1	2·2	1·7	2·4
·2	4·8	<0·5	5·1	2·2	0·9	1·4	2·5
·2	1·8	—	>6	0·1	0·3	0·2	0·8
·3	0·4	<0·3	<0·5	1·1	0·3	0·9	1·2
·7	0·8	—	>2	0·3	0·2	0·3	0·2
·4	0·6	<0·3	<0·5	3·0	0·8	0·7	1·2
·2	0·3	—	>8	0·3	0·3	0·3	0·2
·5	6·8	7·8	11	2·1	1·7	2·0	4·4
·5	3·0	—	>4	0·7	0·4	0·8	0·5
·2	0·7	—	>8	0·9	0·2	0·3	0·3
·1	1·0	—	>6	0·2	0·3	0·2	0·3
·3	0·6	—	—	—	0·7	—	—
·5	2·6	—	—	—	2·5	—	—
·5	0·2	<0·5	<0·5	1·6	1·2	0·3	1·0

Experiments by Cormack, Lemay and MacLachlan in 1963 were made with radioactive $^{45}CaCl_2$ to study the effects of calcium on growth of mustard, maize or tomato root hairs. Radioactive calcium was translocated from the seed treated with $CaCl_2$ to root hairs of the radicle in moist air. Calcium was located in increasing concentration backwards along the root hair wall but was absent at the tip, where growth originated (Plate 18). When seedlings were grown in a solution of $CaCl_2$ (5 mM) the root hair tips contained the most calcium and growth in length was much decreased. Walls contained more calcium than the cytoplasm. Experiments by Borström with wheat roots suggest that cell expansion is inhibited by calcium deficiency to a greater extent than in cell division for which calcium requirements may be 100 times greater, but the level of iron provided at the same time appears to have a modifying effect on the calcium requirements for cell division. Burström concluded that calcium hardened the cell walls and induced the production of an elastic condition.

Calcium deficiency suppresses seed development, and necrosis of cotyledons occurs before seed maturation in pods of beans and peas. In tomato fruits, the pericarp and epidermal cells become necrotic. Root nodule development in legumes shows high calcium requirements which are some ten times greater than those needed for normal growth of the host plant with a fixed nitrogen source. Calcium tends to be immobilised in older tissues so that young leaves suffer from deficiency whereas older ones may remain normal. The gynophore of the ground-nut requires an independent calcium supply after reaching the ground and cannot obtain calcium from the root system of the parent plant.

Effects of calcium supply on histology and ultrastructure

Calcium supply has profound effects on several aspects of cell structure. Florell observed that quite small increments of calcium resulted in considerable stimulation of formation of mitochondria in wheat roots and their protein content. The effect on mitochondria was more pronounced than that on root-cell expansion. Classical studies by Sorokin and Sommer showed that severe lack of calcium in pea roots caused failure of normal mitosis. Pseudomitotic division of nuclei showed incomplete separation of chromosomes, spindle abnormality, aggregation of chromatin and failure to produce the cell plate for new cell-wall formation so that binucleate cells were produced. Differentiation was suppressed but vacuolation was accentuated. As little as 0·06 p.p.m. calcium permitted mitotic division but the axis was abnormally orientated so that lateral swelling rather than axial extension occurred. At this concentration mitosis was still abnormal in lateral primordia. Tetraploid nuclei were still observed after more prolonged growth with 0·25 p.p.m. calcium. In maize calcium deficiency inhibited cell-plate formation and so prevented the middle lamella from being laid down. In *Spirogyra* the characteristic lobes of the spiral chloroplast were suppressed by lack of calcium and a substance resembling lecithin accumulated around the nucleus. Low levels of calcium may cause lack of lignification in pericycle and vascular elements and redistribution of dry matter between cells of different differentiation, increasing cell-wall thickness in the cuticle, epidermis, collenchyma or hypodermis depending on the plant species studied. Calcium deficiency appears to induce fairly consistent and similar cytological and mitotic abnormalities in several species but the concentrations at which such effects appear differ considerably between species.

A long-established idea originated by Payen in 1846, Mangin, in 1892 and Hansteen in 1910 of the role of calcium is that calcium combines with pectic acid to form calcium pectate in the middle lamella. The observation by Bennet-Clark that EDTA promotes cell extension, as also does ammonium oxalate, is consistent with the view that calcium pectate limits cell-wall plasticity. Other divalent or trivalent metal ions including iron, magnesium and copper may have synergistic effects with calcium in forming pectate bridges with non-methylated carboxyl groups according to Ginzburg. Adamson in 1962 showed very elegantly that the processes of cell division and expansion in artichoke tuber tissues could be controlled relative to each other by the concentrations of calcium ions. At a calcium ion concentration of 50 mEq/1, cell expansion was suppressed and division proceeded rapidly, but at 0·1 mEq/1 expansion was fast and mitotic frequency was low.

Magnesium also had this effect but less markedly. It was considered that formation of calcium-uronic acid salts which stiffened the cell wall was the most likely explanation.

The role of calcium in the organisation of chromatin which comprises the deoxyribonucleic acid (DNA) structures of nuclei has been shown by studies of several workers. Chelating agents such as EDTA or citrate induce dispersion of the chromosomes. Low-calcium levels and chelating agents increased chiasmata, and calcium-deficient *Tradescantia* and *Plantago* cells and pollen were more susceptible to irradiation changes which caused chromosomal abnormalities. The molecular basis for these conditions is not known but the divalent metal may orientate DNA in chromatin by forming ionic bridges.

Marinos in 1962 described electron microscope studies on the effect of calcium deficiency on the ultrastructure of barley stem apex cells (Plate 87). An early symptom appeared to be the separation of plasma and vacuole membranes into two layers. Other symptoms developed rapidly and included fragmentation of the nuclear membrane into vesiculated or hollow fragments of membrane with frequent, large irregular gaps. The plasma membranes become irregularly lobed because parts are detached from the cell wall. Plastids disintegrate and plasma double membranes fragment. The cell walls themselves become opaque, or 'electron-dense' but gaps also appear between adjacent walls. The importance of calcium for membranes is certainly indicated by these studies, and the role of calcium in mitochondrial formation was described by Florell and later by Lindblad in 1959. Similar investigations by Vesk, Possingham and Mercer on tomato chloroplasts showed the presence of large starch grains, decreased numbers of grana and a tendency for the dense lamella packing of the grana to expand into a diffuse fret similar to the interconnecting frets. In these respects they resembled older normal chloroplasts.

The hypothesis developed by Bennet-Clark (Chapter 4) that a lecithinase system may be involved in ion uptake and transport suggests an additional role of calcium. This enzyme is activated by calcium and the optimum concentration of calcium is o·oi M. Calcium salts of lecithin may be components of membranes thus accounting for the effects of calcium on mitochondrial formation.

Calcium is probably multifunctional and required for middle lamellae of cell walls, organelle membranes, nuclear substructure and as a base equivalent for inorganic and organic anions of the cell.

Magnesium

The presence of magnesium in chlorophyll (Chapter 8) is a determining feature of the effects of magnesium deficiency. Chlorosis (loss of chlorophyll) occurs as expected and appears first in the oldest leaves (Plate 19). Other pigments, orange, pink, red, but not chemically characterised often appear as the chlorophylls disappear. Cell breakdown later causes necrotic areas in the chlorotic leaves. There are wide variations in the patterns of chlorosis which occur in different plants.

There is another type of symptom of interest which appears in *Phaseolus* (beans). This starts as regularly arranged rows of purple-brown spots adjacent to the main leaf veins of older leaves and originating in the basal areas of the leaflets. Later yellow, green or yellow-chlorotic areas and necrotic patches develop. The symptoms are of interest because almost identical effects occur in young trifoliate leaves of plants deficient in manganese. As manganese and magnesium are interchangeable elements required by many dissociable metal enzyme systems (see Chapter 8) it is possible that in young leaves manganese, and in older leaves magnesium is the metal of preference for one or more of these enzymes whose defection in beans lead to the symptoms described. Differential requirement for the two elements would result from differences in affinity for either metal in competing systems.

Cytochemical and ultrastructural aspects of magnesium

Magnesium has a critical role in the structure of the ribosomal particles responsible for protein synthesis. The ribosomes consist of two or more subparticles whose association in a functional manner is dependent on the correct magnesium concentration. The first recognition of the critical importance of magnesium in this respect is credited by Petermann to the work of Chao in 1957 on yeast microsomes. Similar requirements for pea seedling microsomes were observed by Webster in 1957 and T'so, Bonner and Vinograd in 1958. The binding of magnesium is decreased by chelating agents and by high ionic strength of the medium. The polyamines spermine and spermidine may at least partly replace magnesium in this system. Calcium may also replace magnesium for binding but less effectively for protein synthesis, whereas manganese may be less effective in binding but more effective in protein synthesis *in vitro* and mixtures of the three metals may be still better. In addition to binding the structural units of the ribosomes, magnesium at 10^{-2} to 10^{-3} M probably also binds the transfer RNA which conveys an amino acid to the ribosome and may similarly assist in binding the template or messenger RNA which codes for a specific transfer RNA, to the ribosomal complex where protein synthesis takes place. Dilution of the magnesium ions causes dissociation of the ribosomes. The optimum concentration *in vitro* is about 0·01 M and below this the sub-units begin to dissociate. The aggregate ribosome in peas (or 80 Svedberg sedimentation units (80S)) has a molecular weight of about 450 000 and the sub-units have molecular weights of about 300 000 (60S), 150 000 (41S) and 75 000 (26S). In *Escherichia coli* the proportion of fully aggregated dimeric ribosomes (100S) is a function of the fifth power of the magnesium ion concentration and dissociation is complete at $2·5 \times 10^{-4}$ M. T'so and Bonner concluded that when associated into the single particle, about half the phosphate groups of RNA in the particles were combined with magnesium and that there was six times more magnesium than calcium in the ribosomes.

Marinos in 1963 described effects of magnesium deficiency on ultra-structural changes in the apex of barley shoots. These were similar in general aspects to effects of phosphorus and nitrogen deficiencies noted already. The principal feature was the development of granules about 80 nm across in the mitochondria. As the granules appeared the 'cristae' or 'tubules', inverted membrane structures characteristic of the mitochondria, disappeared. Cytoplasmic inclusions which reacted with manganese (as $KMnO_4$) and associated with Golgi bodies were also more numerous in phosphorus, nitrogen and magnesium deficiencies, but the abnormal appearance of starch granules in plastids observed with phosphorus deficiency did not occur with magnesium and nitrogen deficiencies. Comparable studies on *Phaseolus vulgaris* were described by Thomson and Weier (1962) and Whatley (1971) with particular reference to the structure of chloroplasts (Plates 79 and 80). The grana were decreased in numbers, irregular in shape, and the compartmentation of the grana was reduced or absent. The interconnecting frets were reduced or absent and starch was accumulated. Vesicles appeared and were probably cross-sectional veins of swollen fret channels. Vesk, Possingham and Mercer noted that the effects in maize chloroplasts were quite similar to those described by Thomson and Weier for bean plastids. Spinach chloroplasts were similarly affected and these also had large starch grains. Excessive starch accumulation in chloroplasts of cauliflower was also observed by Hewitt and Hucklesby as magnesium deficiency developed. It has been calculated that the *in vivo* concentration of chlorophyll, and therefore of magnesium in chloroplasts is about 0·2 M. This is some twenty times greater than the average cell concentration and it is not surprising therefore that the first effects of deficiency are often symptoms of chlorosis.

Iron

Effects of iron deficiency on chlorophyll and chloroplasts

The most obvious and immediate effect of iron deficiency is the appearance of chlorosis in the young leaves of the shoot. The leaf veins often remain pale green thereby producing a fine 'net' pattern over the whole leaf of a typical dicotyledon, or green 'tramlines' in monocotyledons such as cereals. When acute, the whole leaf may be pale yellow or almost white with or without necrotic breakdown. Chloroplasts are reduced in size and lack chlorophyll. Chloroplasts may disintegrate or vacuolate and in cauliflower leaves the starch grains shrink and disappear.

Changes in chloroplasts of iron-deficient plants were first observed by Gris in 1844. The structural details as revealed by electron microscope studies were described by Bogorad, Piper, Swift and Melbrath in 1959, Lamprecht in 1961, and Vesk, Possingham and Mercer in 1966. In *Xanthium pennsylvanicum* the principal changes were in the lamellar structure as iron deficiency developed. Lamellae were reduced in number, and occurred in groups of two or three. They often extended across the whole span of the chloroplast. The interlamellar regions were more granular and coarse and the fine lamellar stacking of normal chloroplasts was lacking. Chloroplasts as such did not differ appreciably in size with regard to iron supply. In *Tradescantia*, lamellae were elongated and plastids were amoeboid. Osmiophilic (lipid?) granules increased in size and numbers. Large electron transparent spaces appeared and lamellae tended to fuse together or to form long double lamellae which then broke up. In tomato the numbers of grana were reduced and the stroma area was increased. The relatively rectangular stacks of lamellae in normal plastids were reduced in height and the numbers of compartments in the grana were decreased from ten or so to five or less and these were often swollen. The frets connecting the grana were reduced in number and formed swollen compartments. Starch grains were more numerous and larger. In iron-deficient spinach the chloroplasts were initially abnormally small and resembled the proplastids of etiolated plants. In more acute deficiency the plastids had no grana and only a short length of swollen lamellae with double membranes. Numerous small vesicles developed and fused into irregular tubules embedded in electron-transparent stroma. In maize the changes in moderately chlorotic tissues are similar with respect to decrease in grana size and number and in swelling or disappearance of intergrana frets. When more chlorotic, the grana disappear and the frets are replaced by lamellae which are arranged in parallel layers around the plastid membrane or by vesicles. The relationship to each other in origin of the vesicles and the lamellae adjacent to the membrane is not established.

Effects of iron on growth and respiration

The work of Brown and Possingham in 1957 indicated that root tip meristems in pea and tomato are especially sensitive to iron deficiency. When grown in iron-free media all division ceased abruptly within seven days. The processes subsequent to cell division were less dependent on iron and so continued when division was no longer observed. Protein synthesis also continued so the protein content per cell tended to be higher in the iron-deficient meristems in spite of a drop in total protein per root. Tomato stem apex meristems ceased to produce leaf primordia when severely deficient in iron. The effect of iron deficiency in maize is shown in Plate 32.

Respiration of root tips studied by Possingham and Brown and of sunflower leaves examined by Glenister was depressed by iron deficiency. This response would be expected if the principal respiratory system operating under normal conditions were that dependent on the cytochrome oxidase, cytochrome c, b-cytochromes and succinic dehydrogenase sequence. Nevertheless it was also shown by Possingham and Brown that after three days of iron deficiency the cyanide sensitivity was relatively much greater in the normal than in the iron-deficient tissues. This was considered to mean that a different (cyanide-insensitive) respiratory mechanism had partially taken over from the normal cytochrome system. A flavin-dependent system would be consistent with these observations. Welkie and Miller in 1960 have shown that riboflavin and ribo-flavin phosphate (FMN) increase tenfold in iron-deficient tobacco leaves and Lenhof, Nicholas and Kaplan in 1956 showed that a flavin-dependent respiration replaces an iron-dependent system in *Pseudomonas fluorescens* when deprived of iron. A remarkable change in sensitivity to cyanide by entire soybean plants was found. The normal plants were severely injured by cyanide in the nutrient solution but chlorotic plants deficient in iron were relatively cyanide tolerant.

The role of iron in cell division may be more direct than through an effect of respiratory energy availability. Protein synthesis is dependent on respiration in terms of production of ATP and other nucleotide triphosphates and maintenance of ribosomal RNA. However the direct effect of iron on cell division may be the result either of a direct dependence of this process on the cytochrome oxidase pathway or because iron has an additional role in mitosis. Loring and Waritz and Possingham and Brown in 1957 both showed that iron is heavily concentrated in meristematic nuclei. Cohn in 1959 concluded similarly that iron is involved in chromosome structure and that cytochrome oxidase activity was directly concerned. Amoore in 1962, 1963 reported that pea root-tip respiration was sensitive to cyanide in darkness and light, and to carbon monoxide, the effect of which was reversed by light, indicating the activity of cytochrome oxidase. Although mitosis was also sensitive to both inhibitors the effects of cyanide were also reversed by light, from which it was concluded that a ferrous-iron complex was specifically concerned in mitosis independently of reversible oxidation and reduction of iron in cytochrome oxidase. Kohlman in 1957 and Cohn in 1961 found that cyanide and α, α'-dipyridyl caused chromosome breakage. An iron compound probably in the ferrous state could therefore be involved in chromosomal structure.

Manganese

Effects of manganese supply on chloroplasts

Manganese deficiency caused the appearance of paired or tetrad groups of chloroplasts in *Elodea canadensis* and in *Lemna minor* studied by Brown, Eyster and Tanner, possibly because subdivision was arrested. The electron microscope investigations of Possingham, Vesk and Mercer are illustrated in Plates 74 and 75. In spinach, at first the lamellae connecting the grana become separated from and are more sensitive to deficiency than the grana themselves. The lamellae are decreased in number and fuse together to form vesicles which finally represent all of the lamellar material. The compartments are reduced from as many as twenty-five to only four and increased in length. The contents of the plastid become vacuolated, and mitochondria and other cell organelles appear to become trapped in extruded tails of amoeboid chloroplast material. This situation could be expected to have devastating effects on cellular metabolism. The sharp decrease in oxygen evolution from chloroplasts of plants only slightly deficient in manganese corresponds to the stage at which grana are reduced in numbers and the grana compartments are also reduced. Nevertheless, these workers do not consider that the impaired oxygen evolution is directly the result of structural breakdown because disintegrated chloroplasts still show high oxygen evolution activity. Changes in tomato chloroplasts are generally similar to those described for spinach.

Symptoms of manganese deficiency

Leaves are often chlorotic but the rapid appearance of numerous, initially small, necrotic brown areas frequently distinguishes the symptoms from those of iron deficiency. Manganese deficiency may appear first in young or old leaves but iron deficiency almost invariably appears first in young expanding leaves. A characteristic effect known as 'marsh spot' occurs in cotyledons of ungerminated seeds of peas, broad beans, haricot beans and much more rarely in dwarf or climbing french beans. The symptoms include a shrinkage and browning of the central tissue of the cotyledons and a browning of the radicle and plumule of the embryo (Plates 43 and 44). Two other well-known field disorders are grey-speck in oats where leaves show grey necrotic lesions (Plate 42), and speckled yellows of sugar beet and an analogous necrosis in table beet. In cacao leaves a unique condition of combined iron and manganese deficiency has been found to cause a change in leaf morphology so that the usually slightly serrated leaves become markedly dentate.

Copper

Visible effects of copper deficiency

Several important field disorders are caused by copper deficiency, more especially in some tropical and subtropical tree species. 'Exanthemata' or bark blisters which exude gum occur in citrus, plums, olives, pear and apple. Shoot dieback with S-shaped growths appear in apple, and scorching of young leaves or chlorosis is common. Production of vigorous 'water shoots', with brown stains in the bark and later multiple shoots called 'witches broom' occurs in citrus. Symptoms commonly appear in the younger leaves of herbaceous species, tomato, beans, pea, clovers and lucerne. In cereals the conditions called 'white tip' or reclamation disease prevails on peaty soils and calcareous shell sands. Young leaves are chlorotic, have ring-like kinks at intervals, remain rolled, show a spiral coiling like a spring, sometimes reversed along its length, and remain trapped at the apex in the subtending leaf. Ear and grain formation are severely reduced. Spiralling and kinking of needles occurs in Sitka spruce. The purple brown pigment in flowers of broad beans is pale or bleached, presumably indicating a defective phenol oxidase activity (see Chapter 8). Flower colour of some irises and dahlias may depend on the supply of copper. Copper content of seed has a considerable effect on the appearance of deficiency in beans and peas. Difference in field performance between rye and oats in copper-deficient soils is related to differences in seed copper content. Effects of copper deficiency are shown in Plates 34 to 41, and 45.

Histological effects of copper deficiency

Reed studied changes caused by copper deficiency in tomato leaves. Palisade cells below the stomata separated, causing abnormally large intercellular spaces. The separating cells became isolated and then shrank and collapsed. Plastids were large and thus aggregated and the contents became fluid with lipid droplets. Rather curiously chloroplasts of tomato and spinach remained normal when the plants were deficient in copper except for lack of starch grains. Vesk, Possingham and Mercer concluded that this result indicated suppression of photosynthesis.

Zinc

Effects of deficiency on growth

Several of the effects of zinc deficiency are very characteristic and well known in the field including 'little leaf' of citrus (Plate 49), 'sickle leaf' of cocoa, 'bronzing' of tung, 'rosette' of pecan, and 'white bud' of maize. Severe re-striction of leaf size to as little as 5% of normal and shortening of internodes are the most obvious symptoms, usually accompanied by various types of chlorosis, which may be highly contrasting or diffuse and indistinct. The permeability of leaf-cell membranes appears to be impaired and cell contents leak out to the surface and provide a medium for fungal growth as for example of *Oidium heveae* on rubber leaves and other fungi on leaves of maize and tomato and in roots of water cress causing 'crook root'. Seed formation is particularly sensitive to zinc deficiency in peas and beans and subterranean clovers. Absence of micropyle, integument and embryo sac nuclei occurs. Tomato roots produce irregular swellings behind the apex where root hairs normally occur. These are short and crooked. The effects of zinc deficiency on tomato, red clover, apple and citrus are shown in Plates 45 to 49.

Cytological effects

Abnormal enlargement of decreased numbers of leaf palisade cells was observed in tomato, walnut and apricot plants and was associated with delayed or incomplete differentiation. In clovers palisade cells divide in the plane of the lamina and irregular protrusions appear from epidermal cells. In leaves of many species the plastids become agglutinated, vacuolated and filled with tannin-lipid complexes or undergo lysis. Calcium oxalate crystals appear and cell membranes lose their semi-permeable properties as noted above in other species. Thomson and Weier described electron micrographic studies of zinc deficiency in bean chloroplasts (Plate 84). There was a progressive loss of the grana relative to the stroma. The compartments of the grana were initially clearly defined but there were few intergrana connections. Grana of younger leaves became disorganised, the frets disappeared and the compart-ments of the grana appeared to become isolated or split open. The plastids became vacuolated and electron transparent in confirmation of the earlier light microscope studies of Reed.

Metabolic changes related to zinc deficiency

Zinc deficiency may have effects on auxin metabolism, as first recognised by Skoog. Peroxidase, which is one factor in the widespread indoleacetic acid oxidase system, usually increases markedly in zinc-deficient tissues, and auxin destruction is accentuated. Auxin content is often less than 10% of the usual level in tomato stem apex and increases rapidly after restoring the zinc supply. An independent effect of zinc may be on auxin synthesis according to Tsui who considered that zinc is required for synthesis of tryptophan, a probable precursor, and the tryptophan synthetase system of *Escherichia coli* appears to be activated by zinc.

Amides and several amino acids accumulate in tissues of tomato and tobacco plants. Increased concentrations of inorganic phosphate in several plants is associated with increased activity of acid phosphatase in cases of zinc deficiency but neither of these types of response is specific. Relationships between zinc and enzyme action are considered in Chapter 8.

Boron

Symptoms of boron deficiency

Visible symptoms of boron deficiency include death of the primary growing point and when more severe, of the root apices also. This is usually preceded by deformation, suspended growth or blackening of the *basal* marginal areas of the very young expanding leaves (as contrasted with the *apical* marginal areas in calcium deficiency) and may be accompanied by production of surface corky lesions as in beet, or 'bark measles' in apple, and cross-splitting of vascular bundles as in 'stem crack' of celery. Dormant axillary growing points often develop for a time or may take over while the central crown of the plant is dead as in 'crown rot' of sugar beet. The breakdown of the growing point leads to infection by *Phoma betae*, and in kale, cracked stems lead to *Bacterium (Erwinia) carotovorum* infection in the central pith tissues. Effects of boron deficiency are shown in Plates 58 to 62.

Histological symptoms initially include proliferation of cells in cambial tissues and disorderly and uncontrolled cell expansion, producing giant thin-walled cells. This causes collapse of groups of neighbouring cells which become necrotic regions. Pectic compounds and then cellulose appear to be withdrawn from cell walls and tannins accumulate in the vacuoles. In stem apical cells of peas the period between cell division was found to be doubled and cell division was prevented in the roots, and the root meristematic cells were irreversibly damaged by deficiency conditions exceeding 48–72 hours.

In roots, procambial cells become necrotic, or proliferate and phloem cells enlarge and xylem is poorly differentiated. Apical enlargement is caused by irregular proliferation of the plerome (prevascular) tissues. Differentiation although poor is often premature.

The changes in cell-wall structure may depend on their location. Spurr found that in collenchyma of celery petioles the cell walls decreased in thickness from 9 μm to less than 4 μm and the number of cellulose lamellae revealed by swelling in sulphuric acid decreased from sixty to about twenty, and were also individually thinner. In phloem and ground parenchyma however the cell walls increased from 1 μm to as much as 4 μm in boron-deficient tissues. Impaired translocation of carbohydrates may have been a contributory factor. In general boron deficiency affects cells in cambial and apical meristematic regions of stems and roots. Proliferation and uncontrolled expansion lead to tissue collapse, necrosis and malformation. Differentiation is inhibited and cell-wall dimensions change. Maximal sensitivity occurs in those tissues where differentiation has or would have normally been in progress and when the purely meristematic phase is past.

Effects of boron on cell ultrastructure

Lee and Aronoff (1966) reported the effects of boron supply on the cells of the highly sensitive indicator plant, sunflower. Changes in leaf mesophyll cell ultrastructure occurred before macroscopic effects were detected. Chloroplasts of cells in basal areas of young leaves were the first organelles to show changes. Starch increased and almost all chloroplasts in randomly distributed cells accumulated quantities of an osmiophilic (osmium-tetroxide reactive) compound. Myelin structures appeared in mitochondria and rhombohedral masses of osmiophilic material were deposited in nuclei. The cell walls became thickened and had roughened irregular surfaces consistent with the light microscope observations made on celery by Spurr in 1957. Ultimately cells were entirely filled by osmiophilic particles and probably therefore lipid droplets, while the mitochondria disintegrated. In spinach, chloroplasts were again the most sensitive to boron deficiency and were reduced in size before mitochondria showed any changes.

Molybdenum

Effects of molybdenum deficiency

Symptoms of molybdenum deficiency may be of two types. One type which may be referred to as 'primary' symptoms, is associated with growth of plants under severe deficiency conditions with nitrate as the source of nitrogen. Lettuce, spinach, cauliflower and other brassicas, radish, beet and tomato are especially susceptible. Older leaves, but often not the cotyledons, become chlorotic, particularly interveinally, membranous at the margins, and rapidly scorch. These symptoms progress with younger leaves, until the plants are killed. The symptoms are associated with accumulation of nitrate in the leaves which may attain 15% of the dry weight. This is a direct result of lack of nitrate reductase of which molybdenum is a component. Other species such as beans and pea may not show any symptoms in the first generation. Plants raised from seed grown under deficiency conditions may show moderate symptoms in the next generation and severe symptoms in the third generation. Plants raised from such molybdenum-deficient seed are entirely normal if sown in the presence of the element. Cereals show comparable symptoms but are intermediate in sensitivity between the small-seeded and larger-seeded plants. The other type of symptom has been referred to as 'secondary' and is confined almost entirely to brassica species, especially broccoli, cauliflower and some cabbage and kale varieties (Plates 54, 55 and 56). These secondary symptoms known as whiptail are produced either (1) when the plants are grown with ammonium sulphate, urea, nitrite and some other non-nitrate sources of nitrogen or (2) when grown with nitrate and a molybdenum concentration above that which is associated with the primary symptoms. This level is about 0·000 05 p.p.m. compared with 0·000 005 p.p.m. which causes severe primary symptoms or 0·0005–0·0001 p.p.m. which may permit normal plants slightly restricted in growth.

In Mo deficient cauliflower young leaves suffer loss of the mesophyll of the leaf lamina leaving an irregular margin of tissue along the midrib or only the bare midrib itself, which can continue to elongate into a twisted habit. This type of leaf malformation originates in the breakdown of lamina initially in localised areas near the base of a partially expanded leaf. In later stages the breakdown occurs in progressively younger leaves and finally causes disintegration of primordia and death of the growing point. Partially deformed primordia develop into enlarged but severely distorted tissue masses.

The whiptail symptoms were recognised in field conditions but the cause was unknown for many years before it was reproduced experimentally by Hewitt and Jones in 1947 and identified as molybdenum deficiency in confirmation of conclusions of Davies and Mitchell in 1945 who found responses to molybdenum by field plants. The symptoms may prove to be useful in illustrating an important principle concerning the role of metals in the synthesis of the metallo-proteins in which they are combined (see pages 27 and 203).

Histological effects of molybdenum deficiency

The initial stages of whiptail in leaves of molybdenum-deficient cauliflower grown with ammonium sulphate were investigated by Hucklesby and Hewitt with the light microscope. Collapse of the chloroplasts was followed by disintegration and dispersion into the cytoplasm and erosion of liberated starch grains. Grana lost their dehydrogenase capacity to reduce tetrazolium dyes by NADPH. Chlorophyll disappeared and peroxidase activity increased markedly. Reactions for protein, ribonucleic acid and lipid decreased, and lipid droplets appeared in the cytoplasm. Epidermal cells collapsed and palisade and spongy mesophyll cells enlarged and vacuolated or collapsed in successive layers which became desiccated and fused together. In young leaves of plants grown with nitrate, large starch grains expanded, distending the chloroplasts before chlorosis appeared. Ruptured chloroplasts, lipoprotein and starch grains spread into the cytoplasm.

Spinach chloroplasts of nitrate-grown plants showed similar vacuolation around the thylakoids and breakdown of chloroplast membranes.

Electron micrographs obtained at Long Ashton of chloroplasts from cauliflower leaves grown in a nitrate medium with and without molybdenum are shown in Plates 88 and 89. In molybdenum deficiency vesiculation of the chloroplast membrane occurred, the tonoplast disintegrated and vacuoles appeared along the cell walls. Thylakoid stacking in grana was reduced or indistinct, and thylakoids became suspended in vacuoles. In the nitrate medium, whiptail symptoms were not induced (see page 167) but the plants became very chlorotic. With a molybdenum-deficient ammonium medium, whiptail symptoms appeared and the sequence of chloroplast breakdown in the lesions was similar to that observed for the nitrate treatment. With both nitrogen sources, extreme deficiency caused chloroplast rupture (Plate 90). Mitochondria and nuclei appeared most resistant to breakdown.

Chlorine

Chlorine deficiency

The essential nature of chlorine was discovered as recently as 1954 by Broyer, Carlton, Johnson and Short as the result of detective work on an unidentified suspected deficiency in tomatoes. Apical leaflets wilted and ceased expansion, locally becoming stunted. Injections of 2 μg Cl^- cured the disorder. More advanced symptoms consisted of chlorosis, necrosis and bronzing of the tissues behind the wilted regions. The bronze pigments were associated with locally coagulated cytoplasm and exuded into intercellular spaces. The pigment was insoluble in all solvents tested including alkali, acid and xylol, or alcohol. Roots became stunted and lateral branching was suppressed, or multiple branching with root tips which were club-shaped developed. Lettuce and cabbage (Plate 63) were susceptible species whereas larger seeded cereals and beans were resistant. Bromide partially substituted for chloride. A field response to chloride was reported in Western Australia by Ozanne.

Other elements

Beneficial and restricted effects of sodium, cobalt, aluminium, silicon, selenium and vanadium

The possible or restricted importance of some other element has been noted in the second chapter. The beneficial effects of sodium or rubidium in the absence of adequate potassium are well known. The explanation may be in the ability of these elements to substitute for potassium in some enzyme system but not in all its functions (Chapter 8). In some species sodium may be independently essential. This has been proved beyond doubt by Brownell for *Atriplex vesicaria* a salt-marsh species, but the amount of sodium required is very small, in the micronutrient range of concentration. The explanation of the requirement in addition to potassium has not been elucidated. *Anabaena cylindrica* was shown by Allen and Arnon to require sodium, and this is especially important when it is dependent on nitrogen fixation. One other example of a specific sodium requirement is directly explained by a biochemical condition. *Salmonella typhi* and *Aerobacter aerogenes* when grown on citrate as carbon source produce an alternative metabolic pathway dependent on a different type of oxaloacetic decarboxylase enzyme from the normal. The latter is activated by divalent metals, especially manganese, but the citrate-induced enzyme is specifically dependent on sodium and this element becomes essential for citrate-grown cells.

Cobalt is required by many micro-organisms which depend on vitamin B_{12} or the cobamide co-enzyme for one or more aspects of metabolism (Chapter 7). Cobalt, probably in the form of a B_{12}-type structure is essential for nitrogen-fixing organisms in root nodules of legumes (*Rhizobium*) or the non-legumes (probably Actinomycetes) (Plates 27, 28 and 29).

Therefore cobalt is essential for legumes and the root nodulated non-legumes when these species are dependent on atmospheric nitrogen fixation. Ahmed and Evans, and Bond and Hewitt first showed the importance of cobalt in these circumstances for the two respective classes of plants.

However Wilson and Nicholas observed effects of cobalt deficiency on chlorosis when clover and wheat were grown in aseptic cultures with exclusion of atmospheric contamination. Bolle-Jones and Mallikarjuneswara reported a small growth response in rubber seedlings and Maskell, Evans and Murray reported leaf symptoms in cocoa in relation to deficient cobalt supply. These reports will need to be substantiated, but it is quite possible that only some species require the element. In some enzymic systems concerning glutamine, cobalt influences the direction of optical activity of the products.

Aluminium was reported to be required by *Polygonum sachalinense* and *Miscanthus sinensis* which grow on Japanese volcanic soils. Chenery concluded that the tea plant, which is an aluminium accumulator actually requires the element. The blue colour of hydrangea flowers and some other related species depends on aluminium. Aluminium was also reported to antagonize toxic effects of copper in citrus grown in water culture.

Silica comprises a large proportion of plant ash and is located in the cell walls of leaves and stems in cereals, hairs of the stinging nettle (*Urtica*) (Plate 7), the cell walls of diatoms (Plate 8), etc. and probably fulfils an essential structural role. Attempts to prove that silicon is generally required by plants have not been unequivocally successful. Rice and gherkins appeared to have a specific need as judged by visible symptoms of deficiency reported by Wagner. The form and crystalline structure of silica in carefully ashed plant tissues or natural deposits were investigated by Lanning, Ponnaiya and Crumpton. Opal and α-quartz were found in different species and dumb-bell-shaped silica residues occurred in ashed leaf skeletons. The significance of silicon in plants has been recently reviewed by Lewin and Reimann (1969).

Accumulator plants

Some plants accumulate or incorporate unusual elements into their cells in abnormally high concentrations. The poisonous South African species *Dichapetalum cymosum* (Plate 12) and *D. toxicarium* synthesise fluoro-acetic and fluoro-oleic acids which are highly poisonous to animals consuming them (see page 252). Accumulator plants which absorb abnormally high concentrations of certain elements, which are often toxic to many other species are especially interesting in connection with the possibility of certain elements being essential for particular species.

Accumulation of barium by Brazil nuts, of aluminium by tea, and of selenium by *Astragalus* and some other plants are examples. Sub-species of some plants, particularly the Gramineae become adapted in a short period by genetic selection to soils having excesses of zinc, copper, lead, nickel, chromium, etc. In a few instances they appear to become partially dependent on these soil conditions and these habitats are usually the sources of possible selections for the development of essential requirements for metals such as chromium, nickel or cobalt.

The selenium accumulators are especially interesting (Plate 10). According to Trelease and Trelease, and Levine, low concentrations of selenium were necessary for maximum growth of *Astragalus racemosus*, *A. pattersonii* and also for *Lupinus albus*. Some species, e.g. *A. racemosus* and *A. bisulcatus* accumulate over 1000 p.p.m. Se on a dry weight basis, but *A. missouriensis* contains only 1 to 5 p.p.m. The accumulators are highly adapted to the poisonous seleniferous soils (causing 'alkali disease' of animals) but other species either tolerate them and do not accumulate, or cannot grow in these soils. Selenium can replace sulphur in certain sulphur amino acids giving seleno-cystathionine, selenomethionine, selenocysteine and methylselenocysteine and these compounds are potentially poisonous. Some of these have also been isolated from wheat grown in a seleniferous soil. Selenomethionine competes with methionine in the synthesis of protein.

Mineral element interactions

Several important types of interaction are known. These include the following relationships or associations: $Fe/K/PO_4$, Ca/K, Mg/N, Fe/Mn, $HCO_3/Fe/Mn$, or Cu or Zn or Co or Ni or $Cd/Fe/Mo$, Al/PO_4, NH_4 or NO_3/Mo, Mn/Mg, Cu/N and Ca/Mn. A few of these are considered in more detail below. Certain species or even varieties are especially susceptible to the imbalanced conditions associated with many of these interactions and these have therefore often been recognised first or elucidated only for particular species.

Iron is involved in several types of interaction. In each, chlorosis which is usually visually indistinguishable from that produced by simple iron deficiency is one of the most obvious symptoms. In the $Fe/K/PO_4$ interaction which is associated with potatoes, mustard, maize, sugar cane and some other graminaceous plants a deficiency of potassium causes the appearance of iron deficiency. In potatoes, iron tends to be retained in tubers and roots and in maize and sugar cane iron accumulates in the stem nodes of potassium-deficient plants. The effect of potassium deficiency appears to be related to phosphorus metabolism. This relationship could be a consequence of the potassium requirement in the pyruvic kinase system which controls the reversible formation of ATP from phosphoenol pyruvic acid and ADP, or in the acetothiokinase system which catalyses the following overall reaction:

$$\text{Acetic acid} + \text{ATP} + \text{HSCoA} \rightleftharpoons \text{CH}_3\text{COSCoA} + \text{AMP} + \text{pyrophosphate}$$

Another potassium-requiring enzyme (phosphopyruvate synthetase) which is particularly associated with graminaceous tropical species, e.g. sugar cane, catalyses the reaction:

$$\text{pyruvate} + \text{ATP} \rightleftharpoons \text{phosphopyruvate} + \text{AMP} + \text{Pi}$$

Inhibition of these enzymes could indirectly influence the level of inorganic phosphate, since ATP utilisation would be prevented. The observations made on potato plants showed that potassium deficiency is associated with a low ratio of organic (ester) to inorganic phosphorus and with an increased total phosphorus uptake. Thus there is a large increase in the amount of inorganic phosphorus. This may be located in certain organs or regions and in some manner immobilises iron. The enzyme, ferrochelatase, which inserts iron into porphyrins and may be needed for early stages of chlorophyll synthesis, will function only with ferrous iron. Ferric iron is inactive and ferric phosphate or complexes therewith are not available for translocation to young leaves. Increasing iron supplies to potassium-deficient potato plants was found by Bolle-Jones to result in apparent retention of potassium in the old leaves instead of the normal translocation to young leaves which occurs when potassium is deficient. An associated feature of this relationship was that potassium-deficiency symptoms were delayed by increasing iron supply, were ultimately more severe and tended to appear in the upper before the lower leaves, contrary to the normal manifestation of the effects of potassium deficiency at normal or low iron levels.

Iron-deficiency symptoms are induced in several plants by excesses of manganese, copper, zinc, cadmium, cobalt and chromium. Experiments by Hewitt with beet showed that the order of severity of the induced deficiency can be closely related to the order of stability constants of several chelate-metal complexes, with the exception of cadmium. Since then this relationship has been widely confirmed with other plants, e.g. oats and tomatoes. It might be thought that the induced iron deficiency which inhibited chlorophyll formation could be the result of inhibition of the ferro-chelatase system which controls insertion of ferrous iron into protoporphyrin perhaps by competition for the enzyme. Other enzymes which are iron dependent, e.g. aconitase, could be inhibited under these circumstances but the role of this enzyme in chlorophyll formation is not apparent. The severity of the induced iron deficiency is accentuated by molybdenum for unknown reasons but whereas this applies to chromium in the trivalent form, molybdenum decreases the much greater severity of chlorosis induced by chromium as hexavalent chromate.

Bicarbonate ions antagonise the uptake and utilisation of iron in several plants. Soybeans, French beans and mustard are particularly susceptible to this relationship. In some cases increased phosphate uptake is associated with the presence of bicarbonate in the root medium. Bicarbonate inhibits cytochrome oxidase in roots and apparently competes with iron uptake by roots when present in chelated form as an anion. The situation is very complex however as contradictory relationships between bicarbonate and phosphate uptake have been reported. Bicarbonate may be a factor in lime-induced chlorosis in some calcareous soils. The presence of bicarbonate in the root medium may influence carbon dioxide metabolism of roots as for example the fixation of carbon dioxide by phosphoenolpyruvate to form oxaloacetate with the release of inorganic phosphate.

The oxaloacetate could then produce malic acid by reduction in the malic dehydrogenase system, or citrate by condensation with acetate. The aconitase system which converts citrate to isocitrate via aconitase is now beyond much doubt shown to be dependent on ferrous iron so that when iron is deficient citric acid might accumulate as is often observed. The inconsistent changes in malate/citrate ratio also reported could be explained by the relative extent to which malate is formed as described above or from citrate by the tricarboxylic acid cycle.

A relationship between iron and manganese was originally proposed by Shive with Somers and Gilbert in 1942 on the basis of experiments with soybeans. They suggested that manganese inactivated iron (considered then to be 'active' in the ferrous form) by promoting its oxidation to ferric iron, which was immobilised as a phosphate complex. The hypothesis was based on the fact that the simple ionic couples have a redox potential such that iron would tend to accumulate in the ferric state and

$$Mn^{3+} + e^- \rightarrow Mn^{2+} (E_0 = + 1\cdot51 \text{ V})$$

$$Fe^{3+} + e^- \rightarrow Fe^{2+} (E_0 = + 0\cdot77 \text{ V}).$$

The relative iron/manganese status of the plants was a function of the ratio of these elements so that excess iron could induce manganese deficiency and excess manganese could induce iron deficiency. There are several difficulties about this hypothesis which have been reviewed by Hewitt (1963). However a mechanism by which manganese can be oxidised to a short-lived trivalent or higher valency state in plant tissues is known. This depends on the peroxidation of mono-phenolic or meta di-phenolic compounds which yield oxidising-free radicals that can oxidise manganese. Oxidation of manganese to the trivalent state stabilised by pyrophosphate has also been observed in illuminated chloroplast systems and also in pea plants given excess of the element. One of the main objections to the acceptance of the Shive hypothesis is that metals which cannot undergo oxidation-reduction are active in inducing chlorosis, as already pointed out. Also the relative redox potentials of the simple ion pairs of several of these metals do not conform to the relative extent to which they induce chlorsis which is, however, closely related to their typical stability constants in several metal-organic complexes.

Soluble-nitrogen fractions and nutritional status

Plants contain a wide variety of soluble-nitrogen compounds. These include nitrate, nitrite, hydroxamates, ammonia, ureides, amides, amino acids, amines, nitrosamines, purines and pyrimidines and guanidino derivatives. Several of these compounds show large changes in concentration when certain plants are grown under deficiency or excess conditions of mineral elements.

Nitrate accumulates in plants when molybdenum is deficient and concentrations may reach 10–15% of dry weight. Similar but less dramatic accumulation occurs in some plants, e.g. cauliflower, wheat and tomato, when deficient in manganese. Deficiencies of sulphur, phosphorus and calcium also frequently result in nitrate accumulation. The role of molybdenum in nitrate reductase (described in Chapter 7) is an obvious reason for nitrate accumulation in deficient plants. No such explanation is available to account for the effects of the other elements. The postulated calcium-dependent nitrite permease in chloroplasts is thought to control movement of nitrite into chloroplasts before reduction by nitrite reductase. Under deficiency conditions nitrite produced from nitrate might repress the formation of nitrate reductase. As this enzyme is often short-lived in the cell with a half-life of a few hours its activity may be suppressed by this mechanism and nitrate would accumulate for a period, until the nitrite level again decreased. Manganese affects many aspects of metabolism including oxygen evolution by chloroplasts. It is possible that interference in this reaction leads to nitrite accumulation and a feedback repression of nitrate reductase. Several other sites of manganese activity could however be involved. Deficiencies of sulphur and phosphorus would inhibit protein synthesis and could be expected to exert indirect control on nitrate reduction.

The changes in amino acid and amide concentrations which occur in plants deficient in several different elements are shown in Table 6.2. Where comparisons between species are possible it appears that the pattern of amino acid changes for a given element is quite different for different species. Correspondingly the pattern for different deficiencies in a particular species is also fairly distinct in one or more respects. It may be noted that practically all deficiencies cause increases in amino nitrogen compounds and this is irrespective of the source of nitrogen. Molybdenum deficiency however causes depletion of most amino acids with nitrate and generally causes accumulation with ammonia-grown plants. As expected, sulphur deficiency tends to depress the level of the sulphur amino acids and their derivatives but in some species, especially brassicas, other deficiencies, e.g. Mo and Cl cause dramatic increases in the sulphoxides of methyl cysteine and methionine. Another general point is that large changes in ratio can occur in compounds not normally present in appreciable amounts or the changes may be very great in amount for some compounds already present in abundance. Day length, temperature and other factors interact with mineral deficiencies and modify the patterns in other ways. In a few instances amines accumulate, thus tyramine reaches very high concentrations in tobacco deficient in boron, and to substantial if lesser degrees when deficient in iron or manganese. Ethanolamine concentration increases sharply under conditions of iron deficiency in tomato. Putrescine occurs in abnormally large quantities in many plants, e.g. barley and banana when deficient in potassium, and rubidium can reverse this effect (see page 152). Putrescine can yield polyamines such as spermine and spermidine which interact with nucleic acids by ionic bonding and probably function in the

control of growth. Allantoin, $NH_2CONH\ CH$  , a ureide, also accumulates uniquely in leaves of severely potassium-deficient banana plants while allantoic acid is decreased. Pipecolic acid, the next homologue of proline, accumulates in leaves of magnesium-deficient bananas.

The production of nitrosamines is of interest and importance because these compounds are carcinogenic. Dimethylnitrosamine and other nitrosamines have been identified in plant extracts from plants growing in areas of endemic oesophageal carcinoma, where molybdenum deficiency is also prevalent. Some species, e.g. cycads appear to produce nitrosamines as normal metabolites. The origin of these compounds in plants and in animals is probably the result of a reaction between nitrous acid and a secondary amine at low pH:

$$HONO + NHRR' \rightarrow RR'N\text{-}NO + H_2O$$

The secondary amines may occur naturally and proline and pipecolic acid have the required structure to produce nitrosamines. Subsequent decarboxylation of nitrosoproline would yield the highly carcinogenic compound nitrosopyrrolidine. Nitrite can occur in a few plants, e.g. elderberry at certain seasons, possibly after rapid reduction of nitrate accumulated by molybdenum-deficient plants when the molybdenum supply is suddenly improved perhaps in the darkness when nitrite is not reduced. Reduction of nitrate by xanthine oxidase in liver will also yield nitrite.

Further Reading

Bould, C. and Hewitt, E. J. (1963) Mineral nutrition of plants in soils and in culture media. Chapter 1, pp. 15–120 in Vol. III, *Plant Physiology* (Ed. F. C. Steward). Academic Press: New York and London.

Goodall, D. W. and Gregory, F. G. (1947) Chemical composition of plants as an index of nutritional status. *Commonwealth Bureau of Horticulture Tech. Commun. 17.* Commonwealth Agric. Bureaux, Aberystwyth.

Hewitt, E. J. (1963) The essential nutrient elements: requirements and interactions in plants. Chapter 2, pp. 137–329, Vol. III, in *Plant Physiology* (Ed. F. C. Steward). Academic Press: New York and London.

Raheja, P. C. (1966) *Soil Productivity and Crop Growth.* Asia Publishing House: London.

Wallace, T. (1961) *Diagnosis of Mineral Deficiencies in Plants, a Colour Atlas and Guide* (3rd edn.) H.M. Stationery Office. 125 pp.

7
Inorganic Nitrogen Metabolism

'He gave it for his opinion, that whoever could make two ears of corn or two blades of grass to grow upon a spot of ground where only one grew before, would deserve better of mankind, and do more essential service to his country than the whole race of politicians put together.'

Jonathan Swift
Gulliver's Travels, 'Voyage to Brobdingnag'

Sources of nitrogen

Plants obtain most of their nitrogen as nitrate or ammonium ions. Although the ammonia is freely taken up and is often provided in fertilisers the microbial oxidation of ammonia to nitrate (nitrification) in fertile soils is very rapid. The form in which nitrogen is actually absorbed is therefore primarily as nitrate, since ammonia is usually relatively scarce in soils. The assimilation of nitrate by reduction to ammonia is a key process in the nitrogen metabolism of plants and involves at least two enzymes having several interesting features, which are described later (pages 205 and 261).

Nitrogen fixation by free or symbiotic micro-organisms is the other main source of nitrogen available to plants. Part of the nitrogen fixed may be excreted as ammonia direct to the host, or to the soil, where in the latter case it may be nitrified before absorption. Part of the nitrogen fixed by symbiotic bacteria (*Rhizobium* in legumes and probably Actinomycetes in non-legumes, such as species of *Alnus, Casuarina, Myrica, Hippophaë*, etc.) is absorbed directly as amino acids, and probably some nitrogen fixed by free-living species (*Azotobacter* spp., *Clostridium pasteurianum*, etc.) is also absorbed in this form.

Nitrogen fixation

As may be seen in Fig. 7.1 the fixation of gaseous atmospheric nitrogen by free-living and symbiotic micro-organisms has a very important place in the ecological nitrogen cycle. The suggestion that plants might utilise atmospheric nitrogen was first made by Sir Humphry Davy in 1836, and legume nodules were shown to contain a symbiotic association of nitrogen-fixing bacteria by Hellreigel and Wilfarth in 1886–8. In 1893 Winogradsky demonstrated that the soil bacterium *Clostridium pasteurianum* fixes nitrogen, while it was not until 1928 that Drewes showed this ability in the blue-green algae. No higher plant has yet been shown to fix gaseous nitrogen in the absence of a symbiont.

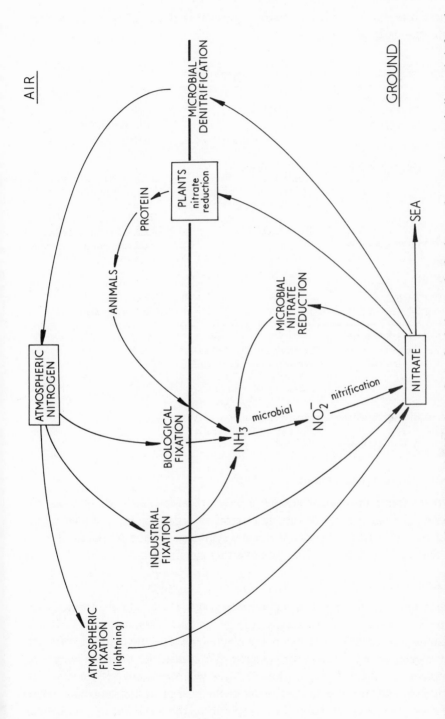

Figure 7.1 The main pathways of nitrogen in the biosphere. Some fixed nitrogen is also lost to the sea where a similar cycle is found.

A list of the classes of nitrogen-fixing organisms is given in Table 7.1, together with some specific examples.

Table 7.1   Examples of nitrogen-fixing organisms

(1) *Symbiotic forms*		
(i) Higher plants		
(a) Legumes	Pisum (pea)	with bacterial symbiont
	Trifolium (clover)	(Rhizobium) in root nodules
(b) Non-legumes	Alnus (alder)	
(over 100	Casuarina	actinomycete symbiont
species)	Hippophaë (sea buckthorn)	in root nodules
	Myrica (bog myrtle)	
	Ardisia	Bacillus ⎫ bacteria in
	Psychotria	Klebsiella ⎭ leaf nodules
(ii) Gymnosperms	Ginkgo	symbiont unknown (non-
	Podocarpus	septate filaments)
	Cycas	blue-green alga
(iii) Pteridophytes	Azolla	
(iv) Bryophytes	Anthoceros	Nostoc
(v) Lichens	Peltigera	blue-green alga
(2) *Free-living forms*		
(i) Bacteria	Achromobacter, Aerobacter, Azotobacter, Beijerinckia, Chlorobium, Chromatium, Clostridium, Klebsiella, Rhodopseudomonas	
(ii) Blue-green algae	Anabaena, Calothrix, Nostoc	
(iii) Yeasts	Pullularia, Rhodotorula	
(iv) Actinomycetes	Nocardia	

Symbiotic-nitrogen fixation

In these forms nitrogen fixation can only proceed when both partners are present, the partnership consisting of a micro-organism and a higher plant. Each partner may live independently and symbiosis is not essential in all cases for the completion of the life-cycle of either symbiont.

(a) *Legumes*

The nodules on the roots of leguminous plants (Plate 23) are formed as a response to invasion by bacteria of the genus *Rhizobium*, members of which commonly occur in the soil. There is a marked host specificity for the varieties and species of *Rhizobium*; for instance the species *R. leguminosarum* will inoculate only the pea group, while *R. trifoli* will infect only the clovers. The bacteria are attracted to the root hairs of the host plant and on colonisation, the root hairs curl, probably as a response to the secretion of the growth substance indoleacetic acid by the bacterium. Invasion then takes place through the root hairs and into host cells within the root. Here the bacteria swell and assume a variety of shapes and they also lose the ability to divide, having first completely filled the host cells.

The mature nodule is composed of an outer cortex, and a vascular region which surrounds the inner infected area. In some species there is also an apical meristematic region. In the *Rhizobium*-infected cells the red pigment haemoglobin is produced, which is almost identical to that found in mammalian blood.

(b) *Non-legumes*

In the non-legume nodules (Plates 24, 25 and 26) the infected cells are external to the vascular tissue, in contrast to those of the legumes where the vascular strands surround the infected root tissue. Since the endophytes cannot be isolated, their exact nature cannot be determined, though in all cases they appear to be filamentous and are probably Actinomycetes.

Primary infection of sterile plants can only be attained by using ground-up nodules of infected plants, but these need not be from the same species. For example, nitrogen fixation in *Hippophaë* and *Elaeagnus* may be due to the same organism and this organism differs from that found in *Alnus*. Like the legume nodules, the non-legume nodule may also contain haemoglobin.

Free-living organisms

(a) *Bacteria*

The widely distributed genus *Azotobacter* is similar to *Rhizobium* and it has been suggested that *Azotobacter* is an ancestral genus of *Rhizobium*. The pigmented photosynthetic bacteria, of which *Chromatium* is an example, and members of the anaerobic genus *Clostridium* also fix nitrogen. It seems unlikely that the free-living nitrogen-fixing bacteria contribute significantly to soil fertility, since they are rather inefficient. Bacteria which fix nitrogen in the free state may also form symbiotic associations with higher plants. In *Dioscorea macroura* nitrogen-fixing bacteria are found in leaf glands, while in *Ardisia hortorum* (Plate 24) they occur in leaf nodules.

(b) *Algae*

The blue-green algae (*Cyanophyceae*) are very important in this group and their activity in the paddy-fields of South-East Asia provides a significant surplus of fixed nitrogen for the rice crop. In ideal conditions blue-green algae can grow as well on gaseous nitrogen as on fixed nitrogen. They may grow symbiotically with fungi, giving lichens; in the liverwort *Blasia*, a *Nostoc* species colonises cavities on the lower surface of the plant; and they are also found in nodules in the roots of Cycads. In *Anabaena* nitrogen is fixed in the heterocysts in aerobic conditions but in the absence of oxygen, nitrogen is fixed in the vegetative cells.

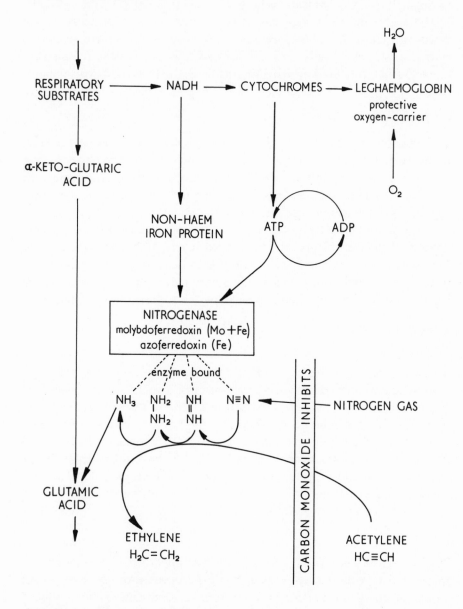

Figure 7.2 Probable mechanism for nitrogen fixation by bacteria of the genus *Rhizobium* in root nodules of leguminous plants. Acetylene is an alternative (non-physiological) substrate for nitrogenase.

Mechanism of nitrogen fixation

The mineral elements closely involved in nitrogen fixation comprise molybdenum, iron, cobalt, magnesium and possibly copper, as well as phosphorus and sulphur.

There are two proteins which make up the nitrogenase complex in all the nitrogen-fixing organisms so far examined (Fig. 7.2). One named molybdoferredoxin by Mortenson, or nitrogenase protein I, has a molecular weight between 100 000 and 300 000. It contains one or two atoms of molybdenum and up to forty atoms of iron tightly bound to the protein. There is also some acid-labile sulphur (yielding H_2S when the protein is acidified). The other, named azoferredoxin, or nitrogenase protein II, has a lower molecular weight of about 50 000. It contains tightly bound iron only (1–4 atom/mol) and an equivalent amount of labile sulphide. The iron in both proteins is non-haem, that is, there are no iron porphyrin complexes and both iron and equivalent amounts of hydrogen sulphide are released on acidification. Both proteins are simultaneously required for any of the characteristic reactions of nitrogen fixation to occur. There are: (1) the hydrolysis of ATP, (2) the evolution of hydrogen and/or the reduction of nitrogen or other nitrogenase substrates, which include acetylene, methyl cyanide, cyanide, nitrous oxide and azide. The phosphorus requirement arises from the fact that energy-rich phosphate in the form ultimately of ATP is essential for nitrogen fixation, in a ratio of 12 to 16 ATP to one N_2 molecule reduced. Experiments with radioactively labelled ATP and labelled methylcyanide as a nitrogenase substrate suggested that ATP was bound by azoferredoxin and the substrate was bound by molybdoferredoxin. This is the first indication of the possible respective Mg complex partial functions of the two protein components of the complex. However, in other experiments, ATP was bound by both proteins. It is probable that the Mo-Fe protein I reduces the substrate, and that ATP hydrolysis assists in reduction of protein I by the Fe protein II. Up to 1g atom/mol of calcium, copper and zinc may be present in protein I.

Magnesium is required for the ATP-ase activity and the ATP-ase activity does not occur unless a reductant or electron source is present. The dithionite molecule $S_2O_4^{2-}$ fulfils the role non-physiologically in all systems investigated, but *in vivo* specific protein carriers and other reductants are involved. In *Clostridium pasteurianum* these are provided by pyruvate and clostridial ferredoxin in normal cells. In iron-deficient cells flavodoxin, a low molecular weight flavoprotein which contains no iron, replaces ferredoxin. In *Azotobacter* the carrier is not ferredoxin although this is present. The primary source of electrons in anaerobic *Clostridium* and aerobic *Azotobacter* can be hydrogen which reacts in the hydrogenase system, thus:

$$H_2 \rightleftharpoons 2H^+ + 2e^-$$

although it is not reversible in *Azotobacter*. Pyruvate provides electrons and ATP for the clostridial system by the following overall but actually complex reactions:

$$CH_3COCOOH + Pi + \text{Ferredoxin ox} \rightarrow$$

$$CH_3CO-PO_4 + CO_2 + \text{Ferredoxin red.}$$

$$CH_3CO-PO_4 + ADP \rightarrow CH_3COOH + ATP$$

The reaction requires thiamine pyrophosphate (co-carboxylase) magnesium, CoA, ADP and inorganic phosphate as well as pyruvic decarboxylase and phospho-*trans*-acetylase. In *Clostridium*, reduced pyridylium (viologen radicals) can replace ferredoxin where this is concerned.

In legume nodule bacteroids the electron source includes an unknown donor which can be replaced by β-hydroxybutyrate and NADH, and an unknown electron carrier which can be replaced by benzyl or methyl viologen and which appears to be a non-haem iron protein with some properties resembling ferredoxin located in the bacteroid membrane.

It is therefore apparent that the electron transport system to the nitrogenase complex can function with low potential electrons (standard redox values about -0.7 V for pyruvate, -0.4 V for ferredoxin and for hydrogenase) or less electronegative systems, e.g. NADH (-0.3 V) or possibly others including a flavoprotein (probably -0.1 to $+0.1$ V) in rhizobia or when flavodoxin is utilised. The actual role of ATP is still unknown, but it may serve as an energy 'pump' to achieve a low redox potential or may conform the protein complex.

In both legume and non-legume root nodules, cobalt is essential for nitrogen fixation by the endophyte. The cobalt requirement was first discovered by Ahmed and Evans for Soybean and by Bond and Hewitt for *Alnus, Casuarina* and *Myrica*. The active compound was characterised as a B_{12} derivative by the relatively specific *Euglena* assay. It was finally identified as B_{12} coenzyme (Fig. 7.3) by Kliewer and Evans using the highly specific assay with *Ochromonas malhamensis* and isolation of the compound, which was characterised by its infrared spectrum and chromatographic behaviour. The B_{12} coenzyme is required for the production of haem compounds, including leghaemoglobin in soybean, but cobalt is also essential for rhizobia when they are cultured in synthetic media containing nitrate nitrogen. However the participation of haem proteins is probably just as necessary under these conditions for growth and the cobalt requirement is not necessarily specific for the nitrogen-fixing condition.

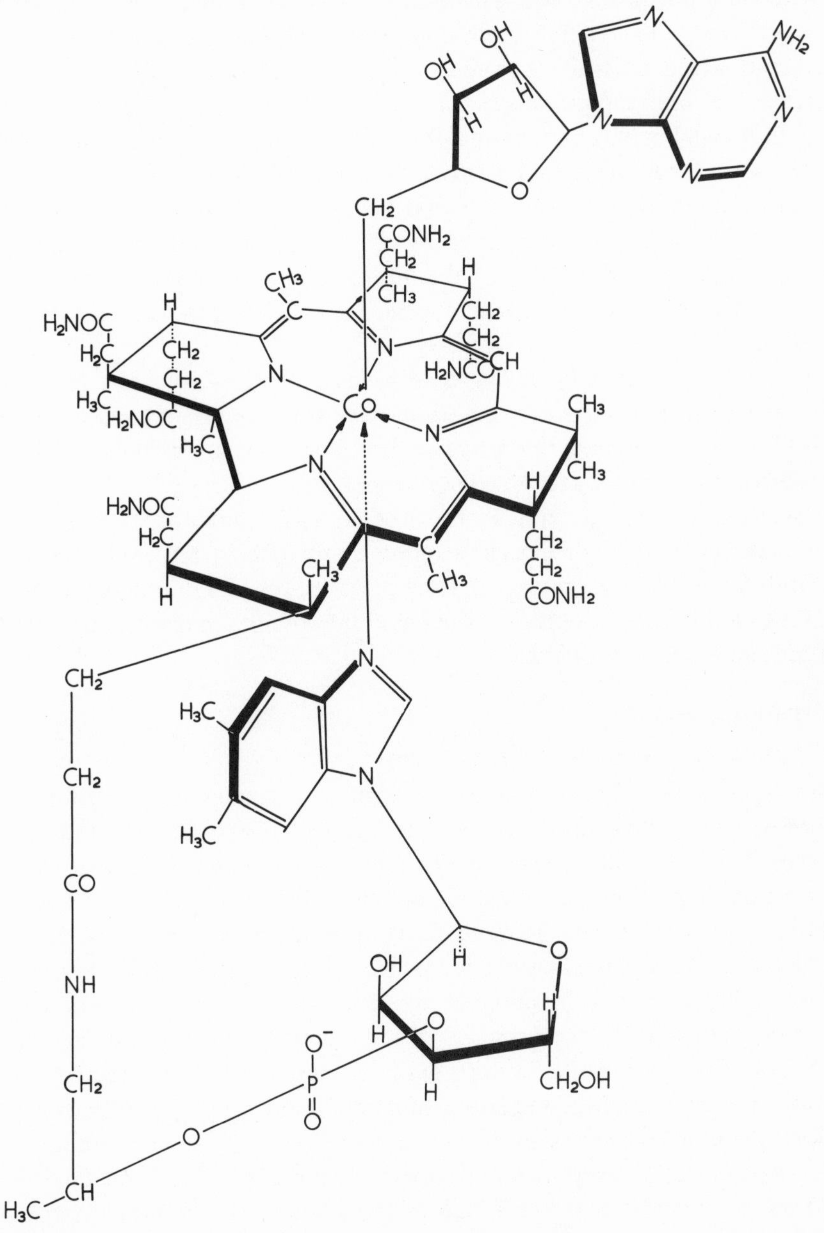

Figure 7.3   The structure of coenzyme B$_{12}$. The cobalt chelated in the corrin nucleus is linked above with adenosine and below with benzimidazole moieties. From Smith (1965) in *Vitamin B$_{12}$*. Methuen, London.

The role of leghaemoglobin in legume symbiotic nitrogen fixation is still unknown. Many nitrogenase systems are very labile in the presence of oxygen and one view is that haemoglobin is an oxygen-scavenging device in legumes and in non-legumes with root nodules. The endophytes, rhizobia and actino-mycetes are aerobic organisms but also produce the oxygen-labile nitrogenase. The haemoglobin may both protect the nitrogenase and mediate oxygen uptake or transport for aerobic metabolism involved in ATP formation.

The technique of *anaerobic* bacteroid isolation, the discovery that acetylene as well as nitrogen can be reduced by the nitrogenase and detected by gas chromatography, and the use of dithionite as a universal single electron donor have considerably facilitated the experimental investigation of nitrogen fixation.

Dixon and Postgate (1972) have succeeded in transferring the genes for nitrogen fixation from *Klebsiella pneumoniae* into the non-fixer *Escherichia coli*. The *K. pneumoniae* was made fertile by introducing a genetic element (plasmid), carrying sex factor activity, from a strain of *E. coli*. This fertile *K. pneumoniae* was mated with a strain of *E. coli* tolerant of foreign gen-etic material in its cell. On conjugation about one in ten million *E. coli* hybrids were able to fix nitrogen. The successful transfer of nitrogen fixation genes to a new species opens up the possibility of obtaining other new types of nitrogen-fixing organisms.

Nitrate reduction

(a) *Nitrate and ammonia as sources of nitrogen*

Most species grow better with nitrate than with ammonium nitrogen even when optimal pH conditions are provided for uptake of each type of nitrogen source (lower pH values favouring nitrate uptake), but it is also clear that when rapidly growing plants are investigated, the differences at the optimal pH values may be greatly reduced. Low light intensities accentuate the un-favourable effects of ammonium compounds, micronutrients such as manga-nese and copper may be required at higher concentrations, and aeration may be more necessary in the presence of ammonium than of nitrate nitrogen supplies. The specific relationships between molybdenum requirements and nitrogen sources are discussed later. Ammonium nitrogen supplies are toxic to many species at concentrations which are quite harmless for nitrate, but a few species, e.g. rice at early stages of growth, maize, *Pinus taeda* and *Pandanus veitchii* may tolerate or thrive better on ammonium than on nitrate nitrogen. An interesting example appears to be that of *Chenopodium album* studied by Marthaler in 1937; this species was reported not to grow with nitrate, which accumulated in the leaves, while with ammonium nitrogen good growth occurred. It is perhaps relevant to point out that no molybdenum was given in the nutrient and an accidental deficiency may have occurred so that the nitrate could not be assimilated. The relative merits of nitrate and ammonia are extensively discussed by Hewitt (1966).

(b) *Nitrate accumulation*

Nitrate accumulation in various parts of plants is recorded quite frequently and in general terms means that rate of uptake exceeds rate of reduction. This may not be particularly important to the plants, but in some instances may be due to the effects of a nutritional disorder, or indicate that reduction cannot occur at a certain stage of development or in certain organs. Some members of the Chenopodiaceae (e.g. spinach) appear to accumulate nitrate readily. Remarkable accumulation up to 20% of dry matter as nitrate were also recorded for species of *Amaranthus* and for *Borago officinalis*. In *Borago* the concentration in dry matter has been found to rise from between 0·5% nitrate in the seedling in April to between 5% and as much as 29% at flowering in June, and to fall to less than 0·1% at fruiting in September. *Amaranthus caudatus* showed similar changes in nitrate content. Most of the nitrate was present in stems and roots. Many other examples are given by McKee (1962).

This behaviour would seem to exclude the possibility that micronutrient or other mineral deficiencies were involved and suggests a real change in the amount, or activity, of nitrate reductase in the plant during development. These species would merit investigation from the point of view of enzyme activity, the inducibility of the enzyme during different stages of growth, effects of light on enzyme activity and products of its activity. Berthelot and André (1884) in fact reported that strong illumination of leaves resulted in the disappearance of nitrate from the tissues of *Borago*.

Nitrate accumulation in food plants may be of particular importance. Spinach sometimes accumulates nitrate to high concentrations, and in babies the nitrate may be reduced to nitrite by micro-organisms in the alimentary tract. This nitrite combines with haemoglobin in the blood to give the chocolate-coloured methaemoglobin which is no longer a functional oxygen carrier, and the babies may suffer severe oxygen deficiency.

(c) *Utilisation of other nitrogen compounds*

Nitrite is severely toxic as undissociated nitrous acid but is tolerated at much higher concentrations at high pH values at which the molecule is fully ionised to NO_2^-. Maize is exceptionally tolerant and is unharmed by 200 p.p.m. nitrite at pH 7 or above. The toxicity or non-availability of hydroxylamine (NH_2OH) contrasts markedly with that of nitrite, as pointed out in the discussion on the status of hydroxylamine as an intermediate in nitrite reduction (see p. 215).

Urea (NH_2CONH_2) is utilised by many plants provided that biuret is absent and the pH is maintained near neutrality. Glutamine is metabolised by tomato and clover in sterile culture, and glutamic acid is an excellent nitrogen source for cauliflower in non-sterile and sterile cultures. Glutamine and glutamic acid may be superior to ammonia for several plants but tobacco seems poorly adapted to using these nitrogen sources. Several amino acids have toxic effects, as was pointed out by Steinberg in 1949 and these compounds may in fact lead to morphological changes in leaves of tobacco and chrysanthemum. Isoleucine and hydroxyproline appear to be two of the most active in this respect.

Physiological factors in nitrogen assimilation

The distribution and activity of nitrate reductase in plants with respect to species, age, organ, time of day and season probably accounts for some of the unusual effects reported above. The principal studies on this subject of physiological interactions in nitrate reductase and nitrate assimilation have been described recently, principally by Pate, Hageman, Losada, Cocking, Miflin and Hewitt and their respective associates.

Some plants such as radish, vegetable marrow, watercress and maize have very high nitrate reductase activity in the leaves. This enzyme is easily extrac-

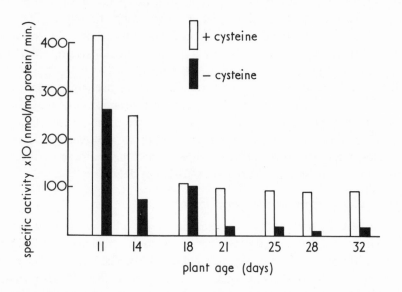

Figure 7.4 The effect of 5×10^{-3} M cysteine in the extracting medium on the specific activity of nitrate reductase of marrow plants. From Cresswell (1961) Thesis, University of Bristol.

ted from radish or marrow but is inactivated in maize extracts unless high concentrations o·05 M) of thiols (cysteine or glutathione) are included in the extracting medium. The amounts of these thiols which give best results vary with species, age, organ and possibly season. An extreme range from nil for *Perilla frutescens* to 10^{-5} M for pea and to 10^{-1} M for cocklebur (*Xanthium pennsylvanicum*) have been recorded.

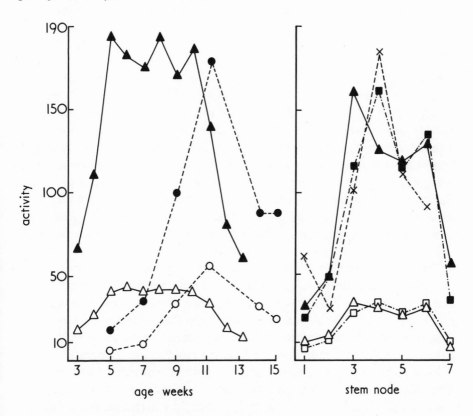

Figure 7.5 *Left*—nitrate reductase in cauliflower leaves (var Tremendous) at different ages and grown with different nitrogen sources, in non-sterile culture.
    Triangles on solid line—nitrate
    Circles on dashed line—ammonium sulphate
    Solid symbols—total activities
    Open symbols—specific activities
Right—nitrate reductase activity in cauliflower leaves at different stem nodes of plants grown with nitrate.
    Triangles on solid line—var Tremendous age 9 weeks
    Squares on dashed line—var Majestic age 8 weeks
    Crosses on dashed line—var Tremendous age 6 weeks
    Solid symbols—total activities
    Open symbols—specific activities
From Afridi and Hewitt (1964) *J. exp. Bot.* **15**, 251–71.

Nitrate reductase activity shows a pronounced relationship with age and leaf position in cauliflower, mustard and marrow plants. The decrease in activity in cotyledons of marrows was associated with the presence of an inhibitor in increasing amounts with time. The importance of cysteine is illustrated in Fig. 7.4. Effects of plant age and leaf position on the distribution of nitrate reductase are shown in Fig. 7.5, from which it appears that large differences in capacity to assimilate nitrate must occur as development proceeds.

Roots

It is relevant here to consider the activity of roots in nitrate reduction since these organs normally grow in complete and continuous darkness. Frank and Ishizuka both in 1897 were probably the first to obtain evidence that roots provide important sites for nitrate reduction. Eckerson stated somewhat dogmatically that in apple trees, nitrate reduction occurs principally in the fibrous roots. Bollard has pointed out that often no nitrate can be detected in the xylem sap of apple tree stems of plants grown with nitrate although abundant soluble nitrogen compounds including amino acids are present. The inference is made that nitrate reduction has occurred in the roots. Moreover it is quite certain that excised roots grown in sterile culture media grow satisfactorily with nitrate as nitrogen source.

The investigations of Willis and Yemm in 1955 and 1956 showed that excised roots of barley seedlings were able to reduce nitrate or nitrite rapidly and to produce substantial amounts of ammonia, glutamine and asparagine in six to nine hours. The assimilation was independent of any requirement for light or exogenous metabolites. Nitrite was scarcely detected in the tissues although uptake was quite rapid, but not as rapid as that of nitrate. Nitrite did not however result in appreciable net protein synthesis when nitrate or ammonia were given. Some glutamine and asparagine were produced in six hours when 5 mM hydroxylamine was given in the external medium. Sanderson and Cocking in 1964 reported that nitrate reductase could be extracted from all parts of the tomato plant including the roots when appropriate conditions were used. Since then nitrate reductase activity has been demonstrated in roots of pea, barley and apple when suitable extraction techniques were adopted though nitrate reductase could not be found in roots of cocklebur. This was correlated with the excretion of only negligible concentrations of amino acids by decapitated cocklebur plants, compared with the presence of abundant amino acids in sap of decapitated pea seedlings. Although the detectable activity of the enzyme after extraction appears to be low in leaves of many plants insufficient attention has been paid in many cases to the need for the protective thiol compounds during extraction. It is probable that all plants able to grow with nitrate contain substantial amounts of the reductase enzyme in leaves. Nevertheless there are good reasons to conclude that its activity does in fact vary with morphology and age, and that the contribution to reduction in the roots is more variable. On the other hand, there is reason to believe that regulated activity *in vivo* may in fact be substantially less than unregulated activity found after extraction, as demonstrated by Ferrari and Barnes (1970) in barley aleurone cells.

Effects of light

Light is an important factor in nitrate reduction. This was first noted by Schimpe in 1888, and is now known to be of varying importance according to species.

The requirement for light as a requisite in nitrate assimilation by different species was critically reviewed by McKee (1962). Many of the experiments are of considerable importance though carried out between 1897 and 1914. One group of experiments between 1897 and 1900 showed that nitrate reduction or assimilation to protein occurred in the dark in the presence of carbohydrate. In another group of experiments on plants including beans and tomato this reaction was additionally stimulated by light or was able to occur in light in the absence of carbon dioxide even more rapidly than with carbohydrate in the dark. A third group of plants including *Pelargonium zonale* and wheat was reported to be entirely dependent on light. In contrast, the conversion of nitrate to protein, and soluble organic fractions in tobacco leaves was found by Delwiche in 1951, from a study with ^{15}N-labelled nitrate, to be unaffected by light or dark. Maize however grown with nitrate is clearly sensitive to light. Figure 7.6 shows the relationship between nitrate-reducing capacity of tissues of two genetic strains and the rate of growth and protein synthesis as affected by light. The time of day, seasonal and climatic conditions of sun and shade, self-shading by foliage or closeness of planting have all been shown to affect nitrate assimilation in a manner wholly explicable by the amount of light falling on the leaves. It is interesting to note that sun and shade as distinct from light and dark were shown to be factors by Schimpe in 1888 who observed that nitrate accumulated in leaves of *Acer negundo* and dandelion far more when shaded than when in full sunlight. It is additionally noteworthy that nitrate reductase in *Ankistrodesmus braunii* shows a comparable seasonal cycle of activity. The relative rates of decline in darkness and restoration of nitrate reductase in light is shown for three species in Fig. 7.7.

Enzymic processes of nitrate reduction described later must depend on the continuous supply of electron- or hydrogen-donating substrates. For this reason nitrate reduction must ultimately stop when reserves of oxidisable substrates or photosynthetically reduced electron carriers are depleted, since these compounds indirectly provide one type of mechanism for production of NADH or NADPH which function as electron (or hydrogen) donors in the nitrate reductase system.*

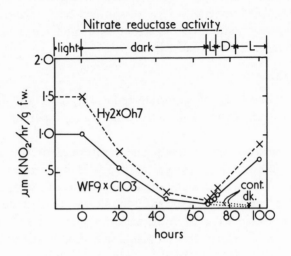

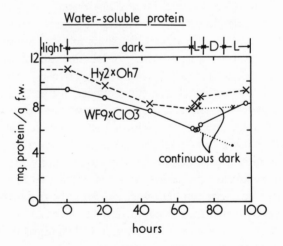

Figure 7.6 Effect of dark treatment on the nitrate reductase and water soluble protein of two varieties of young corn plants. From Hageman and Flesher (1960) *Pl. Physiol., Lancaster* **35**, 700–8. Reproduced by permission of the American Society of Plant Physiologists.

* Dihydroxyacetone phosphate exported from chloroplasts would yield glyceraldehyde-3-phosphate to provide a source of NADH for cytoplasmic nitrate reductase.

The stoicheiometric equations but not the mechanisms for the overall reduction of nitrate to ammonia or to nitrite are shown as follows:

$$NO_3^- + NAD(P)H + H^+ = NO_2^- + NAD(P)^+ + H_2O$$

$$\Delta G^0 = -143 \text{ kJ} \quad \Delta E = +0.74 \text{ V}$$

$$NO_2^- + 3NAD(P)H + 5H^+ = NH_4^+ + 3NAD(P)^+ + 2H_2O$$

$$\Delta G^0 = -392 \text{ kJ}$$
$$(\text{Equivalent } \Delta E = +0.68 \text{ V})$$

Overall $NO_3^- + 4NAD(P)H + 6H^+ = NH_4^+ + 4NAD(P)^+ + 3H_2O$

$$\Delta G^0 = -535 \text{ kJ}$$
$$(\text{Equivalent } \Delta E = +0.69 \text{ V})$$

The suppression of photosynthesis by exclusion of light must inevitably cause the general depletion of those compounds which directly or indirectly provide the reducing potential of the system. Thus Eckerson observed in 1924 that, initially, light or dark made no difference to nitrate reduction in intact tomato plants but the process came to a standstill after thirty days in darkness.

The relationship with light is not, however, quite so simple or direct as this first view would suggest. An early report by Kolesnikov in 1949 which has remained unnoticed until cited in a review by Wood in 1953 appears to have been the first to describe photochemical reduction of nitrate by chloroplasts of barley, with the production of an unidentified product, deemed to be nitrite. Evans and Nason who first isolated nitrate reductase from higher plants in 1953, shortly after the capacity of isolated chloroplasts to reduce NADP *in vitro* had been described by Arnon and by Vishniac and Ochoa, showed quite clearly that nitrate reductase of soybean leaves could be linked to photochemical reduction of NADP by isolated chloroplasts and that this system reduced nitrate to nitrite with a rate comparable to that observed when NADPH was used in substrate amounts.

The stoicheiometry for photochemical reduction of nitrate by NADPH is as follows:

$$NADP^+ + H_2O \xrightarrow[\text{chloroplasts}]{\text{light}} NADPH + H^+ + \tfrac{1}{2}O_2$$

$$NADPH + H^+ + NO_3^- \xrightarrow[\text{nitrate reductase}]{} NADP^+ + NO_2^- + H_2O$$

$$NO_3^- \xrightarrow{\hspace{2cm}} NO_2^- + \tfrac{1}{2}O_2$$

These equations suggest that when catalytic amounts of NADP are used, nitrate should stimulate oxygen evolution of illuminated chloroplasts and in photosynthetic systems. However, as nitrate reductase in most plants is specific for NADH the general physiological significance of this reaction is doubtful and must involve the trans-hydrogenase activity

$$NADPH + NAD \rightleftharpoons NADP + NADH$$

or additional reactions.

Early experiments by Warburg and Negelein in 1920 showed that when *Chlorella pyrenoidosa* cells were illuminated, nitrate reduction was more rapid. Several investigators later showed with *Chlorella* and *Ankistrodesmus falcatus* that addition of nitrate to nitrogen-starved cells in the light changed the progress of gas exchange. More oxygen was evolved and less carbon dioxide was absorbed. The presence of nitrate also caused an increased output of oxygen and decreased carbon dioxide fixation in the light in *Chlorella*, but in *Ankistrodesmus braunii* oxygen evolution was stimulated only slightly by nitrate (although markedly by nitrite) when illuminated in an atmosphere of nitrogen from which carbon dioxide was absent.

The role of light in generating electron or hydrogen-donating substrates which react directly in the nitrate reductase enzyme system was given a different emphasis in other work on wheat by Stoy in 1955 and 1956 which arose from comparisons between the action spectrum for photosynthesis and that for nitrate reduction. Stoy found that NADH and riboflavin phosphate (FMN) or flavin adenine dinucleotide (FAD), the cofactors which are effective in the dark, could be replaced by riboflavin in the presence of ethylenediamine-tetracetic acid (EDTA) as electron donor under anaerobic conditions and blue light from a mercury vapour lamp. This system was nearly twice as active per milligram of enzyme protein as the standard system with NADH and FMN. The anaerobic conditions were necessary because otherwise rapid autoxidation of photochemically-reduced riboflavin would occur with the production of hydrogen peroxide. Stoy's results seemed to provide a further explanation for a direct mechanistic relationship between nitrate reduction and light, though the mechanism involved was different, being directly photochemical without chloroplasts at the flavin stage. However chloroplasts when illuminated are able to reduce the flavin nucleotides, FMN and FAD. Stoy concluded that although nitrite reduction and photosynthesis in wheat leaves showed similar photochemical characteristics in white or red light, blue light stimulated nitrate reduction in an independent manner and the direct role of a yellow pigment was inferred. Work by Losada and his associates has shown that the reduction of nitrate in the presence of nitrate reductase, a flavin nucleotide, and chloroplasts occurred rapidly on illumination, and that FMN was a greatly superior electron donor to NADP or NAD under these circumstances. They suggested that physiological reduction of nitrate to nitrite in the light was mediated directly by FAD or FMN. They also concluded that nitrate reductase is located within the chloroplasts. Studies made by Hageman and his associates using non-aqueous methods of isolation do not support this contention or the role of FMN as a physiological donor. However location on the exterior of the chloroplasts is possible and intact double membrane chloroplasts appear to have significant nitrate reductase activity. Recently Lips has deduced that microbodies and not chloroplasts are the location of the enzyme. The argument continues.

Other studies by Hageman, Hewitt and Woolhouse and their co-workers indicated that these observations were not adequate or the only way to account for the effect of light on nitrate reduction. When either cauliflower, maize or *Perilla* plants were kept in darkness for six hours there was a progressive and ultimately total loss of nitrate reductase activity in cell-free extracts when assayed by the normal means. Moreover when these plants were again exposed to daylight, enzyme activity obtained in leaf extracts was rapidly increased and was restored to normal levels in a few hours, but carbon dioxide was also needed for restoration in *Perilla*. The results of these experiments are summarised in Fig. 7.7. The effect of light on enzyme level may be divided into two components. These are effects on access of nitrate to the site of enzyme induction which is stimulated at low intensities; and on rate of enzyme formation (or activation) which proceeds in darkness after pre-illumination at high intensity. Lips and Roth-Bejeriano have found that kinetin and gibberellin (GA$_3$) are together able to stimulate the formation of nitrate reductase in darkness and appear to substitute for the role of light. Light may thus have two or even three quite independent effects on nitrate reduction in plant tissues; namely on enzyme formation or stability, hormonal activity and on the supply of reductants. The effect of light on activity or amount of enzyme may be related to the presence of free sulphydryl ($-SH$) groups for activity. It is conceivable that some of these are oxidised to disulphide or sulphoxide groups during prolonged darkness. The extraction of the enzyme from different species requires the presence of different specific concentrations of cysteine to obtain optimal activity, and in some cases any activity at all. Mendel and Visser found that whereas nitrate reduction in the light in tomato leaf discs was unaffected by iodoacetate, that which occurred in the dark was inhibited by this compound, indicating either a greater need for free sulphydryl groups in the dark, or that these groups were produced in excess in light. However extraction of enzyme with sulphydryl compounds from dark-grown tissues does not substitute for the effects of light.

The discussion of this work on the role of light is complicated and presents many apparent contradictions. Some experiments followed nitrate

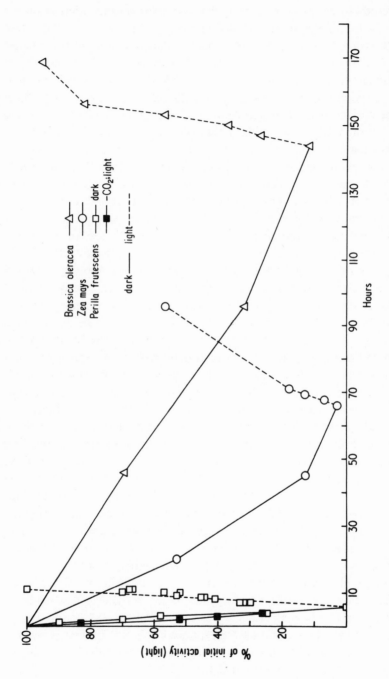

Figure 7.7 Loss of nitrate reductase activity in the dark and regain of activity in the light for three species of higher plants. In the absence of carbon dioxide the enzyme activity declined in *Perilla* on illumination.

disappearance, and some the synthesis of protein and of soluble organic nitrogen fractions. However there are at least two effects of light on nitrate reduction, and another on nitrite reduction described later, p. 211. The magnitude of the effects of light, where demonstrated, varies with different species. Kessler has expressed similar views on the complexity of the effects of light and has suggested that photosynthetic phosphorylation may be a factor involved in the effect of light. The nitrate-reductase system can be resolved into separate proteins mediating the reduction of FAD by NADH or NADPH and the transfer of electrons from the flavin via molybdenum to nitrate. The effects of light on the formation of these two systems is not yet known.

Nitrate respiration

As nitrate reduction involves the oxidation of NADH or NADPH with production of water and nitrite, this process is, in theory at least, capable of fulfilling the functions of a terminal oxidase system, and of playing a part in respiratory activity. Viewed in a different way, it is capable of competing with oxygen for the transfer of hydrogen via NAD or NADP. However these coenzymes are required in their reduced forms in other oxidation mechanisms, possibly those associated with oxidative phosphorylation, and in their oxidised forms with the metabolism of carboxylic acids. It might therefore be expected that the activity of nitrate reduction would interact competitively or synergistically in several other aspects of intermediary metabolism. Nitrate respiration (Satoh, 1956) or dissimilatory nitrate reduction (Verhoeven, 1952) as opposed to nitrate assimilation is associated mainly with bacterial metabolism. In this process the reduction product is usually an oxide of nitrogen (nitric or nitrous oxide), nitrogen gas or nitrite which is excreted without formation of ammonia; otherwise nitrate is reduced to ammonia in complete substitution for oxygen uptake to produce water. Nitrate respiration in bacteria is therefore favoured by low oxygen tension and is a major activity in denitrifying organisms. The stages between oxidation of carbohydrate via NAD(P)H and terminal electron transport to nitrate by nitrate reductase in place of oxygen and cytochrome oxidase allow for oxidative phosphorylation. However the overall energy change is less with nitrate (2280 kJ/mol hexose and yielding N_2O) than with oxygen (2880 kJ yielding H_2O). The biochemical mechanisms may be summarised as being variants of the general scheme in Fig. 7.8. Direct assimilation yields ammonia: microbial dissimilation either yields other products, or else ammonia when nitrate is the terminal electron acceptor. Atmospheric conditions may determine the proportional activities of the different enzymes involved by process of repression and de-repression of enzyme synthesis and probably by inactivation of existing enzymes.

The evidence for true nitrate respiration in higher plants is not so well

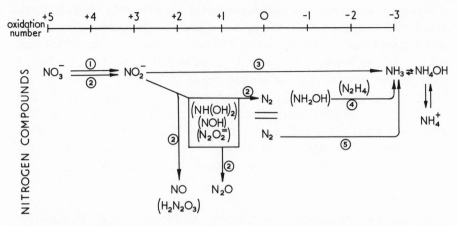

Figure 7.8 Oxidation states of nitrogen and the known pathways of inorganic nitrogen metabolism. Hypothetical intermediates and compounds of unknown physiological importance are shown in parenthesis.

(1) Nitrate reduction: NAD(P)H, FAD(FMN)H$_2$, molybdenum and sometimes also iron.

(2) Denitrification, nitrate respiration: iron and copper.

(3) Nitrite reduction: ferredoxin or NAD(P)H with iron and sometimes copper. Six electrons transferred; free intermediates uncertain.

(4) Hydroxylamine reduction: ferredoxin, NAD(P)H or (FMN)H$_2$, iron or manganese; of unknown significance.

(5) Nitrogen fixation: iron and molybdenum, six electrons transferred without identifiable intermediates.

substantiated as for bacteria. However nitrate assimilation and respiration are interrelated in plant metabolism. In soybean and wheat oxygen reduced the assimilation of nitrate. In soybean this effect may have occurred at the stage of nitrate reduction although it is clear that *in vitro*, activity of the plant nitrate reductase is not immediately affected by oxygen. Radish root slices metabolise nitrate more rapidly when in air than in nitrogen and respiratory activity here is *required* for nitrate reduction, rather than impeding the process. The cauliflower enzyme also declines under nitrogen.

Yemm, Folkes and Willis, between 1952 and 1956, showed that the carbon dioxide output of intact barley seedlings was nearly doubled when nitrate was added to the nitrogen-deficient culture medium. When ammonium chloride was added the stimulation was less but the carbon dioxide production occurred more rapidly than with nitrate although it was not so prolonged. Nitrite similarly stimulated carbon dioxide output by excised barley roots. Oxygen uptake was stimulated greatly by ammonium phosphate and by nitrite immediately whereas nitrate produced initially a small decrease followed after some hours by a marked increase in oxygen uptake. These workers anticipated the later demonstration of the adaptive production of nitrate reductase.

Respiration of cotyledons of *Vigna sesquipedalis* is related to nitrate reduction as a terminal oxidase system. In the presence of nitrate, c-type cytochromes resembling those of *Escherichia coli* were observed for the first two days after germination and nitrate was reduced to nitrite. Later a cytochrome oxidase activity developed and nitrate reduction declined but two nitrate-reducing systems, one of which required anaerobic conditions were at first thought to be present. Recent studies with serological methods suggest however, that only one enzyme is involved, but its control depends on its ultracellular location.

When plants are grown with nitrate in the absence of molybdenum their tissues accumulate high concentrations of nitrate (14–17% of dry weight). On introduction of molybdenum the accumulated nitrate is rapidly reduced with the transitory appearance of nitrite, and more slowly, of ammonia. The respiratory quotient (Ratio CO_2 evolved/O_2 absorbed) of normal cauliflower leaves grown with molybdenum and nitrate or ammonium or other nitrogen sources was about 0·95 to 1·04 and not significantly different for all nitrogen sources. The respiratory quotient (R.Q.) of molybdenum-deficient plants grown with ammonium nitrogen or urea was also about 1·0 and oxygen uptake was similar to that of plants grown with molybdenum, namely about 0·42 µl/hr/g fresh weight. The R.Q. of molybdenum-deficient plants grown with nitrate was significantly higher, about 1·15. When molybdenum was given to the deficient nitrate-grown plants *via* the roots or to the fluid in which excised leaf discs were floating in the Warburg flask, the rate of oxygen consumption fell to 0·26 µl/hr/g fresh weight and there was a marked rise in R.Q. to nearly 1·35. This change was associated simultaneously with the rapid reduction of accumulated nitrate present in the tissues. When all nitrate was reduced the R.Q. fell to nearly 1·04. The change in R.Q. in leaf discs given molybdenum while floating in the Warburg flask was detectable in about one hour and was associated with an increase in rate of carbon dioxide output and a decrease in rate of oxygen uptake. The changes in intact plants were evident in six hours. These changes are shown in Fig. 7.9. High concentrations of nitrate in tissues inhibited oxygen uptake. Rapid nitrate reduction consequent on addition of molybdenum further competed with oxygen for respiratory substrates and stimulated carbon dioxide production. In the barley experiment of Yemm and co-workers, the effects on carbon dioxide output were consistent with these results. The stimulation of oxygen uptake by ammonia or nitrate indicated an energy demand for their assimilation.

Wolfe independently made observations on relationships between nitrogen supply, molybdenum and respiration in the blue-green alga *Anabaena cylindrica*. In these experiments the effects of nitrogen deficiency were first considered. Oxygen uptake was relatively low in nitrogen-starved cells in the

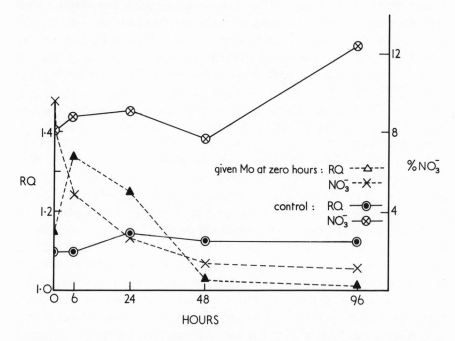

Figure 7.9   Respiratory quotient and nitrate level measured at intervals after giving molybdenum (100 μg) to molybdenum-deficient cauliflower plants. From Ducet and Hewitt (1954) *Nature, Lond.* **173**, 1141-3.

presence of molybdenum but was high in nitrogen-starved cells deficient also in molybdenum. Addition of nitrate to nitrogen-starved cells increased the R.Q. from 1·0 to nearly 2·0 in the presence of molybdenum but had little effect in its absence. Addition of fumarate in the presence of nitrate increased the R.Q. to about 1·8 and promoted nitrate assimilation. These results differed from others obtained with *Chlorella* because although R.Q. was increased by nitrate assimilation in each species, the change was associated essentially with increased carbon dioxide output by *Chlorella*, whereas in *Anabaena* the increased R.Q. was derived sometimes from a marked decrease in oxygen uptake with little change in carbon dioxide production, and sometimes from changes in carbon dioxide output. In cauliflower leaf tissues, darkness increased carbon dioxide output and decreased oxygen uptake, both occurring simultaneously to corresponding degrees.

McKee (1962) represented the relationship between nitrate and nitrite reduction and the utilisation of carbohydrate by the following formulae:

$$HNO_3 + 2(CH_2O) \rightarrow NH_3 + 2CO_2 + H_2O$$

$$2HNO_2 + 3(CH_2O) \rightarrow 2NH_3 + 3CO_2 + H_2O$$

and subtracting one equation from the other gives the following relationship:

$$2HNO_3 + (CH_2O) \rightarrow 2HNO_2 + CO_2 + H_2O$$

Thus wherever carbohydrate is involved, even indirectly, in nitrate or nitrite reduction, additional carbon dioxide production must occur. As however nitrate or nitrite are here substituted for oxygen, it would be expected that oxygen uptake would be simultaneously decreased. Nevertheless, as already noted for *Chlorella* no diminution of oxygen uptake was found when nitrate was added to slightly nitrogen-deficient cells of *Chlorella pyrenoidosa* growing with glucose in darkness but R.Q. was nevertheless increased by extra carbon dioxide production, from already high R.Q. values (1·3–1·5) when glucose was given in the dark.

It is necessary to recognise that when nitrate is reduced to ammonia in a *growing* organism, protein synthesis can then occur and this process requires respiratory energy provided by ATP. The same relationship exists for ammonia assimilation and therefore giving either nitrogen source will result in an increase in respiration, whether it be in maize roots or unicellular algae. The addition of ammonia to nitrogen-deficient *Chlorella* caused a three to sevenfold increase in respiration rate, and the R.Q. fell from about 1·2 to about 0·8 until most of the added ammonia was converted to soluble organic and protein nitrogen. Ammonia assimilation in normal cells was slow in the dark and accelerated by light, while in nitrogen-deficient cells the dark rate was high and light had little effect. The increased respiration probably indicated the role of respiratory ATP utilisation in amide and arginine synthesis. Oxygen uptake was doubled when nitrate was given to nitrogen-deficient *Chlorella* cells but carbon dioxide output increased more and R.Q. rose to 2·5. Reduction of nitrate to nitrite and of nitrite to ammonia were both inhibited by anaerobic conditions in *Ankistrodesmus braunii* and *Chlorella*. Nitrite accumulates in the medium in the absence of oxygen or with added 2,4-dinitrophenol (respiratory uncoupler) when nitrate is present.

Induction and control of nitrate-reductase activity

(a) *Micro-organisms*

The phenomena of enzyme induction or repression and de-repression and substrate stabilisation are most generally associated with micro-organisms, and the capacity for induction or adaptive formation in response to substrates or analogues has not been widely investigated in higher plants. Nitrate reductase is quite readily induced by nitrate in bacteria, fungi including yeasts, and in algae. Induction *in vivo* is repressed by oxygen to a very low basal level in many bacteria able to grow in the presence or absence of oxygen, and oxygen also inactivates the already formed enzyme. Under anaerobic conditions activity increases greatly by induction when nitrate or nitrite are introduced into the medium. Induction can occur under conditions where there is no growth. In several bacteria ammonium nitrogen represses enzyme formation. In some fungi, e.g. *Scopulariopsis brevicaulis* oxygen and ammonia repress formation but in *Neurospora crassa* oxygen and ammonia do not repress when nitrate is present as the nitrogen source for mature mycelia.

In green and blue-green algae, ammonia or products thereof including some amino acids, repress the formation of the enzyme. The enzyme present is then progressively destroyed until no residual enzyme remains.

In *Chlorella fusca* transfer to nitrogen-free media results in rapid de-repression of nitrate reductase formation without added nitrate, but this spontaneous de-repression does not occur in *Chlamydomonas reinhardii*.

In green and blue-green algae, the enzyme may be present in the cells in an inactive form which can be activated. The inactive form may be induced by short treatment *in vivo* with arsenite or ammonia, or during growth with nitrate. Activation *in vivo* can be achieved by short treatments with nitrate after removal of ammonia. Activation *in vitro* can be effected by incubation for prolonged periods with nitrate or instantaneously with oxidants such as ferricyanide, or by controlled heating at about $45°C$. The mechanism of these effects is not known but it seems probable that the dehydrogenase (or diaphorase) site on the enzyme (see properties below) may be the control site. In *Chlorella vulgaris* there is evidence for a low molecular weight protein factor which controls the redox state of the enzyme in terms of $NADH/NAD^+$ ratio and the ratio of ADP to ATP. The role of carbamyl phosphate may be especially important since this compound is a powerful inhibitor of nitrate reductase. However, its hydrolysis product cyanate was shown by Morris and Syrett to be even more inhibitory to the *Chlorella* enzyme in the NADH excess state.

(b) *Higher plants*

The possibility that nitrate reductase might be inducible in plants was first considered by Evans and Nason in 1953 in their work with soybean, but as activities were similar in plants grown in open, non-sterile cultures with either nitrate or ammonia they were obliged to regard the question as unanswered. Hewitt, Fisher and Candela in 1956 and 1957 found that when cauliflower plants were grown in sand cultures with ammonium sulphate, the average level of enzyme activity was substantially lower than that found in plants grown with nitrate or nitrite and suggested that in fact nitrate reductase is an inducible enzyme in higher plants. Similar results were obtained by Hageman and Flesher with maize seedlings in response to nitrate supply. Rice seedlings grown by Tang and Wu (1957) in sterile culture media for seven days were devoid of nitrate-reductase activity when given ammonium sulphate but contained the enzyme when nitrate was given, and Rijven showed induction by nitrate or nitrite when sterile excised embryos of wheat or *Capsella* were exposed to solutions of these compounds for twenty-four hours. Vaidya-nathan and Street found that nitrate reductase was induced by nitrate in excised tomato roots grown in sterile culture. In all these experiments, the induction of the enzyme or the conclusions that it was inducible related to whole plants, excised roots or growing embryos given the inducer for periods of twenty-four hours to several days.

When cauliflower or mustard plants were grown by Afridi and Hewitt in sterile sand cultures with glutamic acid, ammonia or urea no enzyme activity could be detected in leaf extracts. However nitrate reductase was produced at a steady rate for several hours when excised leaf tissues of these plants were infiltrated with nitrate, but nitrite given at comparable concentrations did not result in the induction of activity. The nitrite was also rapidly lost in the illuminated tissues. In other experiments nitrite appeared either to repress or induce nitrate reductase depending on the species when given to plants during growth, or when added to the medium at the time of induction of the enzyme. Ammonium sulphate neither induced nor repressed the induction of activity in such tissues. Several amino acids including alanine, asparagine, methionine, glycine, proline, threonine and valine repressed the formation of the enzyme in tobacco cells grown in isolated cell cultures. Arginine, isoleucine, cysteine and lysine reversed the repression but did not act as independent inducers. Threonine inhibited the uptake of nitrate into the cells which is apparently mediated by a permease system. Afridi and Hewitt found that serine stimulated induction by nitrate but that most amino acids were either inconsistent in effect or tended to inhibit the response to nitrate. Not only does enzyme formation occur as described but enzyme activity already present declines when nitrate supply is removed from growing plants or when excised tissues are held in the absence of nitrate. The excised tissues of such de-adapted plants respond to nitrate when this is introduced by infiltration, in the same manner as excised tissues of plants grown in sterile cultures without nitrate. The instability *in vivo* of nitrate reductase when nitrate is absent or withdrawn has been widely confirmed in several species. The decay follows first-order kinetics and is partly prevented by the presence of cycloheximide which inhibits protein synthesis, but the basis for this is unknown.

The concentration of nitrate in the cells required to produce half-maximal rates of enzyme formation in cauliflower is calculated to be about 10^{-5} M. This concentration was regarded as consistent with the amounts of nitrate available to plants grown in non-sterile cultures as the result of nitrification of ammonia or urea and from which the enzyme could be extracted in relatively normal quantities. The unpredictable extent of nitrification causes

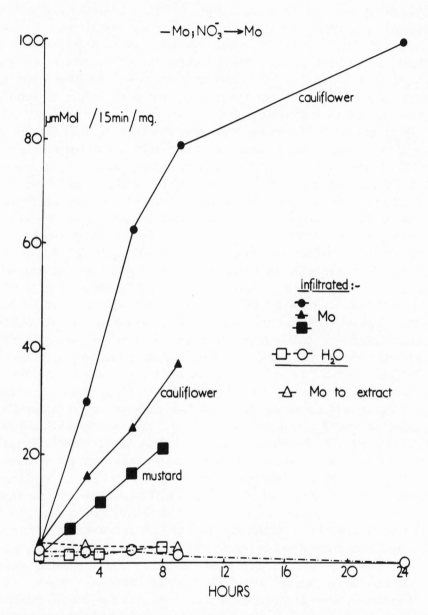

Figure 7.10 Effect of infiltration of molybdenum on the formation of nitrate reductase in excised leaves of cauliflower and mustard. From Afridi and Hewitt (unpublished); cited in Hewitt (1971) *Trace Elements in Soils and Crops*, Technical Bulletin No. 21, H.M.S.O., pp. 21–34.

large differences from time to time in the amount of enzyme present in plants grown under these conditions and probably prevented Evans and Nason from being able to reach any conclusions on the matter.

The presence or absence during growth of molybdenum, which is a component of the enzyme, has a similar effect to nitrate on the production of the enzyme in either fungi or plants. As shown in Fig. 7.10 the vacuum infiltration of molybdenum into leaf tissues of deficient plants grown with nitrate causes the rapid formation of enzyme activity over a few hours. Giving molybdenum to the cell-free extracts is entirely without effect. Plants grown with ammonium nitrogen in place of nitrate and deprived also of molybdenum require both factors simultaneously for full production of activity.

The induction of nitrate reductase has been demonstrated in the field pea, both root and leaf tissues alike showing this response. Other experiments have shown a similar response in the leaves of cocklebur (*Xanthium pennsylvanicum*) which appears not to reduce nitrate at all in root tissues. All species studied, cauliflower, mustard, pea and cocklebur show pronounced effects of age and leaf position on the extent to which induction occurs. The pattern of leaf age effect differs with each species, but reflects largely the distribution of enzyme activity found in plants grown with nitrate.

The formation of nitrate reductase as an inducible response to both nitrate and molybdenum is sensitive to temperature and dependent on oxygen. This dependence on oxygen for maximal rate of enzyme formation is the opposite of that observed for *Aerobacter aerogenes* or for the fungus *Scopulariopsis brevicaulis* where the presence of oxygen suppressed the synthesis of the enzyme. The amount of the enzyme produced in higher plants as represented by maize studied by Hageman and his co-workers is genetically controlled. The same situation probably accounts for large differences found for different varieties of cauliflower by Afridi and Hewitt. Gene control is known to operate in fungi. Some antimetabolites which are effective in inhibiting processes of protein synthesis, nucleic acid synthesis and enzyme induction in other organisms were active inhibitors of nitrate-reductase induction in excised leaf tissues. Examples of effects of some of these compounds on induction in excised leaf tissues are shown in Table 7.2. Among the most active antimetabolites are halogen-substituted uracil compounds, bromacil and isocil, cycloheximide, puromycin, L-azetidine-2-carboxylic acid and patulin. From the work of Fowden and his collaborators it is clear that azetidine-2-carboxylic acid competes in the activation of proline by prolyl-transfer RNA. The action of patulin is not known but its effect on RNA synthesis is even more drastic. There was no clear distinction between the effects of these inhibitors on the formation of active enzyme when induction by nitrate or molybdenum was compared. The conclusion is that both nitrate and molybdenum are required

Table 7.2 Effect of antimetabolites (including inhibitors of protein synthesis) in the infiltration medium of excised leaves on induction of nitrate reductase by nitrite or molybdenum. (From the work of Afridi, Notton and Hewitt)

Compound	Concentration in medium (M)	% inhibition of induction	
		Grown in absence of NO_3 Induction by NO_3	Mo deficient Induction by Mo
Actidione (cycloheximide)	2×10^{-4}	86	58
Patulin	10^{-3}	50	84
Polymyxin B sulphate (cyclic polypeptide)	$1 \cdot 3 \times 10^{-3}$	59	76
Cycloserine	2×10^{-2}	35	56
Bromacil (5-bromo 3-*sec* butyl-6-methyl uracil)	2×10^{-5}	80	84
L-azetidine carboxylic acid	10^{-3}	86	54
L-azetidine carboxylic acid + Proline	$\left. \begin{matrix} 10^{-3} \\ 10^{-3} \end{matrix} \right\}$	25	13
Puromycin	4×10^{-4}	60	93

in the intact cell for the synthesis or stability of the catalytically active polypeptide structure of the enzyme. Serological studies by Notton, Graf, Povey and Hewitt show that partial synthesis may occur in the absence of molybdenum but the stabilisation of the apoprotein seems to depend on the presence of the metal. In *N. crassa* the polypeptide structure of about the same size as the whole enzyme is formed in the absence of molybdenum but activity is only produced in the presence of the metal *in vivo*.

The role of molybdenum in nitrate-reductase formation and activity (so far known in no other plant enzyme except for nitrogen-fixation systems) would suggest that the element should not be required when nitrogen is supplied in a form other than nitrate (see page 27). Molybdenum is still required by cauliflowers when grown with nitrite, urea, ammonium compounds, or glutamate in sand cultures as shown by the appearance of the characteristic symptoms of whiptail (Plates 55 and 56), which appear when molybdenum is deficient. In these experiments sterile conditions were not maintained indefinitely and experience has shown, as already mentioned, that nitrification of urea or ammonium compounds is rapid and sufficient to cause considerable induction of nitrate reductase. Plants grown under these conditions were nevertheless found to contain high concentrations of soluble and protein nitrogen and quite low concentrations of nitrate indicating that a substantial proportion of the ammonia supplied was absorbed before nitrification to nitrate.

It seemed possible that the molybdenum requirement inferred from these experiments was determined by the inducing effect of the nitrate taken up after nitrification on the nitrate-reductase enzyme forming system but in the absence of molybdenum, and that the requirement might be abolished by growing the plants under sterile conditions. An experiment by Gundry and Hewitt (1970) has entirely supported this prediction (see also page 28). Plants grown for up to ten weeks in initially sterile enclosed conditions without molybdenum and with nitrogen as ammonium sulphate remained free of any whiptail symptoms for a further period of four weeks after the cultures were opened until the experiment was concluded. Plants grown with nitrate under these conditions or with ammonium sulphate under non-sterile conditions developed typical whiptail symptoms five days after opening the cultures and symptoms continued to develop for the remainder of the period.

The effects of the herbicide simazine in stimulating the growth of resistant crops, especially of maize, may be noted here in relation to the stability of nitrate reductase. The maximal responses to simazine were obtained with plants grown at somewhat low temperatures or with relatively low levels of nitrate. The effect of simazine in maize appears to be in delaying the breakdown of the enzyme. The enzyme activity is maintained at nearly normal values in plants given simazine after nitrate is removed from the growth medium, compared with the rapid drop in activity which occurs in plants not given simazine. Therefore when the nitrate supply or the temperature are not optimal for formation of the enzyme or for stabilising it in the cells, simazine causes a higher enzyme activity to be built up and maintained. The breakdown of the enzyme which is supposed to occur on removal of nitrate or transfer to darkness is apparently a first-order reaction which is considerably slower when cycloheximide is present. It is probable that the capacity for cell protein synthesis is necessary for enzyme degradation to occur. Hormones such as kinetin may mimic the role of nitrate in enzyme induction and gibberellic acid may act synergistically with nitrate and kinetin in the absence of light.

Reversible regulation of nitrate reductase in higher plants seems certain as nitrate accumulation is a common phenomenon. However, no clear indications of any mechanisms are yet apparent. ADP is an inhibitor of the enzyme from tomato, wheat and spinach and ADP or some other nucleotide may be a regulator of the enzyme *in vivo*. The presence of thiol compounds such as glutathione profoundly influences the effects of ADP. This relationship may indicate another way in which light may be involved in nitrate reduction since thiol concentrations change rapidly in response to light.

Properties of nitrate reductase in fungi and higher plants

The enzyme nitrate reductase in higher plants and fungi was first isolated and characterised from soybean (*Glycine max*) and *Neurospora crassa* by

Evans and Nason in 1953. They showed that the basic system consisted of NADH or NADPH, FMN or FAD and a protein fraction which appeared to involve a metal co-factor. Inhibition by *p*-chloromercuribenzoate and its reversal by cysteine or glutathione indicated that sulphydryl (—SH) groups were required for activity. They were unable to identify the suspected metal component and there was no stimulation from the addition to cell-free extracts of Fe, Mn, Cu, Zn, B or Mo at concentrations effective in other circumstances. The prosthetic metal molybdenum was identified by Nicholas and Nason in 1954 and 1955, and by Evans and Hall in 1955 for fungi, higher plants and bacteria, and is known to be present in all examples so far studied. The product of nitrate reduction *in vitro* is nitrite (Table 8.4).

In soybean and cauliflower NADH and NADPH are about equally effective as hydrogen donors. In most plants the enzyme is relatively specific for NADH. The relative affinities of the enzyme from different sources for NADH or NADPH as revealed by the Michaelis constants (K_m) vary widely, and the optimum concentrations for NADH in spinach leaves, soybean leaves and wheat embryo are 4×10^{-6}, 8×10^{-5} and 4×10^{-4} M respectively. The enzyme from *N. crassa* was nearly specific for NADPH.

Differences in flavin requirements are less clearly established. The soybean leaf enzyme of Evans and Nason (1953) contained FAD as the natural flavin but FMN was able to substitute for FAD at half the efficiency and with an optimum concentration fifteen times higher. The *Neurospora* enzyme described by Nason and Evans showed similar relative specificity and FAD was the natural flavin. The wheat embryo enzyme described by Spencer was FAD-specific. Although addition of flavin was necessary for maximal activity in preparations from soybean, no response was observed on adding flavin to preparations from maize, spinach, vegetable marrow or cauliflower, and *Chlorella* species differ in flavin requirements. Cytochrome-components and/or non-haem ions are present in complex systems in micro-organisms.

Other natural factors

In addition to the nucleotide specificity and molybdenum content already noted, nitrate-reductase enzymes also show an anion requirement most effectively fulfilled by phosphate, which may control the extent of valency change of the molybdenum between 5 and 6. In many nitrate-reductase systems of plants, fungi, algae and bacteria there are two distinct types of activity (Fig. 7.11). Arrows and numerals show the direction of electron transport. Solid lines show the action of inhibitors or heat. A flavin may provide a transition from $2e^-$ to $1e^-$ donation by formation of a semiquinone FADH. Roman numerals I and II indicate the two moieties of the protein complex

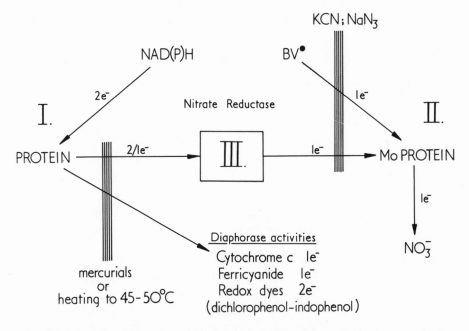

Figure 7.11 Mechanism of nitrate reduction in micro-organisms and plants
Nitrate reductase components I, II and III may form a single enzyme complex in
higher plants. Component III may represent a flavin in soybean and cytochrome b
in *Neurospora*. However component III has not been demonstrated as a separate
entity in other plants. The mechanism of electron donation by BV• (reduced
benzylviologen) is given in Fig. 7.12.

which are possibly separately synthesised in mutant forms, so far observed
only in micro-organisms lacking one or other of the principal activities. The
moieties are inducible by nitrate and can be recombined in heterocaryons or in
extracts of the mutants to produce a complete enzyme. Molybdenum-contain-
ing proteins obtained from plants, liver, or nitrogen-fixing bacteria can yield
an uncharacterised component which can reconstitute the nitrate reductase
activity in extracts of *Neurospora crassa* mutants having only nitrate-induced
dehydrogenase activity.

These experiments, together with the fact that biosynthesis of the enzyme
in an active form depends on molybdenum *in vivo* suggest that a molybdenum-
containing fragment or active precursor is synthesised *in vivo* and is then
united with the rest of the enzyme. Mutant forms of *Escherichia coli* and
Aspergillus nidulans, which cannot normally produce nitrate reductase are able
to do so when given unusually high concentrations of molybdenum, which
have no effect on enzyme activity *in vitro*. It is possible that a 'molybdenum
insertase' enzyme is present, analogous to ferrochelatase, which inserts iron

into protoporphyrin to form haem, a system which occurs in plants as well as in animals. In spinach, the replacement of molybdenum by tungsten results in the formation of a tungsten-protein analogue of nitrate reductase which has normal dehydrogenase but no nitrate-reductase activities.

Artificial electron carriers

The dipyridilium compound benzyl viologen (BV) or methyl viologen (MV) can be reduced to a one e^- donor (BV•, MV•). These are stable free radicals which are readily autoxidisable. These compounds will donate electrons to nitrate reductase in the absence of NADH or FAD (see Fig. 7.12). The action is inhibited by cyanide and most probably occurs as a direct reaction between the donor and the molybdenum atom in the enzyme. Benzyl viologen and ferredoxin (see page 209) are not interchangeable in the reduction of nitrate to ammonia by plants but are apparently interchangeable in the enzyme from *Anabaena*.

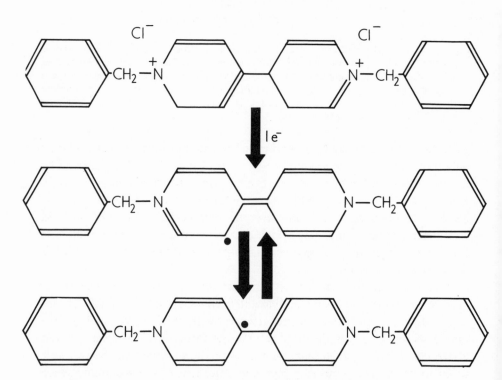

Figure 7.12 Mechanism of production of the free radical reductant benzylviologen (BV•), which occurs in two resonant forms.

Other systems

The early work of Virtanen and Von Hausen indicated that in cotyledons of peas and beans there were nitrate-reducing systems which were dependent on the presence of glutathione or ascorbic acid which were essential for nitrate assimilation during early seedling growth. Vaidayanathan and Street reported that crude extracts of excised sterile tomato roots contained a nitrate-reducing system which was activated by ferrous iron and ascorbate. These systems may be related but have not been characterised. A possibly distinct system known as aldehyde oxidase has been obtained from potato tubers and was first described by Bernheim in 1928. This enzyme reduces nitrate to nitrite under anaerobic conditions with acetaldehyde or other aldehydes as hydrogen donor. In air acetaldehyde is oxidised with the formation of hydrogen peroxide which inactivates the enzyme. It is not known elsewhere in plants and the properties of the enzyme require further study. Peroxidase has also been found to reduce nitrate in the presence of diethyldithiocarbamate and sulphite by an unknown mechanism.

Nitrite reduction in higher plants

The first observations of enzymic systems in higher plants which are able to convert nitrite to ammonia in quantitative yields at rates consistent with the activity of nitrate reductase and with nitrate assimilation by intact plants were made with proteins from vegetable marrow leaf extracts and were described by Cresswell, Hageman, Hewitt and Hucklesby between 1962 and 1965. This system utilised benzyl viologen (BV$^\bullet$) as an electron donor or as a carrier at catalytic concentrations in the presence of a diaphorase enzyme and NADPH. No activity was found on omitting the BV$^\bullet$. The product of the reaction was ammonia and within limits of experimental error the yields were quantitative.

Previously to this, Huzisige and Satoh in 1960 and 1961 had reported a direct photochemical reaction of nitrite in enzymic systems obtained from *Euglena* and spinach leaves. Illuminated spinach leaf homogenates induced rapid loss of nitrite under aerobic conditions. The system could be separated into a grana fraction and a soluble enzymic protein fraction. Grana and light alone were inactive. Huzisige and Satoh noted the similarity in method of preparation of their enzyme system to that used by San Pietro and Lang in 1958 for isolation of the photosynthetic pyridine nucleotide-reductase system now identified with ferredoxin (see p. 281) and a flavoprotein. Davenport, Hill and Whatley in 1952 first reported the function of ferredoxin in catalysing the reduction of methaemoglobin by illuminated chloroplasts. Separate studies by Losada, Hageman, Huzisige and Hewitt with their co-workers have since shown beyond doubt that in leaves, nitrite is reduced in the light by a chloroplast system containing ferredoxin and a protein-nitrite reductase. The nitrite is reduced quantitatively to ammonia. NADPH was shown to be able to reduce nitrite in the presence of ferredoxin and soluble nitrite reductase without the mediation of grana and light.

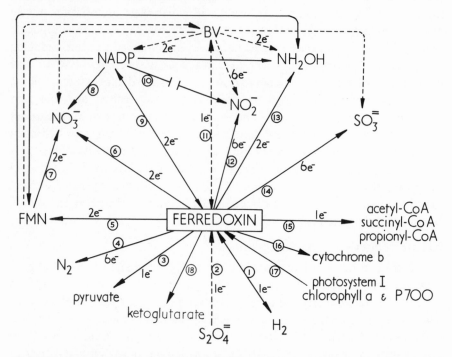

Figure 7.13 Metabolic processes dependent on ferredoxin. Dotted lines indicate the paths of electrons from non-physiological donors. Arrows indicate the likely direction of electron flow in biological systems.

 (1) Hydrogenase in *Clostridium* and some *Chlorella* spp.
 (2) Dithionite—non-physiological donor.
 (3) Phosphoroclastic reaction in *Clostridium* giving acetyl phosphate and CO_2.
 (4) Nitrogenase.
 (5) FMN reduction.
 (6) Nitrate reduction in *Anabaena* only.
 (7) Nitrate reduction in most other plants.
 (8) Nitrate reduction in soybean.
 (9) NAD(P) reduction.
 (10) Unlikely to occur in any photosynthetic organisms.
 (11) Benzylviologen reduction, non-physiological donor.
 (12) Nitrite reduction.
 (13) Hydroxylamine reduction.
 (14) Sulphite reduction (see Chapter 8).
 (15) Reductive carboxylation giving keto acids.
 (16) Cyclic phosphorylation, donation to unknown carrier
   (probably a cytochrome b).
 (17) Photosynthesis. Donation from ferredoxin-reducing substance.
 (18) Assimilation of α-ketoglutarate by glutamine in chloroplasts.

Ferredoxin-dependent nitrite reduction

Ferredoxin is described in detail in Chapter 8. Briefly it is a low molecular weight iron-containing protein occurring in chloroplasts which mediates the direct transfer of chlorophyll-activated electrons to proteins like nitrite reductase or NADP reductase and so is the immediate electron donor for the processes of NADP and nitrite reduction (Fig. 7.13). Because of the auto-oxidisable properties of ferredoxin anaerobic conditions are preferable for the investigation of nitrite reductase and rates are often increased in chloroplast systems when oxygen evolution is suppressed by using chlorophenylmethyl urea, an inhibitor of this process, or by heating the chloroplast grana for five minutes at 55°C. In either case it is then necessary to provide an artificial electron donor in place of water and the chlorophyll b system, and this is usually achieved by adding ascorbic acid and a dye carrier such as dichloro-phenolindophenol.

It may be accepted with reasonable certainty that ferredoxin is the natural carrier in the hydrogen or electron transfer system in which nitrite reduction in the presence of nitrite reductase is achieved in leaves. Ferredoxin is a constituent of chloroplasts, although it was shown to be readily and almost completely released from these particles after cell rupture. Recent evidence favours the view that nitrite reductase itself is also present in, and possibly even confined to chloroplasts in leaves, though other subcellular particles have been suggested as a location. The properties of nitrite reductase are described in Chapter 8 (see p. 283).

Oxygen evolution in the light is stimulated by nitrite in wheat leaves and also in the green alga, *Ankistrodesmus,* and it presumably acts as a Hill reagent, i.e. a terminal electron acceptor allowing the photolysis of water to yield oxygen in accordance with the following equation:

$$HNO_2 + H_2O \rightarrow NH_3 + 1 \cdot 5O_2$$

The partial and overall reactions involved may be represented thus:

$$H_2O \rightarrow OH^- + H^+$$

$$OH^- \xrightarrow{\text{light}} OH^\bullet + e^-$$

$$2OH^\bullet \rightarrow H_2O + 0 \cdot 5\ O_2$$

$$3H_2O \rightarrow 6e^- + 6H^+ + 1 \cdot 5O_2 \tag{1}$$

$$6\ \text{Ferredoxin (Fd)ox} + 6e^- \rightarrow 6Fd.red \tag{2}$$

$$6Fd.ox + 3H_2O \rightarrow 6Fd.red + 6H^+ + 1 \cdot 5O_2$$

$$NO_2^- + 6Fd.red + 7H^+ \rightarrow NH_3 + 2H_2O + 6Fd.ox \qquad (3)$$

Sum $\qquad NO_2^- + H_2O + H^+ \rightarrow NH_3 + 1\cdot5O_2 \qquad (4)$

This system is accompanied by photosynthetic non-cyclic phosphorylation of ADP to ATP when whole chloroplasts are used and therefore nitrite can replace NADP as the terminal acceptor.

Dark nitrite reduction

(a) *Higher plants*

There is adequate evidence to indicate the mechanism involving light in nitrite reduction in leaves under natural conditions. However, other mechanisms may also exist for dark reduction of nitrite. Roots of many plants export amino acids and therefore they can reduce nitrite formed from nitrate. The growth of excised roots with nitrate in sterile media is additional evidence of this activity. Cresswell and Hewitt observed a steady although relatively slow disappearance of nitrite introduced into intact leaf tissues held in darkness, and Huzisige and Satoh observed a slow loss of nitrite in the presence of a homogenate of spinach leaves in the dark. This reaction was regarded as the result of reduction of the intermediate donor normally produced during photosynthesis by substrates of dehydrogenase systems. Many workers have linked glucose-6-phosphate and its dehydrogenase, through NADP, NADPH-ferredoxin oxido-reductase, ferredoxin and nitrite reductase to nitrite reduction, and the above conclusion is probably correct for leaves. Vaidyanathan and Street reported that extracts of excised tomato roots contained an enzyme that caused rapid loss of nitrite in the presence of NADH, FMN (or glutathione) and manganese. The reaction product resembled hyponitrite rather than hydroxylamine, and ammonia formation was negligible. Recent studies by Miflin and co-workers with barley have now shown that dark or non-photochemical systems for nitrite reduction occur in roots and are located in particles which appear to be distinct from mitochondria. Reduced benzyl viologen, ferredoxin or succinate are effective electron donors. It is probable that a one-electron physiological carrier is involved, though ferredoxin has not been detected in roots. However, succinic dehydrogenase systems of yeasts and animal tissues which are present in particles contain a 'built-in' ferredoxin type of protein sub-unit. This could be the carrier involved in the root systems which is still unidentified. Experiments by Hucklesby using radioactive iron have shown this to be incorporated into a purified fraction containing nitrite reductase when the enzyme is induced in plants by nitrate. Studies with some derivatives of *o*-phenanthroline and with carbon monoxide have also indicated the likelihood that this is present but apparently not as a haem compound.

ATP was found to be essential for nitrite reduction to ammonia by cell-free particulate preparations. It was suggested that some aspects of this system may resemble the requirements for ATP and ferredoxin in the transfer of six electrons for molecular nitrogen reduction by nitrogenases.

(b) *Algae*

The experiments of Kessler, and Huzisige and Satoh have shown that in the dark, certain green algae including *Euglena gracilis*, *Ankistrodesmus braunii* and *Scenedesmus obliquus* can reduce nitrite to ammonia in the presence of hydrogen donors such as malate, or in the presence of hydrogen and presumably a hydrogenase system, which in effect achieves the following reaction:

$$H_2 \rightleftharpoons 2H^+ + 2e^-$$

The equation can be written thus:

$$NO_2^- + 8H^+ + 6e^- \rightarrow NH_4^+ + 2H_2O$$

The question of whether ferredoxin is involved was not considered, as its existence was then unknown. However the participation of ferredoxin seems likely by analogy with the work of Tagawa and Arnon who were able to link hydrogen and hydrogenase from *Clostridium* to chloroplasts of spinach in the presence of ferredoxin, so that they carried out reactions in darkness that are normally associated with photochemical systems. Kessler stated that as *Chlorella vulgaris* had no hydrogenase activity it was unable to reduce nitrite in the dark in the presence of hydrogen but *C. pyrenoidosa* has a strong hydrogenase and can do so. An unexplained feature of nitrite reduction by hydrogen in *A. braunii* was discovered by Kessler in 1957. The presence of carbon dioxide greatly stimulated the rate of nitrite reduction and also resulted in raising the quotient H_2 consumed/NO_2^- reduced, from 2·6 to a theoretical value of 3·0. In other words in the absence of carbon dioxide, other hydrogen donors were involved but their participation was inhibited by carbon dioxide even though the overall rate of reduction with hydrogen was increased. No carbon dioxide fixation however could be detected. As noted already for higher plants, iron has also been shown by Losada and his co-workers to be associated with purified nitrite reductase from *Chlorella*.

In intact cells of *Ankistrodesmus braunii*, 2,4-dinitrophenol severely inhibits nitrite reduction at practically the same concentration at which oxygen uptake is characteristically greatly increased by this poison. When oxidative phosphorylation is 'uncoupled', i.e. no longer occurs, this relationship means that nitrite reduction depends on the utilisation of high-energy phosphate bonds generated by normal respiratory activity requiring oxygen uptake. In some strains of *Chlorella*, nitrite accumulates if anaerobic conditions are imposed, but nitrate reduction is unaffected.

Nitrite reduction by *Ankistrodesmus* either utilises hydrogen and hydrogenase or occurs photochemically. Reduction in the presence of hydrogen is independent of light intensity. Under nitrogen the rate rises sharply with increasing light intensity at first, but as light intensity increases still further the rate of nitrite reduction decreases and reaches a constant value equal to that produced with hydrogen in either light or dark (Fig. 7.14). In the presence of 2,4-dinitrophenol the reduction with hydrogen is completely inhibited for reasons at present unknown. With increasing light intensity in the presence of this inhibitor the rate of nitrite reduction increases hyperbolically in the manner expected for a saturation relationship for light intensity instead of showing the peak at 330 lux.

Nason and co-workers obtained an enzyme from *Neurospora* which reduced nitrite to ammonia with NADPH or NADH as hydrogen donor; 3 mols of NADH were oxidised for each mol of nitrite reduced. FAD was required and NADPH was 1·5 times as active as NADH. Further experiments by Nicholas and his co-workers showed that both iron and copper increased activity in extracts when given during growth in the culture medium. Also there was a greater content of both metals in the purified protein fractions as specific

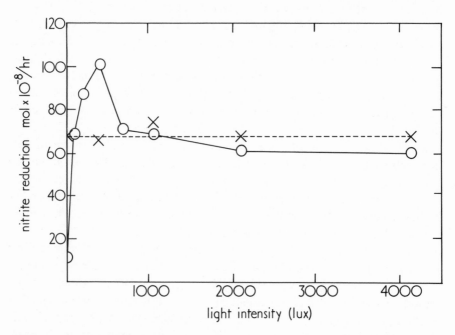

Figure 7.14 The dependence of nitrite reduction on light intensity in the alga *Ankistrodesmus* under hydrogen (crosses) and nitrogen (circles). From Kessler (1957) *Planta* **49**, 505–23.

activity increased. 2,4-Dinitrophenol inhibited nitrite reduction in cell-free systems obtained from *Neurospora*. This compound might be acting either by interference with availability of high-energy phosphate or as a direct inhibitor of nitrite reductase.

Hyponitrite and hydroxylamine as intermediates of nitrite reduction

Biological reduction or oxidation reactions involving a large energy change usually proceed in steps each of smaller energy difference or oxidation-reduction potential than the total change. The reduction of nitrate to ammonia has been represented in classical schemes as involving probably three intermediates and four steps. The scheme proposed by Meyer and Schultze in 1894 involved nitrite; a hypothetical compound at the level of hyponitrite; and hydroxylamine; resulting in four steps of two hydrogen atoms or electrons each. This early hypothesis has been widely accepted without critical evaluation until recently, and is still cited.

The status of hyponitrite ($H_2N_2O_2$) and hydroxylamine (NH_2OH) as intermediates in nitrite reduction (Fig. 7.8) has been a matter of confusion and doubt. Medina and Nicholas reported the reduction of hyponitrite to ammonia by an enzyme system from *Neurospora*, and McNall and Atkinson reported a similar result with *Escherichia coli*. Fearer in 1955 observed that ^{15}N-labelled hyponitrite given to soybean plants was converted to ammonia, but Frear and Burrell were of the opinion that hyponitrite was first oxidised to nitrate or nitrite before ammonia was formed by a different reduction pathway. This reaction could even occur non-enzymically. Vaidayanathan and Street, who thought that hyponitrite or a compound resembling it was the product of rapid nitrite reduction by extracts of tomato roots in the presence of manganese, found that hyponitrite reduction to ammonia by these preparations was extremely slow. It appears from these and other experiments on fungi and higher plants that the rate of nitrite reduction to ammonia exceeds the rate for the suggested intermediate, hyponitrite, at a comparable concentration. Moreover, hyponitrite severely inhibited nitrite reductase although this compound was regarded as the product of nitrite reduction. Nevertheless the possibility—not then investigated—still remained that at much lower concentrations, this compound might be more rapidly reduced and less inhibitory. Neither hyponitrite nor nitrous oxide were reduced by an enzyme obtained from *E. coli* which rapidly reduced both nitrite and hydroxylamine to ammonia. No utilisation of hyponitrite by *Pseudomonas aeruginosa*, *P. stutzeri* or *Micrococcus dinitrificans* has been demonstrated and the purified nitrite reductase from plants is completely inactive towards hyponitrite. Nitric oxide appeared to be metabolised by crude homogenates from plants but no reaction occurs anaerobically with pure enzyme. If nitric oxide is an

intermediate of nitrite reduction, from which it may be formed by denitrification reactions in bacteria, a single-electron step must be involved between
nitrite and nitric oxide:

$$NO_2^- + 2H^+ + e^- \rightarrow NO + H_2O$$

since the overall reaction is a single-electron process (p. 196) at least one more
single-electron step must be involved if two more two-electron steps occur
later in the sequence, including the stage of hydroxylamine reduction.

Nason critically reviewed the evidence advanced for the participation of
hyponitrite in the reduction of nitrite to ammonia by fungi and bacteria. He
could not accept unreservedly current published views regarding the status of
hyponitrite as an intermediate. Nevertheless in enzymic systems obtained
from chicken liver hyponitrite appeared to be formed during nitrite reduction,
and was also thought to be reduced to ammonia by the same complex of
enzymes.

The idea that hydroxylamine is an intermediate in nitrite reduction to
ammonia has been accepted quite widely since the proposal of Meyer and
Schulze in 1894. The evidence for and against this view requires to be assessed
in relation to the observations obtained with plants and with micro-organisms.

In favour of the idea are the following points. Hydroxylamine is enzymatic-
ally reduced to ammonia by systems obtained from a wide variety of organisms
including higher plants. A stoicheiometric relationship between enzymic
hydroxylamine loss and NADH oxidation, and between the latter and ammonia production was found in the *Neurospora* system. The activity of
hydroxylamine reductase in fungi or tomato roots was much greater than that
of nitrite reductase in the same (or similar) preparations in terms of substrate
loss or ammonia production. Hydroxylamine yields ammonia in quantitative
amounts when ferredoxin, benzyl viologen or FMN are used as electron
donors with enzymes from marrow, spinach or maize. Hydroxylamine is
rapidly lost in the presence of ferredoxin, illuminated spinach chloroplast
fragments and a chloroplast protein extract, and the product is ammonia.
Hydroxylamine-reductase activity is present in highly purified nitrite reductase from which it is not entirely lost and not recovered separately during
purification. Distinct haem proteins having hydroxylamine-reductase activity
are also found.

The production of hydroxylamine, oximes or hydroxamic acids has been
observed during nitrite assimilation, and hydroxylamine is utilised for
nitrogen assimilation and ammonia formation in several species, but exceptions
quite definitely occur. Hydroxamate formation from glutamine by exchange
with hydroxylamine may also provide a possible mechanism for direct
assimilation but has not yet been demonstrated. Free hydroxylamine is rarely

identified in plants but has been reported to occur as a product of nitrite reduction. Lemoigne, Monguillon and Desvaux (1935, 1937) reported that oximes or compounds of hydroxylamine hydrolysed by HCl were present in fresh leaves of carrot, spinach, beet and other species, and oximes were reported to be present in lucerne, pea and barley leaves. Lemoigne *et al.* in 1937 found that ascorbate at pH values of *Syringa* leaf sap reduced nitrite chemically to produce some hydroxylamine but the importance of this reaction seems doubtful except as an artefact.

Oxime formation may be important in the pathway from nitrite to ammonia in *Neurospora crassa* mutants. Pyridoxine which is essential for growth of certain mutants with nitrite is converted to pyridoxal phosphate and this compound forms pyridoxal phosphate oxime. The oxime may then be reduced to an amino group and is transferred to a keto-acid by the transamination reaction, and regenerates pyridoxal phosphate. The scheme of Silver and McElroy (1954) is shown in Fig. 7.15.

The evidence which casts doubt on the status of *free* hydroxylamine or any of its derivatives in the free state as potential intermediates in nitrite reduction is summarised below. Spencer, Takahashi and Nason in 1957 were quite definite that although an enzyme preparation from *Azotobacter agile* rapidly reduced nitrite to ammonia in stoicheiometric yields, no ammonia formation could be detected on the disappearance of hydroxylamine which occurred in the same preparations. The product of hydroxylamine loss could not be identified but it was not nitrite, ammonia or oximes and only traces of a hydroxamic acid were detected.

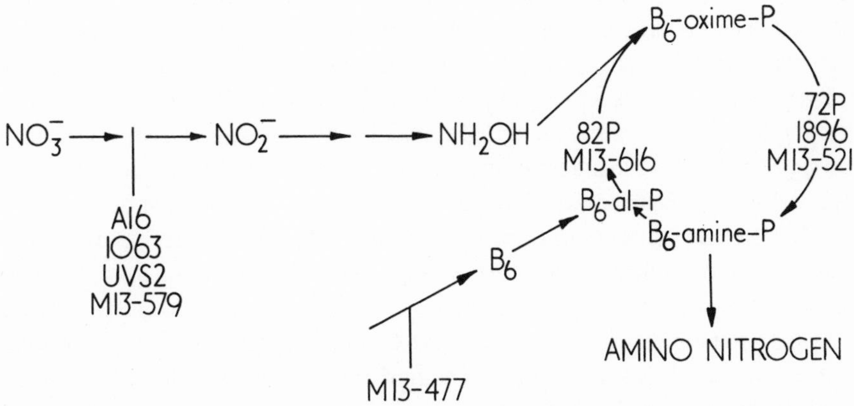

Figure 7.15 Postulated scheme for nitrite reduction in the fungus *Neurospora*, implicating pyridoxal phosphate (B₆). Numbers refer to mutants blocked at the stages shown. From Silver and McElroy (1954) *Archs Biochem.* **51**, 379–94.

Kessler studied the effects of nitrate, nitrite and hydroxylamine addition on hydrogen uptake by *Ankistrodesmus* in the dark. Whereas the uptake was greatly stimulated by nitrite and slightly so by nitrate the effect of an equimolar concentration of hydroxylamine induced an even slower rate of hydrogen uptake. On the basis of the following equations:

$$HNO_2 + 3H_2 \rightarrow NH_3 + 2H_2O$$

$$NH_2OH + H_2 \rightarrow NH_3 + H_2O$$

he calculated that the rate of hydroxylamine reduction to ammonia was only 25% that of nitrite reduction. Moreover hydroxylamine has been shown to be markedly inhibitory to many plants, and it is not utilised for growth in the circumstances so far tested. Steinberg concluded that reports that hydroxylamine accumulates in plants were erroneous and could be explained by assuming that the compound was nitrohydroxylaminic acid (*syn.* oxyhyponitrite, which is a little known compound and relatively unstable). Wood also expressed doubt that reports of the occurrence of hydroxylamine in plants were valid since they depended on the use of an analytical method which would not give unequivocal results in the presence of nitrite or nitrohydroxylaminic acid.

In a study of nitrite and hydroxylamine metabolism in *E. coli* Lazzarini and Atkinson in 1961 and later with Kemp and Ehret in 1963 reached the conclusion that nitrite and hydroxylamine reductase activities were not sequentially involved in the reduction of nitrite to ammonia. They were unable to detect the formation of hydroxylamine as an intermediate when they used ^{15}N-labelled nitrite and attempted to isolate hydroxylamine with unlabelled carrier. They considered that a single enzyme might well be responsible for the reduction of nitrite direct to ammonia without the production of free intermediates. In this system as in *Neurospora* NADPH was the natural electron donor. They also concluded that sulphite, nitrite and hydroxylamine-reductase activities are mediated by the same enzyme in *E. coli* and reiterated their belief that the transfer of six electrons to produce sulphide or ammonia was carried out by one enzyme, the intermediates remaining bound to the enzyme surface in accordance with kinetic studies. Similar conclusions seem valid for enzymes from yeasts described by Naiki in 1965 with respect to all three activities and for nitrite and hydroxylamine-reduction systems studied by Folkes and Sims for several yeasts and now more fully described in the symposium at Long Ashton in 1967.

The kinetic studies of Hewitt and his associates have shown that for the marrow and spinach leaf systems with the *same* preparation nitrite is enzymically reduced quantitatively to ammonia by reduced benzyl viologen or by ferredoxin using chloroplast grana and light, at a much faster rate than hydroxylamine when given at the same molar concentration. This evidence is not however of itself conclusive. The data show that the apparent K_m for nitrite is between 10^{-6} and 10^{-4} M according to circumstances, while that for hydroxylamine is between 5×10^{-5} and 10^{-3} M, i.e. ten to fifty times greater. Hydroxylamine has no inhibitory effect on the activity of either hydroxylamine or nitrite-reductase activities over the whole range up to 10^{-3} M required to obtain saturating concentrations for hydroxylamine reduction. These are about five to ten times greater than the concentration of nitrite which saturates nitrite reductase. Now, at any steady-state condition the concentration of hydroxylamine, if produced as an intermediate, cannot exceed that of nitrite at the beginning of the reaction. During enzymic nitrite reduction, no compound reacting like free hydroxylamine accumulates although the above kinetic data would require such a compound to accumulate appreciably if it were an intermediate. Nitrite at 10^{-5} M severely inhibits the reduction of sixty times higher concentrations of hydroxylamine to ammonia in ferredoxin or benzyl viologen donating systems. Senez and Pichinoty in 1958 also observed a marked inhibition of hydroxylamine reduction by nitrite in the presence of hydrogen and benzyl viologen for cells of *Desulphovibrio desulphuricans*. Other studies by Losada and by Hageman and their associates have yielded similar evidence. The generally favoured view at present for the reduction of nitrite to ammonia by higher plants, bacteria and yeasts is that one enzyme mediates the transfer of all six electrons without either the production of free intermediates, or of intermediates which can equilibrate with free hydroxylamine or other compounds such as hyponitrite. A tentative scheme which accommodates this idea and allows for one and the same enzyme to reduce either nitrite or hydroxylamine is reproduced in Fig. 7.16 as a basis for argument and thought. For simplicity at the time of its conception the reactions were based on a series of two electron steps. If obligatory one electron steps are involved further modification to the scheme will be necessary. An earlier scheme presented by Kemp, Ehret, Lazzarini and Atkinson in 1963 involves similar ideas for the reduction of sulphite and nitrite but does not deal with hydroxylamine and differs in other details.

The oxidation of nitrogenous compounds to nitrate in plants

A specialised aspect of nitrification is the oxidation of ammonia or other partially reduced compounds of nitrogen to nitrite or nitrate in plant cells. Evidence for this, which is based solely on feeding plants with ammonia or nitrite in open culture conditions and observing the appearance of nitrite or nitrate in the tissues, is of little value. Nitrification of ammonia to nitrite and production of nitrate in culture media that are not sterile occurs readily in

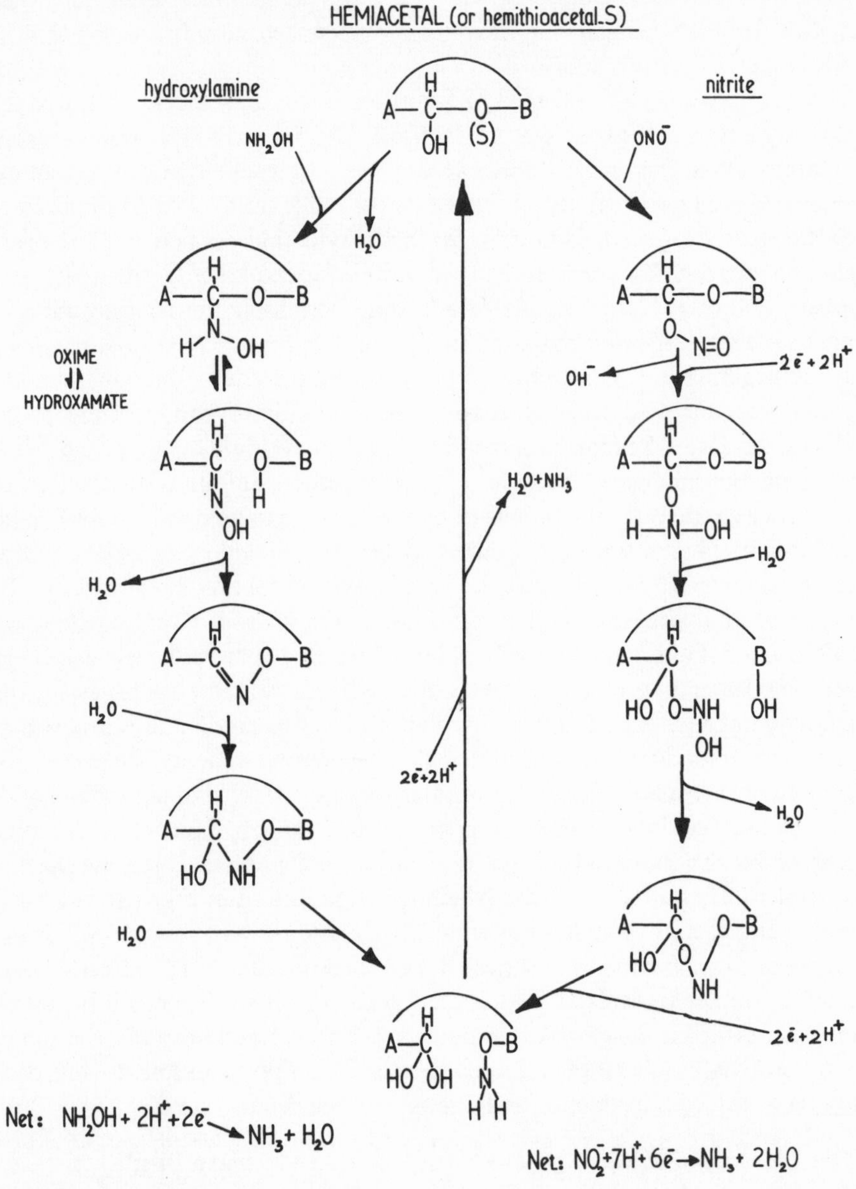

Figure 7.16 Tentative scheme for the reduction of nitrite or hydroxylamine in a sequence of 2e⁻ steps by the same enzyme system having a hemi-acetal prosthetic site and producing no free intermediates. From Hewitt, Hucklesby and Betts (1968) in *Recent Aspects of Nitrogen Metabolism in Plants*, Academic Press, London and New York.

plant or algal cultures. In an 'enriched' environment where organisms responsible for nitrification abound, these reactions take place rapidly after adding the reduced compounds to the culture medium. Evidence for oxidative nitrogen metabolism based on the use of sterile culture media is more satisfactory, but again must only be accepted with caution. When nutrient solutions containing ammonium sulphate are sterilised by autoclaving the oxidation of ammonia to nitrite is sometimes detected. Cauliflower plants grown in these sterilised media often had appreciable nitrate-reductase activity in the leaves. When glutamic acid was used, no nitrite was formed and no nitrate-reductase enzyme activity was found under these conditions. Mazé in 1915 also reported that nitrite was produced from ammonia by oxidation in distilled water at 56°C.

The production of nitrate or nitrite from ammonia within plant tissues should not be in theory so unlikely once the stage of hydroxylamine has been reached. This may arise in the first place from the hydrolysis of oximes which undoubtedly occur. Cresswell and Hewitt in 1959 showed that hydroxylamine is oxidised mainly to unknown products but also to give a small yield of nitrite by peroxidase in the presence of hydrogen peroxide (or a peroxide generating system), manganese, and a monophenol of which several occur naturally. The Kenten and Mann system involved in other analogous reactions is known to operate *in vivo* in certain plants and all the components for such a mechanism are normally present in many plants. Peroxidase, catalase or methaemoglobin will also mediate the oxidation of nitrite to nitrate. Detached (but not surface sterile) leaves which have not otherwise been damaged may gain in *nitrate* nitrogen while being kept isolated from any external source of fixed nitrogen. Such changes have been reported by McKee and Lobb for *Beta vulgaris*, *Vicia cicla*, and tomato; by McKee (1950) for barley, by Vickery, Pucher, Wakeman and Leavenworth, for tobacco; and by Moyse for wheat, buckwheat and *Rumex acetosa*, though the changes were small in some experiments. On the other hand Delwiche (1951) was unable to obtain any evidence for such nitrate production by excised tobacco leaves (*N. tabacum*) when ^{15}N-labelled ammonia was used in more critical work, and Munsche (in 1955) also obtained negative results with *Nicotiana glauca*. Fungi including *Penicillium atrovenetium* and *Aspergillus flavus* and some actinomycetes grown in sterile media readily produce oxidised compounds such as 3-nitropropionic acid, nitrite and nitrate from ammonia; 3-nitropropionic acid has also been found in some higher plants (e.g. *Astragalus* spp.). The possible role of peroxidase and catalase in such oxidative metabolism as distinct from nitrification has been noted earlier, in connection with hydroxylamine oxidation. The production of nitrate, nitrite or nitro-compounds by such means may explain the occurrence of activity of nitrate reductase in circumstances where the enzyme, although inducible, appears under conditions which should have excluded exogenous supplies of nitrate or nitrite.

Further Reading

Beevers, L. and Hageman, R. H. (1969) Nitrate reduction in higher plants. *A. Rev. Pl. Physiol.* **20**, 495–522.

Beevers, L. and Hageman, R. H. (1972) The role of light in nitrate metabolism in higher plants. *Photophysiology* **7**, 85–113.

Bond, G. (1967) Fixation of nitrogen by higher plants other than legumes. *A. Rev. Pl. Physiol.* **18**, 107–26.

Hewitt, E. J. (1974) Aspects of trace element requirements in plants and micro-organisms: the metalloenzymes of nitrate and nitrate reduction. Chapter 6 in *MTP International Review of Science—Biochemistry Section—Plant Biochemistry* (Ed. D. H. Northcote).

Hewitt, E. J., Hucklesby, D. P. and Betts, G. F. (1968) Nitrite and hydroxylamine in inorganic nitrogen metabolism with reference principally to higher plants, in *Recent Aspects of Nitrogen Metabolism in Plants.* (Ed. E. J. Hewitt and C. V. Cutting) Academic Press: London and New York.

Hewitt, E. J. and Nicholas, D. J. D. (1964) Enzymes of inorganic nitrogen metabolism in *Modern Methods of Plant Analysis* Vol. 7, Chapter 2 (Ed. H. F. Linskens, B. D. Sanwal, M. V. Tracey). Springer-Verlag: Berlin.

Kirkby, E. A. (Ed.) (1970) *Nitrogen Nutrition of the Plant.* University of Leeds.

McKee, H. S. (1962) *Nitrogen Metabolism in Plants.* Clarendon Press: Oxford. 712 pp.

Postgate, J. R. (Ed.) (1971) *The Chemistry and Biochemistry of Nitrogen Fixation.* Plenum Press: London and New York. 326 pp.

Steward, F. C. (Ed.) (1965) *Plant Physiology*, Vol. IVa. Metabolism: Organic Nutrition and Nitrogen Metabolism. Academic Press: New York and London. 731 pp.

Stewart, W. D. P. (1966) *Nitrogen Fixation in Plants.* Athlone Press: London. 168 pp.

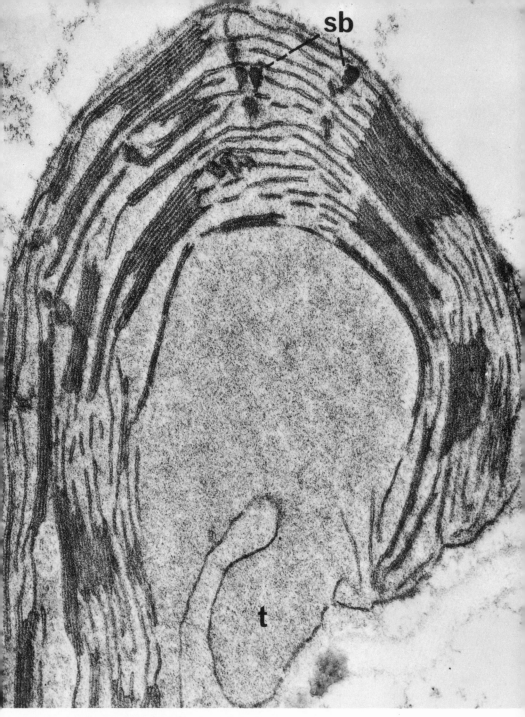

Plate 72 Electron micrograph of chloroplast from normal spinach leaves. The chloroplast is cup-shaped and has a small tail of stroma (t). Some of the grana have compartments while other grana appear diffuse. The fretwork is well developed and several star bodies (sb) occur between the frets. ×56 000. From Possingham, Vesk and Mercer (1964) *J. Ultrastruct. Res.* **11**, 68–83.

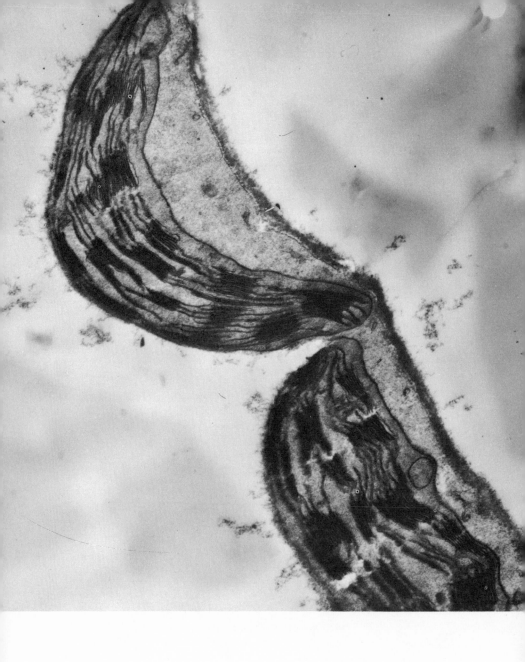

Plate 73 Electron micrograph of chloroplasts from normal spinach leaves. The chloroplasts are long and narrow, slightly concave and contain a regular grana-fretwork system. ×27 000. From Possingham, Vesk and Mercer (1964) *J. Ultrastruct. Res.* **11**, 68–83.

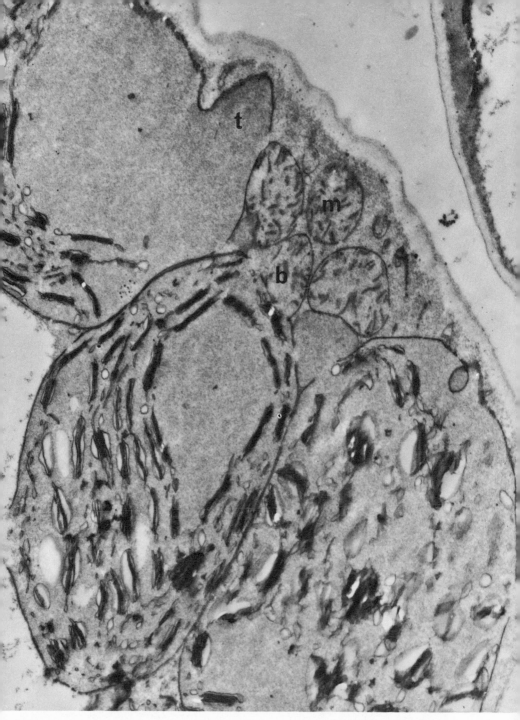

Plate 74 Electron micrograph of chloroplasts from the leaves of manganese-deficient spinach plants. Chloroplasts with tails (t) and buds (b) at the edge of the stroma area. Swelling of both the grana compartments and the frets is particularly noticeable (m, mitochondria). ×15 000. From Possingham, Vesk and Mercer (1964) *J. Ultrastruct. Res.* **11**, 68–83.

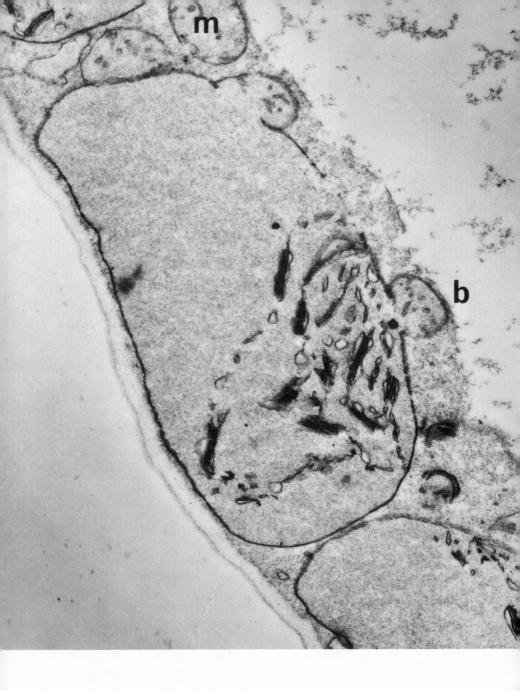

Plate 75 Electron micrograph of chloroplast from the leaves of manganese-deficient spinach plants. The plastids show reduction of the grana-fretwork system. Most of the frets have been replaced by vesicles. At the edge of the stroma area of the plastid are buds (b), which contain short lengths of tubules and bear a strong resemblance to the cristae of mitochondria (m). ×20 000. From Possingham, Vesk and Mercer (1964) *J. Ultrastruct. Res.* **11**, 68–83.

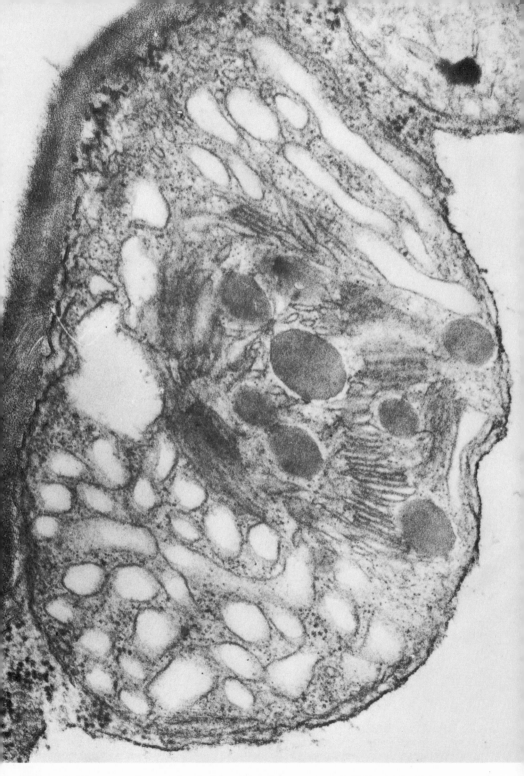

Plate 76 Electron micrograph of chloroplast from a normal (full nutrient) bean (*Phaseolus vulgaris*) plant. By courtesy of Dr Jean M. Whatley (unpublished).

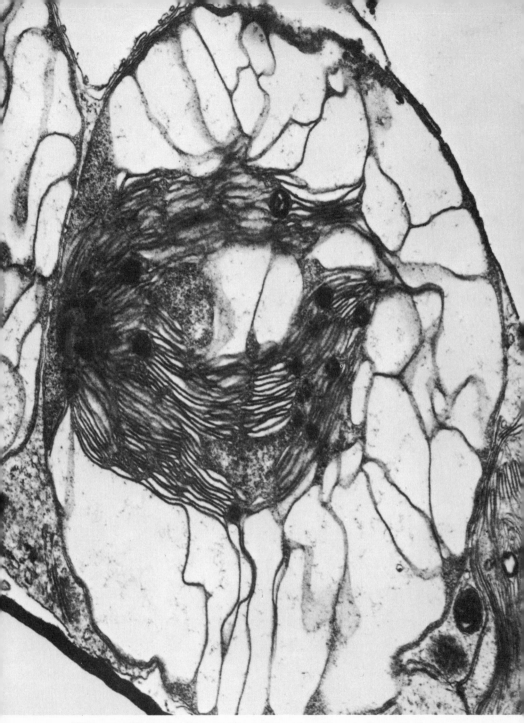

Plate 77 Electron micrograph of chloroplast from primary leaf of a nitrogen-deficient bean (*Phaseolus vulgaris*) plant. Stroma is minimal, and lamellae are aggregated in one area within the plastid. There is a surrounding area occupied by a very swollen lamellar system. ×58 000. From Whatley (1971) *New Phytol.* **70,** 725–42.

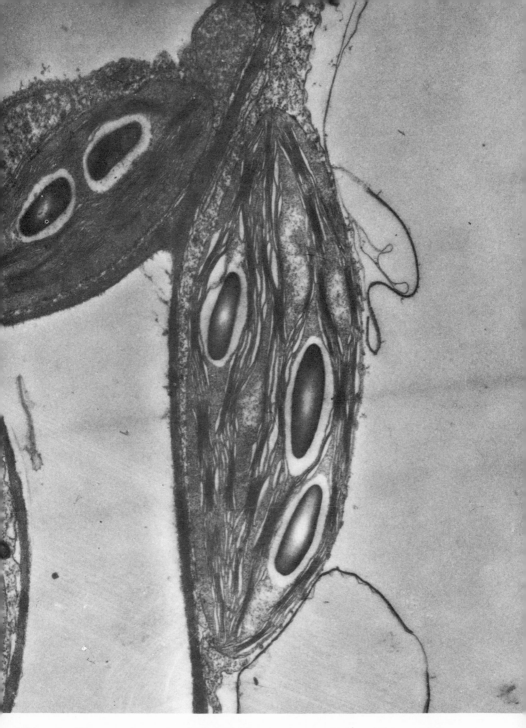

Plate 78 Electron micrograph of chloroplasts from second trifoliate leaf of a sulphur-deficient bean (*Phaseolus vulgaris*) plant. Grana are constricted between swollen upper and lower compartments. ×58 000. From Whatley (1971) *New Phytol.* **70,** 725–42.

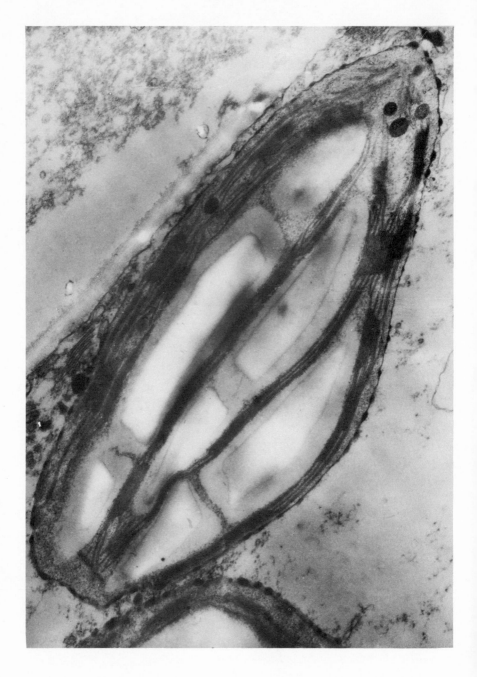

Plate 79 Electron micrograph of chloroplast from first trifoliate leaf of a magnesium-deficient bean (*Phaseolus vulgaris*) plant. Starch has accumulated and there is restricted lamellar development. ×60 000. From Whatley (1971) *New Phytol.* **70**, 725–42.

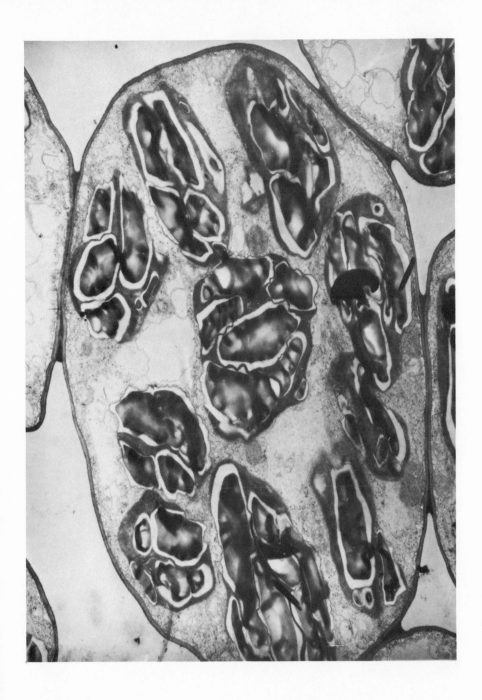

Plate 80 Electron micrograph of chloroplast from primary leaf of a magnesium-deficient bean (*Phaseolus vulgaris*) plant. Starch accumulation is considerable. ×16 000. From Whatley (1971) *New Phytol.* **70**, 725–42.

Plate 81 Electron micrograph of a chloroplast from the leaf of a normal bean (*Phaseolus vulgaris*) plant. The grana fretwork system is well formed (s, starch). ×27 000. From Thomson and Weier (1962) *Am. J. Bot.* **49**, 1047–55.

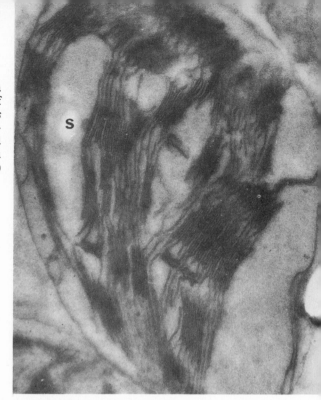

Plate 82 Electron micrograph of chloroplasts from leaves of a phosphorus-deficient bean (*Phaseolus vulgaris*) plant. The lamellar system appears to be loosening (*left*). The grana (g) are recognised by their outline. ×16 000. In the chloroplast shown on the right taken from a plant with severe phosphorus deficiency, the lamellar system shows considerable disruption, and there is an accumulation of star bodies. ×20 000. From Thomson, Weier and Drever (1964) *Am. J. Bot.* **51**, 933–8.

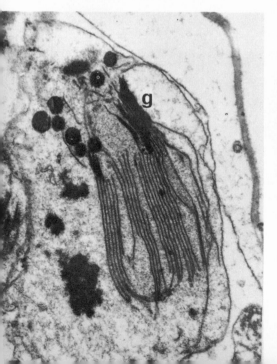

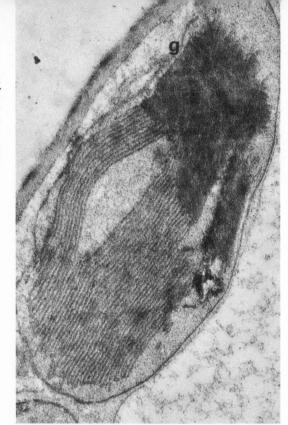

Plate 83 Electron micrograph of a chloroplast from the leaf of a potassium-deficient bean (*Phaseolus vulgaris*) plant. The grana have become large electron-dense masses (g) and an extensive lamellar system has formed. ×32 000. From Thomson and Weier (1962) *Am. J. Bot.* **19**, 1047–55.

Plate 84 Electron micrograph of chloroplasts from middle and upper leaves of a zinc-deficient bean (*Phaseolus vulgaris*) plant. In the chloroplast from the middle leaf (*left*) there is considerable stroma (s), a reduced grana-fretwork system and many vesicles (v) or swollen frets. Some vesicles (m) are associated with the inner layer of the plastid membrane. ×25 000. In the chloroplast from the upper leaf (*right*) there is considerable stroma and a vacuole (h) is present which is bordered partly by grana constituents and stroma. Disorganised grana and compartments are present. ×17 000. From Thomson and Weier (1962) *Am. J. Bot.* **49**, 1047–55.

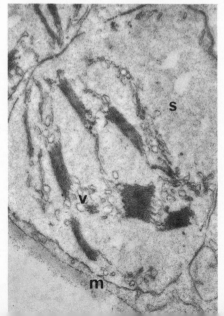
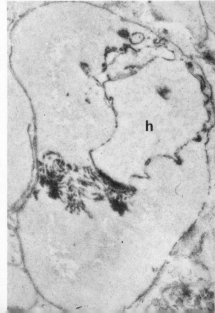

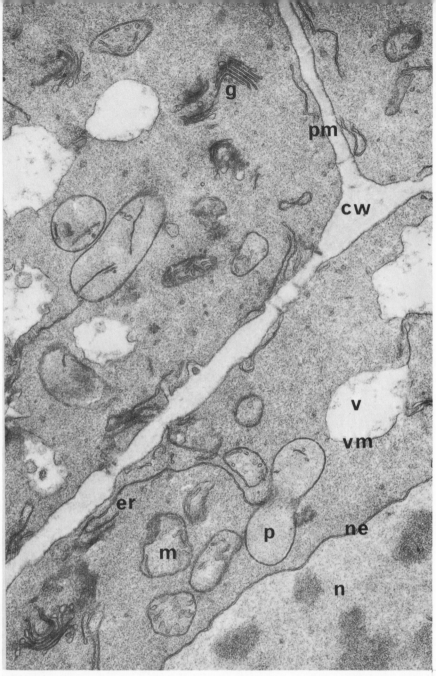

Plate 85 Electron micrograph of corpus meristematic cells from the central region of a normal barley apex at the level of the youngest visible leaf primordium. Initiation of vacuolation is apparent, the membrane (vm) bounding the young vacuoles (v) and the extensions of this membrane into the cytoplasm are clearly defined. Other features include the nucleus (n) with the denser staining chromatic material, the nuclear envelope (ne), plastids (p), mitochondria (m), Golgi apparatus (g), endoplasmic reticulum (er) and the plasma membrane (pm). The cell wall (cw) is electron transparent. ×25 000. From Marinos (1962) *Am. J. Bot.* **49**, 834–41.

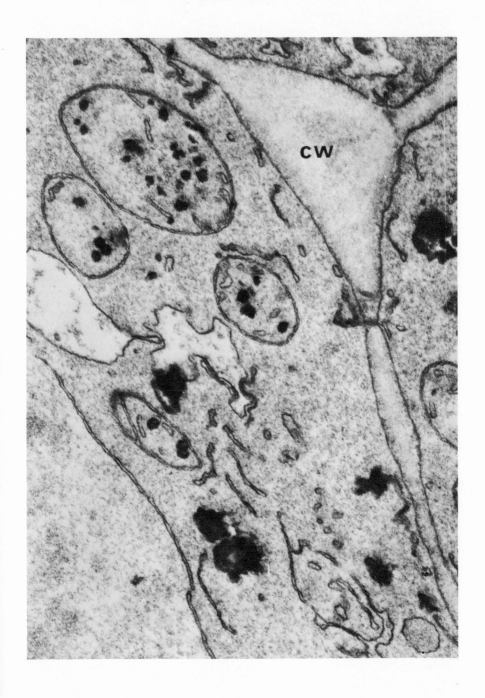

Plate 86 Electron micrograph of apex from a phosphorus-deficient barley plant (cw, cell wall). ×23 000. By courtesy of Professor N. G. Marinos (unpublished).

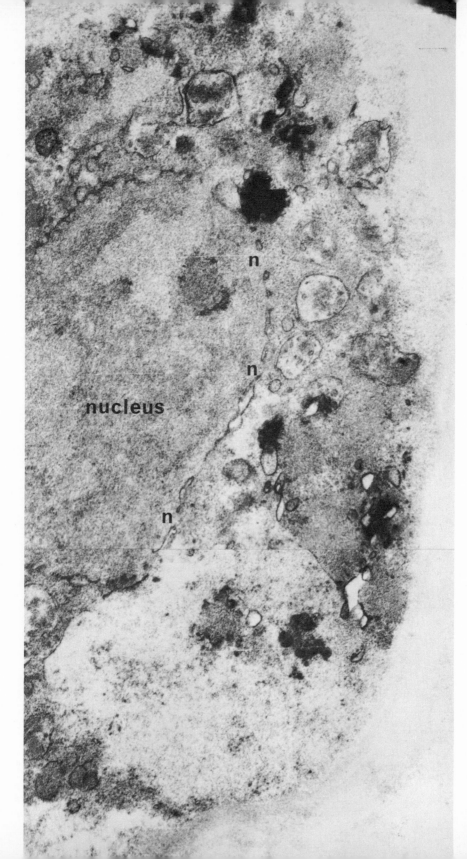

Plate 87 Electron micrograph of a tunica cell from the apex of a calcium-deficient barley plant. The nuclear envelope is vesiculating and breaking up (n). ×15 000. From Marinos (1962) *Am. J. Bot.* **49**, 834–61.

Plate 88 Electron micrograph of a chloroplast from a cauliflower leaf grown in nitrate medium with normal molybdenum level. Large starch grains (s) and mitochondria (m) are visible. ×18 000. Unpublished work of R. J. Fido, C. S. Gundry, B. A. Notton and E. J. Hewitt (Long Ashton Research Station).

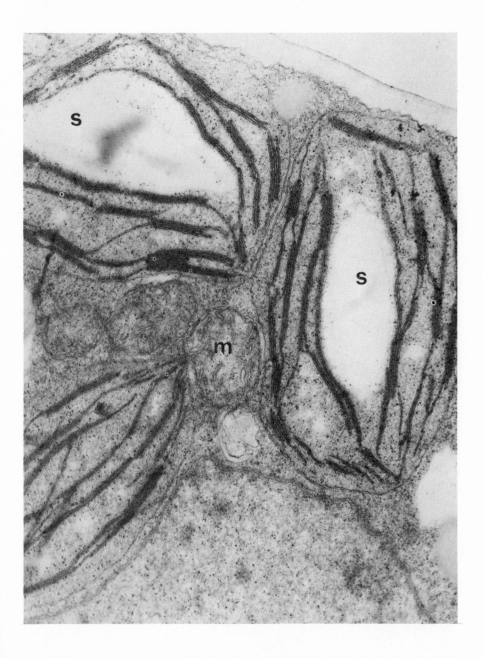

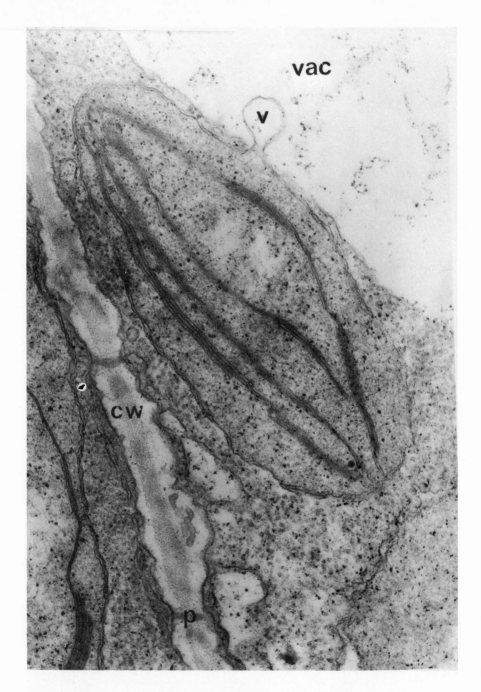

Plate 89   Electron micrograph of a chloroplast from a cauliflower leaf grown in a molybdenum-deficient nitrate medium. The chloroplast has elongated thylakoids and a vesicle (v) extending into the vacuole (vac). Plasmodesmata (p) may be seen in the cell wall (cw). ×28 000. Unpublished work of R. J. Fido, C. S. Gundry, B. A. Notton and E. J. Hewitt (Long Ashton Research Station).

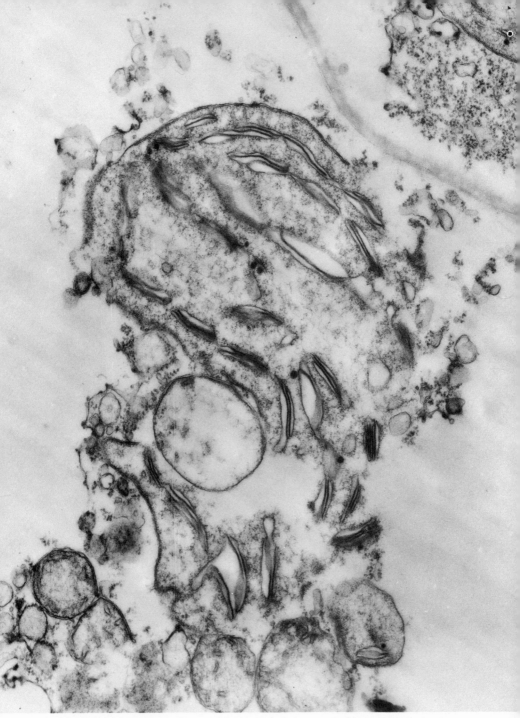

Plate 90 Electron micrograph of a chloroplast from a cauliflower leaf grown in a molybdenum-deficient ammonium medium. The plant showed severe whiptail symptoms (see Plates 55 and 56). Chloroplast disintegration is extreme. ×14 000. Unpublished work of R. J. Fido, C. S. Gundry, B. A. Notton and E. J. Hewitt (Long Ashton Research Station).

8
The Functions and Metabolism of the Elements

'It is necessary for the biochemist to remember that his data gain their full significance only when he can relate them with the activities of the organism as a whole. His may not be the last word in the description of life, but without his help the last word may never be said.'

Sir Frederick Gowland Hopkins

In this chapter it is proposed to review in detail the participation of the elements in metabolism and to survey some of the metabolites of the various elements found in plants. Nitrogen metabolism has been discussed in the previous chapter and will not be considered in detail in this account. The functions and compounds of the essential mineral nutrients are summarised in Table 8.1. Examples of enzymes and electron carriers dependent on metals are given in Tables 8.2 to 8.6 at the end of the chapter. The enzymes given in these tables are numbered. On reference to these enzymes in the text these numbers appear in brackets after the enzymes.

Phosphate

Unlike nitrate and sulphate, phosphate is not reduced to a different oxidation state by plants. Undoubtedly the major pathway by which phosphate enters into organic combination in plants is through esterification with adenosine to form AMP, ADP and ATP. The energy derived from photosynthesis (see page 257) or released in respiration (see page 90) is trapped mainly in the form of the latter compound which is used for energy transfer. The precise way in which ATP is formed in these processes is still largely unknown. The driving force for ATP formation in chloroplasts and mitochondria is probably the pH gradient generated by the mechanism suggested by Mitchell (the chemi-osmotic theory, see page 95). However, one process of ATP generation which has been known in detail for many years is found in the pathway of glycolysis. Inorganic phosphate is esterified during oxidation of glyceraldehyde-3-phosphate by NAD. The 1,3-diphosphoglycerate which is formed donates high-energy phosphate to ADP to form ATP. The reversible phosphorylation of polysaccharides, e.g. by starch phosphorylase giving

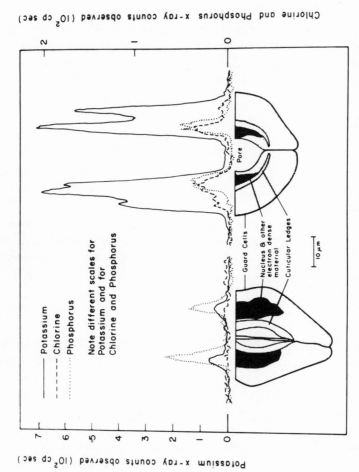

Figure 8.1 Profiles of relative amounts of potassium, chlorine and phosphorus across an open and a closed stoma. The traces are the result of scanning a 0·5 μm diameter beam across the stomata shown diagrammatically below the traces. In order to indicate the profile scanned, the images of the stomata have been cut off in this diagram where the beam crossed the guard cells. From Humble and Raschke (1971) *Pl. Physiol., Lancaster* **48**, 447–53. By permission of the American Society of Plant Physiologists.

glucose-1-phosphate, provides a further pathway for the entry of inorganic phosphate into organic metabolites. The energy in the ester phosphate bond varies widely from 8·4 to 12·6 kJ, as in glucose-6-phosphate, up to 54·6 kJ, as in phosphoenolpyruvate.

Potassium

Probably greater success has been achieved in elucidating the mode of action of some of the micronutrient elements than of potassium, which is required in relatively large amounts for normal growth. The average minimal and maximal concentrations for the percentage of potassium on a dry weight basis for normal plants were 1·7 and 2·8% respectively, and for deficient plants 0·8 and 1·2% respectively, calculated by Evans and Sorger (1966) from fifteen different species. Potassium is considered to function in osmotic processes, in the synthesis of protein and the maintenance of protein stability, in stomatal opening (Plate 12, Fig. 8.1), membrane permeability and in pH control (page 152), though the precise way in which it accomplishes many of these roles is still far from clear. Certainly potassium is known to be an activator of some enzymes (Table 8.2), and in most cases it is more effective than the other univalent cations for this purpose.

Although few plants require sodium, many benefit from the addition of this element even when potassium is supplied at its optimal concentration. Richards (1944) showed that rubidium can partially replace potassium in the growth of barley but addition of sodium, lithium or caesium was ineffective. Sodium is partially effective in suppressing the formation of putrescine in potassium deficient barley (pages 123 and 152).

Activity of potassium for those enzymes involving ATP could be explained by the co-ordinated complex known to be formed between K^+ and ATP which appears to be sterically different to that found with sodium. Some enzymes are known to require potassium at very high concentrations for optimal activity, for instance acetaldehyde dehydrogenase in yeast requires 0·05 to 0·1 M potassium. This is in contrast with the optimal concentration of acetaldehyde (0·0017 M) and NAD (0·005 M) by the same enzyme.

Evans and Sorger (1966) suggest that potassium ions increase the activity of the potassium-requiring enzymes by changing the conformation of the enzyme molecule in a way which increases the exposure of the active sites. It seems likely that one of the reasons for the high potassium requirement of plants may be found in the need for high concentrations of this element by certain enzymes for optimal activity.

Sulphur

The pathway of sulphate reduction is not known in complete detail, and investigation of this field was until recently neglected by comparison with the study of nitrate reduction. Although sulphur is not incorporated into such a wide range of compounds as nitrogen, it is particularly important for the formation of the amino acids cysteine (—SH group) and methionine (—S—CH_3 group), and thiamin (the thiazole ring).

Like nitrogen, sulphur is cycled in the biosphere. Sulphate-reducing bacteria in the sea and soil produce hydrogen sulphide which is oxidised in the atmosphere. The sulphur is re-deposited on the land as sulphate and is returned to the sea in ground water. About one-third of the sulphur reaching the sea now originates from industrial processes, mainly as sulphur dioxide. Sulphur deficiency does not occur in the vicinity of major industrial conurbations and is unknown in the United Kingdom.

The reduction of sulphate to hydrogen sulphide in the process of ATP generation (dissimilatory reduction) is confined to a few anaerobic bacteria (e.g. *Desulfovibrio*) while the reduction of sulphate for the synthesis of sulphur-containing compounds (assimilatory reduction) is universal in the plant kingdom.

The first step in the process of assimilatory sulphate reduction is the formation of an 'active' sulphate by combination with ATP, giving adenosine phospho-sulphate (APS), catalysed by the enzyme ATP-sulphurylase. This enzyme has been found in the chloroplasts of higher plants and in extracts of bacteria, algae, fungi and animals. The equilibrium is highly unfavourable ($K = 4 \times 10^{-8}$).

$$
\begin{array}{c}
\quad\ \ \text{O} \qquad\ \ \text{O} \qquad\ \ \text{O} \\
\quad\ \ \| \qquad\quad \| \qquad\quad \| \\
\text{adenosine—O—P—O—P—O—P—O}^- + \text{SO}_4^{2-} \\
\quad\ \ | \qquad\ \ | \qquad\ \ | \\
\quad\ \ \text{O}^- \qquad \text{O}^- \qquad \text{O}^-
\end{array}
$$

ATP sulphurylase

$$
\begin{array}{c}
\quad\ \ \text{O} \qquad\ \ \text{O} \\
\quad\ \ \| \qquad\quad \| \\
\text{adenosine—O—P—O—S—O}^- + \text{PPi}^{4-} \\
\quad\ \ | \qquad\ \ \| \\
\quad\ \ \text{O}^- \qquad \text{O}
\end{array}
$$

In the next step, APS reacts with additional ATP to give 3'-phosphoadenosine-5'-phosphosulphate (PAPS) and adenosine diphosphate (ADP).

$$\text{Adenine—CH—CHOH—}\underset{3}{\text{CH}}\text{—}\underset{5}{\text{CH}}\text{—CH}_2\text{—O—P—O—S—O}^-$$

The affinity for APS of the enzyme effecting this step (APS-kinase) is very high, and there is also a large negative free-energy change in the process of the reaction which alleviates the unfavourable equilibrium of the previous step. Moreover, the system is coupled with a pyrophosphatase. These three factors allow the reaction to proceed to the right. The overall reaction at this stage may be written:

$$SO_4^{2-} + 2ATP^{4-} \rightleftharpoons PAPS^{4-} + ADP^{3-} + 2Pi^{2-} + H^+$$

ATP sulphurylase, but not APS-kinase, has been demonstrated in spinach. However, APS-kinase has been identified in chloroplasts from French bean and maize leaves by Mercer and Thomas (1969) and this enzyme is almost certain to be present in spinach also since it has been shown that PAPS is a substrate for the next step, i.e. the reductive process. The mechanism for this is complex and only partly understood. The reaction is best known in yeast but it seems likely that a similar process occurs in higher plants.

Overall the reduction may be written:

$$NADPH + PAPS \xrightarrow[\text{protein fraction C}]{\text{enzymes A and B}} NADP^+ + PAP + HSO_3^-$$

The sulphite remains bound in protein fraction C, apparently attached to a sulphydryl group of an amino acid, and it does not appear in the free state. In higher plants a co-factor, possibly the same fraction C, is also required.

Sulphite reductase (39), which appears to be a haem protein in spinach leaves, yields hydrogen sulphide, with the transfer of six electrons by one enzyme without the appearance of free intermediates.

$$HSO_3^- + 7H^+ + 6e^- \rightarrow H_2S + 3H_2O$$

The sulphide may also remain enzyme-bound (see below); there is a clear analogy with nitrite reductase here. The studies of Atkinson and co-workers, and Siegel and Kamin indicate that in *Escherichia coli* the same enzyme mediates both nitrite and sulphite reduction with NADPH as electron donor. The enzyme (mol. wt. 670 000) appears to be very complex and contains FAD and FMN, non-haem iron, labile sulphide and possibly an unusual haem constituent (Table 8.3, I). In higher plants separate enzymes are involved in nitrite and sulphite reduction, and the physiological electron donor for both is probably ferredoxin in chloroplasts. Bandurski and co-workers find similar evidence for an unusual haem in the plant enzyme.

In roots, the electron donor for both enzymes, which appear from work of Miflin, Mayer and Hucklesby, to be located in mitochondria or other particulate organelles, is still unidentified. Ferredoxin cannot function, but *in vitro* reduced pyridilium dyes are effective.

The compound *N*-ethylmaleimide reacts with sulphide and sulphite. In experiments of Ellis, when *Lemna* fronds were plunged into ethanol containing this compound after being allowed to reduce added radioactive sulphite, only very faint traces of radioactively labelled sulphide could be detected in the frond extract. In the absence of *N*-ethylmaleimide no sulphide was found, but in both cases there was abundant radioactivity in cysteine and residual sulphite. The conclusion is that the trace of sulphide was released from a low level of enzyme-bound intermediate and that free sulphide does not accumulate *in vivo* although it is readily produced *in vitro* in the absence of further metabolic activity. It is not certain that free H_2S appears at all during sulphite reduction *in vivo*. The conversion of sulphide to cysteine can occur in higher plants by enzymic reaction of H_2S with serine, as has also been found with yeast.

$$
\begin{array}{l}
CH_2OH \\
| \\
CH-NH_2 \\
| \\
COOH
\end{array}
+ H_2S \rightarrow
\begin{array}{l}
SH \\
| \\
CH_2 \\
| \\
CH-NH_2 \\
| \\
COOH
\end{array}
+ H_2O
$$

However, the mechanism which appears to operate in bacteria utilises *O*-acetyl derivatives of amino acids and is catalysed by the enzyme *O*-acetylserine thiolase.

$$O\text{-acetylserine} + H_2S \rightarrow \text{cysteine} + \text{acetate}$$

In spinach, the sulphur atom of methionine originates in cysteine. *O*-acetylhomoserine combines with cysteine to give cystathionine, which splits to form homocysteine and serine. The homocysteine is methylated with methyltetrahydrofolic acid (MeTHFA) as the donor.

$$
\begin{array}{lllll}
& & \text{COOH} & \text{CH}_2\text{SH} & \\
& & | & | & \\
\overset{\displaystyle \text{O}}{\overset{\displaystyle \|}{\text{CH}_2\text{OCCH}_3}} & & | & | & \\
| & & | & | & \\
\text{CH}_2 & +\ \text{CH}_2\text{SH} & \text{CHNH}_2 & \text{CH}_2 & \text{CH}_2\text{OH} \\
| & | & | & | & | \\
\text{CH}{-}\text{NH}_2 & \text{CHNH}_2 \rightarrow & \text{CH}_2 \rightarrow & \text{CHNH}_2 + & \text{CHNH}_2 \\
| & | & | & | & | \\
\text{COOH} & \text{COOH} & \text{S} & \text{COOH} & \text{COOH} \\
& & | & & \\
& & (\text{CH}_2)_2 & \text{homocysteine} & \text{serine} \\
\text{\textit{O}-acetyl-} & \text{cysteine} & | & & \\
\text{homoserine} & & \text{CHNH}_2 & & \\
& & | & & \\
& & \text{COOH} & & \\
& & \text{cystathionine} & & \\
\end{array}
$$

homocysteine → (MeTHFA) →

$$
\begin{array}{l}
\text{CH}_3 \\
| \\
\text{S} \\
| \\
(\text{CH}_2)_2 \quad \text{methionine} \\
| \\
\text{CHNH}_2 \\
| \\
\text{COOH}
\end{array}
$$

It is of interest to note that the work of Ellis with *Lemna* demonstrated strong feedback inhibition of sulphate assimilation *in vivo* by cysteine or the oxidised form, cystine, but not by glutathione, methionine or sulphide. *In vitro* cysteine does not inhibit any of the stages between ATP sulphurylase and *O*-acetylserine thiolase. However, cysteine appears to inhibit sulphate uptake by a permease system. In more highly organised plants other control mechanisms may be involved, as inorganic sulphate is often the major form of sulphur in the leaves and accumulates under unfavourable physiological conditions, except in sulphur deficiency.

Ester sulphate, unlike ester phosphate, does not occur frequently in nature. However, it is found in the polysaccharide, agar, extracted from seaweed (especially *Gelidium* spp.). The sulphate comprises 4–10% of the weight of the acidic agaropectin component and does not occur in the neutral agarose fraction. Ester sulphate is also found in carrageenin, a polysaccharide similar to agar extracted from the seaweed, *Chondrus crispus*.

Selenium

The element selenium is closely related to sulphur, and probably enters the plant by a similar mechanism to form the selenium-containing analogues of cysteine and methionine (see page 170). Distinct from its toxic and antagonistic properties in the production of the Se-amino acids already mentioned, selenium is essential for *Escherichia coli* when grown with nitrate. It is incorporated into the formate dehydrogenase hydrogen-lyase complex (see page 286) which is associated with nitrate reductase activity. Selenium will also replace sulphur as labile selenide in parsley ferredoxin and putidaredoxin of *Pseudomonas putida*. The putidaredoxin resembles ferredoxin but catalyses hydroxylation of a methylene carbon in camphor. Selenium is an analogue for vitamin E function and has been shown to be an essential constituent of the enzyme glutathione peroxidase present in mammalian blood.

Magnesium

Magnesium is a readily dissociable ionic activator for many enzymes (Table 8.2, Classes II and III) and it stabilises ribosomal particles in the configuration necessary for protein synthesis (page 262). However, perhaps its best-known role is in chlorophyll where it is complexed in a tetra-pyrrole ring. About 10% of total leaf magnesium is incorporated in chlorophyll, and 2·7% of the weight of the chlorophyll molecule is magnesium. Magnesium enters protoporphyrin IX which is then condensed with phytol to form chlorophyll a, which may be further converted to chlorophyll b. In chlorophyll a, group R is —CH_3 while in chlorophyll b this is —CHO (Fig. 8.2).

Boron

There is no evidence that boron is a component or an activator of any enzyme and its role is still the least understood of all the essential elements. This is despite the great diversity of effects of boron deficiency. Although changes in the activities of certain enzymes have been found in boron-deficient plants these changes also occur with deficiencies of other elements. The borate ion is outstanding for its ability to complex with various polyhydroxy compounds, notably with certain carbohydrates and phenols.

Complexes of boron with *cis* configurations of polyhydroxy compounds may be generally of three forms.

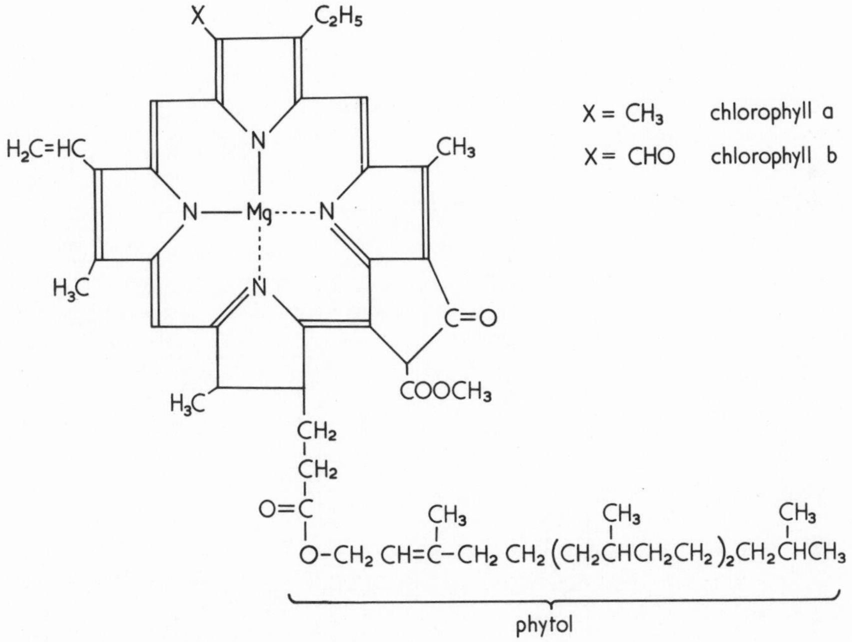

X = CH₃   chlorophyll a
X = CHO   chlorophyll b

Figure 8.2   The structure of chlorophylls a and b.

These include compounds of *o*-diphenols, some carbohydrates and some sugar phosphate esters where the 6 or 5C is esterified. The complexes are more dissociated than the parent compounds and may have increased permeability in membranes and thereby facilitate carbohydrate transport. The fact that some sugars and sugar phosphate esters migrate differently on electrophoresis or chromatography when borate is added to the system illustrates the changed properties of the borate complexes.

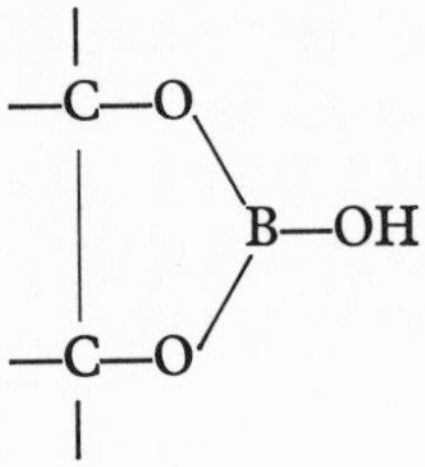

$$
\begin{array}{c}
| \\
-\text{C}-\text{O} \\
|\diagdown \\
\text{B}-\text{OH} \\
|\diagup \\
-\text{C}-\text{O} \\
|
\end{array}
\qquad (1)
$$

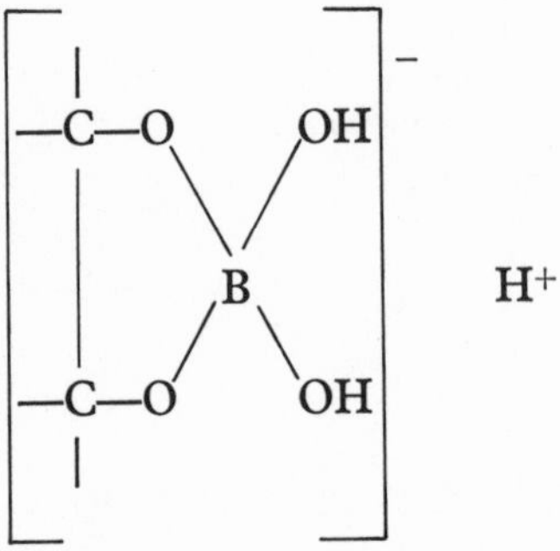

$$
\left[
\begin{array}{c}
| \\
-\text{C}-\text{O}\text{OH} \\
|\diagdown\diagup \\
\text{B} \\
|\diagup\diagdown \\
-\text{C}-\text{O}\text{OH} \\
|
\end{array}
\right]^{-}
\quad \text{H}^{+}
\qquad (2)
$$

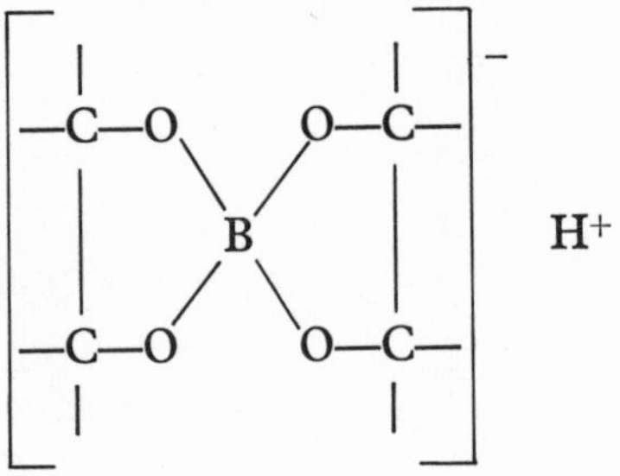

$$
\left[
\begin{array}{c}
|| \\
-\text{C}-\text{O}\text{O}-\text{C}- \\
|\diagdown\diagup| \\
\text{B} \\
|\diagup\diagdown| \\
-\text{C}-\text{O}\text{O}-\text{C}- \\
||
\end{array}
\right]^{-}
\quad \text{H}^{+}
\qquad (3)
$$

In the reaction for sucrose synthesis:

$$\text{UTP} + \text{Glucose-1-PO}_4 \rightleftharpoons \text{UDPG} + \text{PPi} \qquad (1)$$

$$\text{UDPG} + \text{Fructose} \rightleftharpoons \text{UDP} + \text{Sucrose} \qquad (2)$$

10 mM borate favoured reaction (1) and inhibited reaction (2).

Phenol oxidases increase abnormally in boron-deficient tissues but mono-phenols and *o*-diphenols, e.g. chlorogenic and caffeic acids, also accumulate and the overall picture is complex. The monophenols are auxin oxidase (peroxidase) activators and the *o*-diphenols are inhibitors. The boron may influence their ratio by controlling (inhibiting) some aspects of phenolase activity and thereby indirectly influencing auxin oxidation, lignin synthesis and other reactions.

Iodine

Iodine is accumulated by seaweeds, especially the Laminariales (large brown seaweed, Kelp) and this element was first characterised on extraction from *Laminaria digitata* (Plate 9) by Courtois in 1811. Until recently, seaweeds were a major source of iodine, the content ranging up to 0·6% of the dry matter. Fries (1966) has shown that iodine is an essential element for the sea-weed *Polysiphonia*. There was a linear correlation between the amount of added iodide and growth for thirty days over the range from 1 μmol up to at least 8 μmol per litre. After nineteen days the culture to which no iodide had been added darkened and died. Some iodine in marine algae is incorporated into iodo-amino acids (mono- and di-iodotyrosine) probably by the action of an iodide peroxidase, like that which has been characterised from the green seaweed *Enteromorpha linza* by Murphy and hEocha (1970). Iodide is also incorporated into iodo-amino acids on being fed to higher plants. Fowden (1959) has demonstrated that both barley and mung bean seedlings, and especially the maritime plants *Salicornia perennis* and *Aster tripolium* incorporate iodine into a variety of tyrosine derivatives.

Chlorine

Although the chloride ion is known to be essential for photosynthesis (see page 257) only a few compounds containing covalently-bound chlorine are found in higher plants. These include acutumine and acutumidine from *Sinomenium acutum* and *Menispermum dauricum*, a sesquiterpenoid lactone from *Eupatorium rotundifolium*, and the alkaloid jaconine from *Senecio jacobaea*. A chloride-containing gibberellin from *Phaseolus multiflorus* is probably formed as an artefact during extraction. More recently, Gandar and Nitsch (1967) and Marumo and co-workers (1968, 1969) have isolated a chlorine-containing auxin from *Pisum sativum* which was shown to be 4-chloroindolyl-3-acetic acid. In immature seeds this apparently takes the place of IAA, which cannot be found. This discovery may give an additional reason for the essentiality of this element in plants. Chlorine is also combined in a sulpholipid from the alga, *Ochromonas danica*. Many chlorine-containing compounds are found in fungi and bacteria.

Fluorine

Although there is evidence that fluorine is an essential element for higher animals, it does not appear to be essential for plants. However, fluoride is accumulated and metabolised by a number of plant species. Certain ornamental Camellias may contain up to 3000 p.p.m. dry weight, while the tea plant contains 70 to 300 p.p.m. dry weight. In the toxic South African plant *Dichapetalum cymosum* (Gif blaar; Afrikaans for poison leaf) (Plate 11) and the West African plant *D. toxicarium* fluoride may accumulate to 200 p.p.m. dry weight. In the toxic Australian plant *Acacia georginae* investigated by Peters and Shorthouse (1967), inorganic fluoride was incorporated into an organic form by leaf extracts on incubation with ATP, pyruvate and Mn^{2+}. Some of the fluoride was found in monofluoroacetone, but other unidentified organic fluorine compounds were also detected.

The naturally-occurring toxic principle in all these plants is fluoroacetate which may comprise up to 50 p.p.m. of the dry weight. Fluorocitrate is not accumulated by these species. Fluoroacetate, however, is converted to fluorocitrate on ingestion by animals, and this substance acts as a competitive inhibitor of aconitase in the Krebs cycle. The mechanism for the toxicity of fluoroacetate in animals was established by Sir Rudolph Peters in 1949. It is known that *Dichapetalum cymosum* has an active Krebs cycle, and the means by which the plant avoids damage is not known with certainty. Results obtained by Eloff and Sydow (1971) suggest that either the acetic thiokinase or citrate synthetase enzymes of *D. cymosum* discriminate against the fluorinated derivatives. The fact that *D. toxicarium* contains ω-fluoro-oleic and ω-fluoro-palmitic acid makes it likely that a blockage in fluoroacetate metabolism occurs at the point of citric acid formation in this plant. Peters and Shorthouse (1972) have shown that fluorocitrate is formed in certain food plants, e.g. oats, soybean and tea. However, a person drinking eight cups of tea per day would only absorb about 3·4 µg/kg body weight, which is well below the toxic dose.

Calcium

Almost certainly calcium has many functions which are at present unknown, but it is likely that it is implicated in some way with membrane stability, with the maintenance of chromosome structure and with the activation of many enzymes (Table 8.2, Classes II and III).

Calcium may be found in high concentrations in the cell walls as the insoluble salt of pectic acid in which it links adjacent chains. Treatment of plant tissues with the chelating agent EDTA causes loss of calcium and polysaccharide and results in increased cell-wall plasticity. It appears that calcium

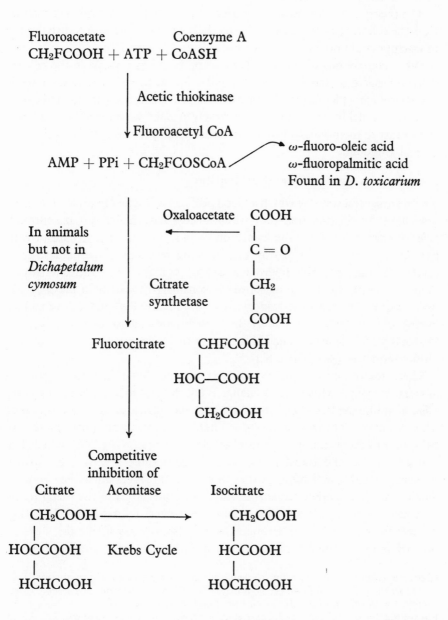

Fluoroacetate   Coenzyme A
$CH_2FCOOH + ATP + CoASH$

Acetic thiokinase

Fluoroacetyl CoA

$AMP + PPi + CH_2FCOSCoA$ → ω-fluoro-oleic acid
ω-fluoropalmitic acid
Found in *D. toxicarium*

Oxaloacetate   COOH

In animals
but not in
*Dichapetalum
cymosum*

$C = O$

Citrate CH_2
synthetase

COOH

Fluorocitrate   CHFCOOH

HOC—COOH

CH_2COOH

Competitive
inhibition of
Citrate   Aconitase   Isocitrate

CH_2COOH ⟶ CH_2COOH

HOCCOOH   Krebs Cycle   HCCOOH

HCHCOOH   HOCHCOOH

pectate acts as a cementing agent in the cell wall and increases the rigidity of the structure (see page 157).

The theory that IAA causes extension of plant tissues by removing calcium from the cell walls now appears to be unlikely since no release or redistribution of calcium could be found on treating coleoptiles with IAA.

Other compounds of calcium likely to be found as crystals in the cell include the calcium salts of phytic acid and oxalic acid, and in certain seaweeds (e.g. *Corallina*) (Plate 6) calcium carbonate provides a hard articulated external casing. Calcium salts do not occur widely in plants as supporting structures, in contrast to their widespread use as skeletal and protective structures in the animal kingdom.

Functional aspects of metal activation

There are several ways by which a metal performs its activating role. The most obvious is by electron transport which occurs with many systems through valency change involving the transition metals. This is the mechanism with iron in the cytochromes (29 to 35), in some reactions of peroxidase (27), catalase (28) and probably hydrogenases (50), as many are sensitive to carbon monoxide. Valency change of copper is considered to occur in plastocyanin (63), laccase (60), ascorbic acid oxidase (61) (Table 8.5) and in the copper linking cytochromes a and a₃ in the cytochrome oxidase complex (34, 35) (Table 8.3). A valency change also occurs in molybdenum ($Mo^{6-} \rightleftharpoons Mo^{5-}$) in nitrate reductase (54) (Table 8.4).

There are, however, electron transport enzymes containing metals capable of valency change, where such a change is not thought to take place. Examples include amine oxidase (62), tyrosinase (59) and galactose oxidase (66), all of which contain copper (Table 8.5). There is some uncertainty about the behaviour of the iron in the chloroplast ferredoxin (44) (Fig. 8.3), which has two iron atoms and transfers electrons singly (Table 8.3, 11). Mossbäuer resonance studies indicate that one iron atom is converted to Fe^{2+} on reduction, while the other remains in the ferric state. Most of the metal redox enzymes transfer electrons singly but the bacterial ferredoxin (Fig. 8.4) appears to transfer two at a time. There is controversy about the electron stoicheiometry of spinach plastocyanin (63) which has two atoms of copper,

Figure 8.3 (*above*)   Model of the iron–sulphur group in higher plant ferredoxins. Two iron atoms and two labile sulphur atoms occur in ferredoxins from this source. From Hall, Cammack and Rao (1971) *Nature, Lond.* **233**, 136–8.

Figure 8.4 (*below*)   Structure of bacterial ferredoxin having seven iron atoms linked with acid labile and cysteinyl sulphur. There are fifty-five amino acids (aa) of which eight are cysteine residues. The ferredoxins are electron carriers with very low redox values. From Tanaka, Benson, Mower and Yasunobu (1965) in *Non-Heme Iron Proteins* (Ed. San Pietro), Antioch Press, Yellow Springs, Ohio, pp. 221–4.

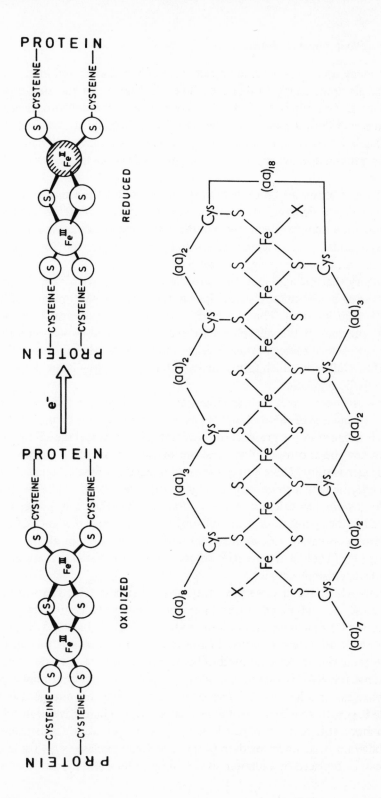

unlike many other plastocyanins which have only one atom and undoubtedly transfer electrons singly (Table 8.5). The mechanisms of the zinc proteins are diverse. Zinc binds NAD(H), the coenzyme of the dehydrogenases for glutamic acid (80), alcohol (78), glyceraldehyde-3-phosphate and lactic acid (76) (Table 8.6) and probably also in other analogous enzymes. Many of the dehydrogenases contain more than one atom of the metal per molecule of enzyme.

A charge transfer action probably explains the role of the zinc in fructose-1,6-diphosphate aldolase (79) which occurs in yeasts and bacteria (Table 8.6). Electron attraction may be involved in the hydrolytic or isomerase activities of carboxypeptidase (74), alkaline phosphatase (73), hexose isomerase and carbonic anhydrase enzymes (72) (Table 8.6).

A theory that metallo-substrates are the true substrates of some enzymes is supported by the close relationships between activity and the ratio of ADP or ATP to magnesium. The Mg–ADP complex may be the true substrate of several enzymes of the phosphokinase type. It is possible that the cellular control of some of these enzymes is related to the ADP/Mg ratio, as well as to the ATP/ADP ratio which forms the basis for the 'energy-charge' hypothesis of metabolic regulation.

Some enzymes which are dependent on magnesium (e.g. fructose diphosphate phosphatase of chloroplasts) appear to undergo a conformational change which is induced by the presence of the metal. This increases the affinity of the protein for the substrate. The presence of calcium in plant glutamic acid dehydrogenase (80) (Table 8.6) causes the aggregation of the protein sub-units of the enzyme with a consequent change in the substrate K_m. The amylase of *Bacillus subtilis* has calcium at the hydrolytic site while zinc is separately involved in the aggregation of the sub-units into the active oligomeric form of the protein. Separate zinc atoms fulfil separate functions in alkaline phosphatase (73) (Table 8.6); one pair influences structural stability and another pair effects catalytic activity.

Metals which are in close proximity in the periodic table can sometimes replace the 'normal' metal in certain enzymes. For instance tungsten can be substituted for molybdenum in nitrate reductase (54) (Table 8.4) when plants are grown with excess tungsten in the nutrient medium and the resulting nitrate-reductase enzyme is found to be inactive in nitrate reduction but still functional for NADH diaphorase activity. However vanadium may replace molybdenum in the molybdoferredoxin component of nitrogenase (56) (Table 8.4) with about 70% of the normal activity. There have been reports which have still to be confirmed that tungsten can weakly substitute for molybdenum in xanthine oxidase (57) or aldehyde oxidase (57) (Table 8.4). Zinc can be replaced by cadmium in carboxypeptidase and the zinc in alcohol dehydrogenase (78) (Table 8.6) can be replaced with cobalt with reduced activity.

Superoxide dismutase (71) effects the following reaction:

$$2H^+ + 2O_2^- \cdot \rightleftharpoons H_2O_2 + O_2$$

This enzyme, which is widely distributed in micro-organisms and plants, may contain Fe, Mn or Cu and Zn, depending on source. It probably protects macromolecules against free radical oxidations.

Photosynthesis

Figure 8.5 summarises the probable relationships of mineral element function in photosynthesis in higher plants.

The evolution of oxygen in photosynthesis is considered to result from the decomposition of a peroxide complex which is produced by combination of OH radicals, which are formed from OH^- ions by transfer of an electron to chlorophyll b. The oxygen evolution step is dependent on manganese and chlorine, probably as Cl^-. The loss of oxygen evolution as the result of manganese deficiency was discovered by Brown and Hendricks and by Kessler who proposed a role in decomposition of a peroxide. Manganese is probably concerned in a redox reaction in which Mn^{2+} and Mn^{3+} are produced reversibly in an electron transport sequence, possibly at the point of peroxide breakdown. Gerretson in 1950 first observed that addition of Mn^{2+} to chloroplasts caused a large rise in electrode potential during illumination, which was reversed in the dark. In the absence of Mn^{2+} a small potential rise occurred followed by a decrease while still illuminated.

Kenten and Mann in 1949 showed that illuminated chloroplasts oxidise Mn^{2+} to Mn^{3+}, and Ben Hayyim and Avron have proposed that Mn^{2+} ions can function as the direct electron donor for activated chlorophyll b (Chl*$^-$). The following reactions may be visualised:

$$Mn^{2+} + Chl + hv \rightarrow Mn^{3+} + Chl^{*-}$$

$$2(Mn^{3+} + OH^-) \rightarrow 2(Mn^{2+} + OH \cdot) \rightarrow H_2O_2$$

$$2Mn^{3+} + H_2O_2 \rightarrow 2Mn^{2+} + O_2 + 2H^+$$

or overall $\quad 2Mn^{3+} + H_2O_2 \rightarrow 2Mn^{2+} + O_2 + 2H^+$

The net result is the transfer of electrons from OH^- ions of water to chlorophyll b via manganese and elimination of oxygen.

The work of Haberman with pokeweed chloroplasts and ^{18}O labelled oxygen or water indicate that manganese catalyses both oxygen uptake and oxygen evolution as simultaneous activities. Cheniae and Martin in 1967 were probably the first to identify the direct relationship between a manganese chlorophyll

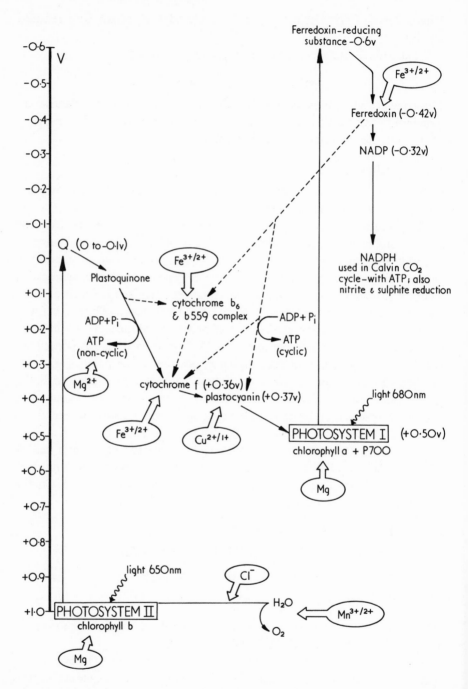

Figure 8.5 Involvement of the mineral elements in electron transport processes in chloroplasts.

complex and oxygen evolution. In later work they found that extraction by Tris or by hydroxylamine readily removed two-thirds of the manganese in the chloroplasts and this decreased oxygen evolution by 80%. The last one-third part of the manganese was only removed by exhaustive extraction, and oxygen evolution was then decreased by 95% of normal activity. Restoration of depleted manganese occurs when chloroplasts are incubated with Mn^{2+} and illuminated at the same time. The ratio of manganese was about 3 atoms: 200 chlorophyll molecules. It was concluded that each oxygen-evolving centre contained three manganese atoms. Two of these were considered to be linked reactively in a symmetrical way to the third which was thought to be more closely linked to the chlorophyll-photochemical centre.

The role of chlorine was first suspected by Warburg in 1946 who found that oxygen evolution by chloroplast fragments was stimulated by Cl^- ions with a saturating concentration of 7 mM. Absence of Cl^- ions causes irreversible photo-inactivation of chloroplasts with time. Studies by Hind, Heath and Izawa on the fluorescence reactions of photoactivated chlorophyll b indicates that Cl^- has a function which is closely related to the carrier which transfers electrons from OH^- ions to the chlorophyll b molecule. Absence of Cl^- diminishes the yield of fluorescent emitted energy when chlorophyll b is illuminated, and illumination in the absence of Cl^- causes inactivation of chloroplasts. It is considered that the monovalent anion is associated with the reactions involved in the penetration of H^+ ions into chloroplasts on illumination.

Light-activated chlorophyll b (Photosystem II) donates an electron at an energy of about 0 volts to plastoquinone via an uncharacterised factor Q and from here to cytochrome f (30) (Table 8.3, I) which is a haem iron-containing protein. The electron then probably passes to plastocyanin which is a copper protein. The energy gap (0·4 volts) between plastoquinone and cytochrome f, is barely sufficient to allow esterification of ADP to produce ATP by non-cyclic photophosphorylation by the transfer of a single electron, since about 31·5 to 33·6 kJ are required for this process. However a $2e^-/ATP$ ratio would allow $\Delta 0·75eV$ or about 71·2 kJ, which would be sufficient. The chlorophyll a, in photosystem I and an associated pigment (P_{700}) accept an electron from plastocyanin. The photosystem I pigment complex when activated by light is able to reduce ferredoxin (44) which is a non-haem iron-containing protein of low redox potential close to that of molecular hydrogen. There may also be an intermediate stage represented by a protein called 'ferredoxin reducing substance'. Ferredoxin and a flavoprotein enzyme can reduce NADP to NADPH for utilisation in the Calvin carbon dioxide fixation cycle or it can recycle electrons back to cytochrome f for cyclic photophosphorylation.

There are at least two other haem (iron) proteins, cytochrome b_{563} and cytochrome b_{559} (identified by their light absorption maxima) (32) (Table 8.3 I) which may function together or separately in the electron transport systems. However their present significance and sequential location are still controversial.

An excess of ATP over NADPH is needed for carbon dioxide reduction which requires the utilisation of $1·5$ mol of ATP per mol of NADPH.

Cyclic electron flow from reduced ferredoxin ($E_0' - 0·42$ V) to cytochrome f ($E_0' + 0·36$ V) provides adequate energy for cyclic photophosphorylation with a $1e^-/ATP$ ratio.

Ferredoxin in the reduced form is an activator of one of the enzymes (fructose diphosphate phosphatase) involved in the Calvin cycle. The phosphorylation and several steps in the Calvin cycle involving transformations of phosphate esters require magnesium. An enzyme able to hydrolyse ATP also occurs in chloroplasts and is dependent on calcium. The role of zinc is uncertain in this system. Aldolase which reversibly converts fructose diphosphate to glyceraldehyde-3-phosphate and dihydroxyacetone phosphate probably does not contain zinc in chloroplasts unlike the muscle enzyme.

The reversible hydration of carbon dioxide to produce bicarbonate is catalysed by carbonic anhydrase (72) (Table 8.6) and this contains zinc in plants as well as in micro-organisms and animals. Carbonic anhydrase seems to be relatively abundant in the leaves of aquatic species, but it is also present in the chloroplasts of terrestrial species and has been purified from parsley.

The metal-dependent enzyme systems noted above are mainly bound to the chloroplast structure. Therefore the chloroplasts tend to retain metals after isolation from the leaves in isotonic-extracting media which preserve their integrity. When the chloroplasts are ruptured by dilution of the suspending medium, particles of different sizes and centrifugal sedimentation properties are obtained. They tend to separate into two main size groups, larger particles sedimenting at around 10 000 g and a progressive series of smaller particles sedimenting between 30 000 and over 140 000 g. On analysis of these particles notable differences are found in the metal concentrations relative to chlorophyll, and also differences in the ratios of chlorophyll a/b. Chlorophyll a with an associated pigment absorbing principally light of 700 nm wavelength is involved in the light reactions in photosystem I resulting in the reduction of ferredoxin with electrons provided by plastocyanin. These are found in particles sedimented at high centrifugal fields (140 000 g). Chlorophyll b which absorbs light of shorter wavelength is involved in oxygen evolution, for which manganese is required. These components are found predominantly in larger particles (sedimenting at 10 000 g).

Nitrogen assimilation

Nitrate reductase (54) (Table 8.4) contains molybdenum in tightly bound form as a specific part of the enzyme (see Chapter 7). The nitrate-reductase complement is in part associated with chloroplasts obtained by methods which preserve the double membrane. Nitrite is the first free product of nitrate reduction and is further reduced to ammonia by a single enzyme, nitrite reductase. The experiments of Hewitt, Hageman and Losada and their respective collaborators have shown that hydroxylamine and hyponitrite are not involved as *free* intermediates in the reactions in which 6 electrons are required to reduce nitrite to ammonia. Nitrite reductase (48) (Table 8.3) in plant leaves is located in chloroplasts from which it may be removed by prolonged washing. The pure enzyme (mol. wt. 64 000) is brown in colour with marked light absorption at 380 nm and a weak band at 560 nm in addition to the characteristic protein band at about 280 nm. It contains labile sulphide and two atoms of non-haem iron and is not a flavoprotein as first thought. In fungi and dinitrifying bacteria, iron or copper or both occur together with cytochromes and flavins.

At least two proteins function as hydroxylamine reductases (41) yielding ammonia (Table 8.3). One may be identical with nitrite reductase while the other may be quite different, being half the molecular weight and behaving like a b-type cytochrome. Hydroxylamine-reductase activity is also closely associated with chloroplasts. Ammonia is incorporated into amino acids principally by glutamic dehydrogenase (GDH) (80) working in the reverse direction to the indication of the name of the enzyme (Table 8.6). In chloroplasts the GDH is NADPH specific and the role of a metal has not been shown. Most NADPH dependent dehydrogenase enzymes are activated by magnesium or manganese and sometimes by calcium, the ions being readily dissociable from the protein (Table 8.2). Outside chloroplasts the NADH specific GDH (80) is located in mitochondria. This enzyme is most probably a zinc metalloprotein similar to nearly all NADH-specific dehydrogenases (Table 8.6).

Many but by no means all the essential protein amino acids are produced from glutamate by the action of transaminase enzymes which catalyse the reversible reaction between an amino acid (e.g. glutamate) and a keto acid (e.g. pyruvate). These enzymes require pyridoxal phosphate but do not appear to contain or depend on metal activators.

Both DNA and RNA polymerases appear to be zinc-containing enzymes. Amino acids are united by peptide bonds on the messenger RNA templates to yield specific proteins. The amino acids are first activated as amino acyl-AMP compounds and are then combined with transfer RNA(t-RNA) by enzymes (amino-acyl t-RNA synthetases) specific for each type of transfer RNA appropriate to a particular amino acid. The reaction catalysed by a given synthetase requires ATP and proceeds as follows:

$$\text{amino acid} + \text{ATP} \underset{\longleftarrow}{\overset{\substack{\text{K}^+ \text{ with} \\ \text{Mg}^{2+} \text{ or Mn}^{2+}}}{\longrightarrow}} \text{amino-acyl AMP (enzyme bound)} + \text{PPi}$$

$$\text{amino-acyl AMP (enzyme bound)} + t\text{-RNA} \underset{\longleftarrow}{\overset{}{\longrightarrow}} \text{amino-acyl } t\text{-RNA} + \text{AMP}$$

Magnesium and potassium or ammonium ions are needed together for the transfer of the amino acid from the amino-acyl t-RNA to the growing poly-peptide chain. The Mg^{2+} requirement has a sharp optimum, the concentration depending on the species. The metals are freely dissociable and are required in concentrations of about 5 to 10 and 30 to 200 mM respectively. Sodium is relatively ineffective in replacing potassium in this function, unlike the pyruvic kinase or starch synthetase system of plants in which either rubidium or sodium are fairly active. In intact tissues K^+ or NH_4^+ are relatively specific activators. The specific site of the K^+ activators appears to be at the stages of binding of the amino-acyl t-RNA to the ribosomes, possibly the hydrolysis of guanosine triphosphate and the amino-acid residue transfer to the peptide chain.

Carbohydrate and carboxylic acid metabolism

The metal requirements for the metabolism of carbohydrates and carboxylic acids are mainly fulfilled by potassium and magnesium. Other monovalent cations can substitute for potassium in varying degrees. Ammonium ions are often equally effective, with rubidium, sodium and lithium in order of decreasing activity and sometimes in order of increasing inhibition. Many phosphokinase systems depend on both a monovalent ion and on magnesium or manganese, which function with varying degrees of efficiency (Table 8.2, Class II).

Many of the enzymes in this class show similar metal activation patterns in a wide range of organisms; plant, animal and bacterial, but some interesting differences in detail also occur. Thus the pyruvic kinase system (11)

$$\text{Phosphoenolpyruvate} + \text{ADP} \rightarrow \text{pyruvate} + \text{ATP}$$

found in seeds and seedlings of several species is activated by most monovalent ions in decreasing order of effectiveness; potassium, rubidium, ammonium, sodium and magnesium or manganese (Table 8.2).

The acetic thiokinase system (5) (Table 8.2, Class II) which also occurs in higher plants depends on both mono- and di-valent ions. The reaction is shown below

$$ATP + acetate \underset{\longleftarrow}{\overset{Mg^{2+}}{\longrightarrow}} acetyl\ AMP + PPi$$

$$Acetyl\text{-}AMP + CoASH \underset{\longleftarrow}{\overset{K^+}{\longrightarrow}} acetyl\ CoA + AMP$$

The acetic thiokinase differs from many other enzymes in this activation class with respect to the effect of sodium which is inactive on substitution for potassium and moreover inhibits the action of potassium competitively. However, the acetic thiokinase system is not completely specific for potassium, since rubidium and ammonium ions are both able to activate the enzyme. The true ATP substrate may be Mg-ATP.

It is interesting to consider the possible significance of sodium in halophytes in some of the systems where monovalent cations are required (see also page 22). No clear evidence for a specific role of sodium in an enzyme system is yet reported even though the element has been shown to be essential by Brownell for some species (e.g. *Atriplex vesicaria*). Ahmed and Hewitt investigated the possibility that pyruvic kinase (11) (Table 8.2, Class II) may require sodium instead of potassium in some halophytes, but no evidence was found for the displacement of potassium as the principal cation. However, other workers have demonstrated some differential effects of sodium in halophytes. Thus, whereas some marine plants, including *Zostera marina*, and certain red and brown algae normally fix carbon dioxide in darkness into amino acids, cell-free preparations of spinach leaves fix carbon mainly into carboxylic acids unless provided with high sodium, when fixation tends to predominate in the amino-acid fraction. If the concentration of NAD^+ is also increased the normal pattern is again observed. Brownell (1972) has shown that those species (mainly tropical Gramineae, e.g. millet, and halophytes, e.g. *Atriplex vesicaria*) having the C_4 supplementary photosynthesis pathway are clearly dependent on sodium for growth.

The carboxylic acid dehydrogenase utilising NADP and decarboxylases, and other enzymes of the carboxylic acid cycle, including the condensing enzyme, are generally activated by magnesium or manganese. These metals are readily dissociable from the enzymes and are usually interchangeable while retaining comparable activity, though K_m values for manganese tend to be smaller than for magnesium. One key enzyme in the tricarboxylic acid cycle of higher plants, aconitase (53), however, appears from the work of Palmer and DeKock to be specifically dependent on ferrous iron as a dissociable co-factor (Table 8.3). The NAD-linked dehydrogenases, in most tissues (bacterial and animal), and by inference in plants, are zinc proteins (Table 8.6) in which the metal is tightly combined and links the coenzyme to the protein, which often exists in up to four sub-units. Jefferies, Laycock, Stewart and Sims in 1968 showed that calcium ions favour the aggregation of malic dehydrogenase, extracted from *Lemna minor*. This effect of calcium could also be observed *in vivo*, and different strains responded to calcium ions at widely different levels. Other enzymes of *Lemna* with allosteric properties and subject to feedback control, including NAD-glutamic dehydrogenase (80), NADP isocitric dehydrogenase (16) (Table 8.2, Class III), and glucose-6-phosphate dehydrogenase were also reported to be subject to the effect of calcium ions with respect to their allosteric properties.

Several enzymes which catalyse reactions of sugar phosphate esters and related compounds are activated by magnesium and often by manganese in plants, animals and micro-organisms.

This survey of metal-activation patterns illustrates the great diversity of examples which may occur. There are those in which only a single metal is required and is tightly combined. Here there may be one or several atoms and their forms of combination or redox action may differ within the same enzyme (e.g. some of the copper proteins). Copper may undergo redox changes in some enzymes but not in all, even though these mediate oxidation. Copper and iron, or molybdenum and iron may be associated in one protein in closely bound form and each can also be the only metal present. In other enzymes, iron may be found as haem, as iron-sulphur or as other linkages, or the relatively freely dissociable form in different enzymes. In some enzymes one of two metals, i.e. iron, zinc or manganese is tightly bound, and another, e.g. magnesium, potassium or manganese is relatively dissociable, both being needed. In other systems dependent on two metals both the mono-valent and di-valent ions are dissociable and usually but not always non-specific. In enzymes where only a dissociable metal is required, specificity ranges from extreme in the case of manganese to wide interchangeability in several enzymes of phosphate ester or carboxylic acid metabolism. In some, cobalt is more effective than manganese as an alternative to magnesium.

In the single metal-dependent metalloproteins where zinc is normally present, cobalt or cadmium may be substituted in some cases *in vitro* to produce an active enzyme, and cobalt may replace zinc *in vivo* in alcohol dehydrogenase.

In some metal-dependent enzymes additional prosthetic groups are present such as flavins, nicotinamide nucleotides, pyridoxal phosphate, thiamine pyrophosphate and sometimes two haem groups are present in one protein, as in sulphite reductase of *Escherichia coli* and possibly in nitrite reductase of *Pseudomonas aeruginosa*.

Other variants in the patterns of metal activation may be expected to come to light with further investigations.

Further Reading

Bandurski, R. S. (1965) Biological reduction of sulphate and nitrate. Chapter 19, pp. 467–90 in *Plant Biochemistry* (Ed. E. J. Bonner and J. E. Varner). Academic Press: New York and London.

Bendall, D. S. and Hill, R. (1968) Haem-proteins in photosynthesis. *A. Rev. Pl. Physiol.* **19**, 167–86.

Caughey, W. S. (1967) Porphyrin proteins and enzymes. *A. Rev. Biochem.* **36** (2), 611–44.

Evans, H. J. and Sorger, G. J. (1966) Role of mineral elements with emphasis on the univalent cations. *A. Rev. Pl. Physiol.* **17**, 47–76.

Evans, H. J. and Wildes, R. A. (1971) *Colloquium Proceedings: Potassium in biochemistry and physiology*. International Potash Institute.

Falk, J. E., Lemberg, R. and Morton, R. K. (1961) *Haematin Enzymes*. Pergamon Press: Oxford London.

Federation of American Societies for Experimental Biology (1961). Proceedings of conference on biological aspects of metal binding. *Federation Proceedings* **20**, No. 3, part 2 (supplement No. 10), pp. 1–273.

Hall, D. O. and Evans, M. C. W. (1969) Iron-sulphur proteins. *Nature* **223**, 1342–6.

Hewitt, E. J. (1958) The role of mineral elements in the activity of plant enzyme systems in *Encyclopaedia of Plant Physiology* (Ed. W. Ruhland). Springer-Verlag: Berlin, vol. 4, pp. 427–81.

Hewitt, E. J. (1959) The metabolism of micronutrient elements in plants. *Biol. Rev.* **34**, 333–77.

International Potash Institute (1971) 8th Colloquium, *Potassium in Biochemistry and Physiology*, pp. 244.

Miller, L. P. and Flemion, F. (1973) The role of minerals in phytochemistry in *Phytochemistry III Inorganic elements and special groups of chemicals* (Ed. L. P. Miller) Van Nostrand Reinhold Company: New York. pp. 1–40.

Peisach, J., Aisen, P. and Blumberg, W. E. (1966) *The Biochemistry of Copper*. Academic Press: London and New York. 588 pp.

Price, C. A. (1968) Iron compounds and plant nutrition. *A. Rev. Pl. Physiol.* **19**, 239–48.

Pridham, J. B. (Ed.) (1963) *Enzyme Chemistry of Phenolic Compounds*. Pergamon Press: Oxford and London. 142 pp.

Richmond, D. V. (1973) Sulfur compounds in *Phytochemistry III Inorganic elements and special groups of chemicals* (Ed. L. P. Miller) Van Nostrand Reinhold Company: New York. pp. 41–73.

Rosenfeld, I. and Beath, O. A. (1964) *Selenium: Geobotany, Biochemistry, Toxicity and Nutrition*. Academic Press: New York and London. 411 pp.

Smith, E. L. (1965) *Vitamin B$_{12}$* 3rd edn. Methuen: London. 180 pp.

Thompson, J. F. (1967) Sulfur metabolism in plants. *A. Rev. Pl. Physiol.* **18**, 59–84.

Valentine, R. C. (1964) Bacterial ferredoxin. *Bact. Rev.* **28**, 497–517.

Vallee, B. W. and Williams, R. J. P. (1968) Enzyme action: views derived from metalloenzyme studies. *Chemistry in Britain* **4**, 397–402.

Williams, R. J. P. (1968) Role of transition metals in biological processes. *Roy. Inst. Chem. Revs.* **1**, 13–38.

Table 8.1 The functions and compounds of the essential mineral nutrients occurring in plants

Element	Probable functions	Examples of compounds
Nitrogen	Major metabolic importance as compounds	Amino acids (proteins), purines, pyrimidines (nucleic acids), amines, alkaloids, ureides, amino sugars, flavins and other coenzymes, porphyrins
Phosphorus	Energy transfer, structural	Sugar phosphates, ATP, GTP, etc., nucleic acids, coenzymes, phytic acid, phospholipids, acetyl phosphate, phosphoenol pyruvate, coenzyme A, thiamine pyrophosphate
Potassium*	Osmotic relations, protein conformation and stability, stomata, membranes and pH control	Probably occurs predominantly in the ionic form
Magnesium*	Enzyme activation, pigments and ribosomal stability	Chlorophyll
Calcium*	Enzyme activation, cell walls	Calcium pectate, calcium phytate, calcium carbonate
Sulphur	Active groups in enzymes and coenzymes	Cysteine, cystine, glutathionine, methionine, S-adenosyl methionine, thio-glucosides, polysaccharide sulphates (agar), lipoic acid, coenzyme A, thiamine, adenosine phosphosulphate, sulpholipids
Iron*	Active groups in enzymes and electron carriers	Cytochromes, ferredoxin, catalase, porphyrin synthesis, nitrogenase, nitrate, nitrite and sulphite reductases, ferritin
Copper*	Enzymes, photosynthesis	Polyphenol oxidase, amine oxidase, plastocyanin
Manganese*	Photosynthesis, carboxylic acid metabolism	Manganin
Molybdenum*	Nitrogen fixation and nitrate reduction	Nitrate reductase, nitrogenase
Zinc*	Enzymes	Carbonic anhydrase
Sodium*	Enzyme activation	

Element	Probable functions	Examples of compounds
Cobalt*	Nitrogen fixation	Vitamin B_{12} in nitrogen-fixing micro-organisms only
Silicon	Structural	Hydrated silicon dioxide
Chlorine	Photosynthesis (as Cl^-), also in compounds	Chlorinated indoles, alkaloids
Boron	Sugar transport, co-ordination with phenols	Borate ion; no naturally-occurring organic compound established with certainty

* See also Tables 8.2 to 8.6

Table 8.2 Some enzymes dependent on monovalent or divalent cations (K^+, NH_4^+, Ca^{2+}, Mn^{2+}, Mg^{2+})

CLASS I: single monovalent cations required

Trivial name	Source	Reaction	Metal requirements, etc. (Concentrations M)
(1) Aldehyde dehydrogenase	Yeast	$CH_3CHO + NAD^+ + H_2O \rightarrow CH_3COOH + NADH + H^+$	K or Rb equivalent in effect. NH_4 30%, Na 4% of effectiveness of K
(2) Tryptophanase	Escherichia coli	Tryptophan $\rightarrow$ indole + ammonia + pyruvic acid	K opt. 7×10^{-2}; pyridoxal phosphate coenzyme also needed. NH_4 and Rb also activate in decreasing degree
(3) Deoxyguanylate kinase	E. coli	Deoxyguanosine monophosphate + ATP $\rightarrow$ Deoxy-GTP + AMP	K opt. 0·3, NH_4 and Rb 50%, Na, Cs, Li 5–10% of effect of K. Infection of the bacterium by T_2 strain bacteriophage modifies the protein and eliminates the cation requirement for activity
(4) Inosine-5-phosphate dehydrogenase	Peas, Aerobacter sp.	Inosinic acid + NAD^+ + $H_2O \rightarrow$ xanthylic acid + $NADH + H^+$	K opt. 6×10^{-2}, K_m 10^{-3}; NH_4 50%, Na 6% of effect of K

CLASS II: monovalent and divalent cations required

Trivial name	Source	Reaction	Metal requirements, etc. (Concentrations M)
(5) Acetic thiokinase	Plants	I. ATP + acetate $\rightleftarrows$ adenylacetate + $P_2O_7^{4-}$ II. Adenylacetate + coenzyme A $\rightleftarrows$ acetyl-CoA + AMP	Two reactions are catalysed by this enzyme. Reaction I is dependent on Mg and inhibited by Na or K; reaction II is dependent on K whereas Na is inactive

Table 8.2—continued

Trivial name	Source	Reaction	Metal requirements, etc. (Concentrations M)
(6) Glutathione (GSH) synthetase	Wheat germ, yeast, *Escherichia coli*	γ-Glutamyl cysteine + glycine + ATP $\rightarrow$ GSH + ADP + PO_4^{2-}	K or Rb (15% effect of K); Mg four times as effective as Mn in wheat germ. K opt. 0·02, NH_4 75% effect of K, Na inactive. Mg and Mn equivalent in *E. coli* enzyme. Mg specific for yeast enzyme
(7) Aldolase	Yeasts (*Candida utilis*), Bacteria, Fungi, *Euglena*, Blue-green algae	Fructose-1,6-diphosphate $\rightleftarrows$ glyceraldehyde-3-phosphate + dihydroxyacetone phosphate	K opt. 0·1. K dissociable and specific (Na inactive) plus Zn tightly combined, 1 atom per mol enzyme; Mg, Mn or Co inactive
(8) β-Methylaspartase	*Clostridium tetanomorphum*	L-threo methylaspartate $\rightarrow$ mesaconitate + NH_4^+	K opt. 10^{-2}, K_m 3×10^{-3}; NH_4 65%, Rb 55%, Li 35%, Na 10% of effect of K; Mg opt. 2×10^{-3} K_m $1 \cdot 2 \times 10^{-4}$; Mn, Zn inactive, unless crystalline enzyme is pretreated with EDTA. Ca inhibits competitively 95% at 10^{-3}
(9) Methionine-activating enzyme	Yeast	Methionine + ATP $\rightarrow$ S-adenosyl methionine + $P_2O_7^{4-}$	K or NH_4 opt. 0·2, K_m $2 \cdot 5 \times 10^{-2}$, Rb 85%, Li, Cs, Na 10% of effect of K or NH_4. Mg and Mn equivalent, opt. 0·1, K_m 6×10^{-3}
(10) ATPase	Carrot and pea roots	ATP $\rightarrow$ ADP + Pi	Stimulated by Na, K, Rb, Li, NH_4 ions with separate requirement for Mg ions replaced by Ca, Fe or Mn with varying degrees of effectiveness
(11) Phosphoenolpyruvate phosphotransferase (pyruvic kinase)	Widespread in seeds, leaves, yeast, bacteria, etc.	$CH_3COCOOH + ATP \rightleftarrows CH_2{=}CO(H_2PO_3)COOH + ADP$	Requires K or Na and Mg or Mn. Relative effectiveness of Mn or Mg varies considerably between different plants

CLASS III: divalent cations only required

Trivial name	Source	Reaction	Metal requirements, etc. (Concentrations M)
(12) Phosphoenol pyruvate carboxytrans-phosphorylase	Propionic bacteria	Overall reaction $CH_2=CO(H_2PO_3)COOH + Pi + CO_2 \rightarrow COOHCH_2COCOOH + PPi$	Bound metal probably Mn and dissociable metal either Mg or Mn having separate roles in the mechanism
(13) Hexokinase	Yeast	Glucose + ATP → Glucose-6-PO_4 + ADP	Mg opt. 10^{-2}; K_m $2·6 \times 10^{-3}$
(14) Enolase	Yeast	2-Phosphoglycerate → phosphoenolpyruvate + H_2O	Mg opt. 10^{-2}; K_m $2·8 \times 10^{-3}$; Mn opt. $1·7 \times 10^{-4}$; K_m $3·8 \times 10^{-5}$; Zn opt. 2×10^{-5}; K_m 5×10^{-6}. Mn and Zn produce 40% of max. rate with opt., Mg and compete with Mg
(15) Inorganic pyrophosphatase	Yeast	$P_2O_7^{4-} + H_2O \rightarrow 2HPO_4^{2-}$ $PPi + H_2O \rightarrow 2Pi$	Mg opt. 2×10^{-3}; K_m 7×10^{-4}. Mg nearly specific but Co can activate slightly
(16) NADP isocitric dehydrogenase	Yeast	Isocitrate + NADP → oxalosuccinate + NADPH	Mg opt. 2×10^{-3}; m $3 \times 10 K^{-4}$; Mn opt. $1·5 \times 10^{-3}$; K_m $2·5 \times 10^{-4}$. Mn about two times as effective as Mg
(17) NAD isocitric dehydrogenase	Yeast	Isocitrate + NAD → oxalosuccinate + NADH	Mg opt. 5×10^{-4}; K_m 5×10^{-5}; Mn opt. 10^{-4}; K_m 2×10^{-5}. Mn more effective than Mg
(18) Carboxylase (pyruvate decarboxylase)	Yeast	Pyruvate → acetaldehyde + CO_2	Mg opt. 2×10^{-4}; K_m 4×10^{-5}; Mn opt. 2×10^{-4}; K_m 4×10^{-5}. Mg and Mn equally effective

Table 8.2—continued

	Trivial name	Source	Reaction	Metal requirements, etc. (Concentrations M)
(19)	Phosphopyruvate synthetase (pyruvate phosphate dikinase)	Sugarcane Maize Sorghum	Pyruvate + ATP + Pi → phosphoenolpyruvate + AMP + PPi	Mg cannot be replaced by Ca or Mn. Key enzyme in the C_4 dicarboxylic acid photosynthetic pathway
(20)	Isocitric dehydrogenase	*Avena* coleoptile	Isocitrate + NADP → oxalosuccinate + NADPH	Mg opt. 10^{-3}; Mn opt. $4 \cdot 5 \times 10^{-4}$; K_m $1 \cdot 5 \times 10^{-4}$; Co opt. $7 \cdot 5 \times 10^{-4}$; K_m 2×10^{-4}. Co and Mn slightly more effective than Mg
(21)	Enolase	Pea seeds	2-Phosphoglycerate → phosphoenolpyruvate + H_2O	Mg opt. 10^{-3}; K_m 2×10^{-4}; Mn opt. 10^{-4}; K_m 10^{-5}; Co opt. 4×10^{-4}; K_m 10^{-5}; Zn opt. 3×10^{-5}. Ca inhibits competitively Zn 7%, Co 30%, Mn 40% of activity of Mg
(22)	Uridine diphosphate glucose pyrophosphorylase	Pea seeds and other species	UDPG + $P_2O_7^{4-}$ ⇌ UTP + Glucose-1-PO_4	Mg opt. 5×10^{-3}; K_m 8×10^{-4}; Mn opt. 10^{-3}. Co and Ni also active. Mn and Mg equally effective
(23)	(i) Glutamyl synthetase (ii) Glutamyl transferase enzyme	Pea seeds	(i) Glutamate + NH_3 ⇌ glutamine (ii) Glutamine + hydroxylamine (or NH_3) ⇌ glutamohydroxamate or NH_3 exchange	(i) Mg opt. 4×10^{-2}; K_m 5×10^{-3}; Mn opt. 4×10^{-3}; K_m 10^{-4} (ii) Mg opt. 2×10^{-2}; K_m 8×10^{-3}; Mn opt. 10^{-3}; K_m 2×10^{-4}. One protein having two functions and different metal activation patterns for each
(24)	ATPase (Apyrase)	Potato tubers	ATP → ADP + Pi	Activated by Ca
(25)	α-Amylase	Barley	Starch hydrolysis	Ca probably needed for activation and stability
(26)	Phospholipase D	Cabbage leaves	Lecithin + H_2O → choline + phosphatidic acid	Ca opt. $0 \cdot 1$; Sr 67%, Ba 34% of activity with Ca

Notes on Table 8.2

Class I: single monovalent cations required

The variable extent to which other monovalent cations replace potassium may reflect small differences in the affinity of the enzymes for certain ions. Steric relationships of certain configurations or ionised sites in the protein may determine the optimum ionic radius for hydrated ions. It may be that on infection of *Escherichia coli* by T_2 phage, deoxyguanylate kinase (3) combines with the substrate without the need for a metal ion which is apparently necessary for the enzyme obtained from the uninfected cells.

Class II: monovalent and divalent cations required

It will be seen that several enzymes require both a divalent cation, Mg^{2+} or Mn^{2+}, and a monovalent cation, usually K^+ or NH_4^+. In at least one case—the acetic thiokinase of plants—the reaction proceeds in two steps. One step is dependent on the divalent cation and the other requires the monovalent ion. In this class of enzymes the effectiveness of Na^+, NH_4^+, Rb^+, etc. compared with K^+ ranges from equivalent to negligible. Only rarely however does potassium appear specific, and its essential character in plants must depend on those instances where other metals do not replace it or on a unique integrated effect of the ion on several systems.

Class III: divalent cations only required

The concentration ranges for optimal activity and K_m values are two-hundred-fold for magnesium and about tenfold for manganese for the examples from yeast in the series of enzymes in which a single divalent ion is required for activity. For most, magnesium is more efficient than manganese at the optimal concentration, but in a few (certain peptidases and arginase), manganese is equally or more effective than magnesium. Similar ratios of Mg to Mn concentrations are effective at optimal values for enzymes from plant sources. One enzyme—the glutamyl transferase-synthetase (23) of peas, purified about 1000 times—catalyses two distinct reactions for which the metal activation patterns differ appreciably.

The phosphoenol pyruvate carboxytransphosphorylase (12) of propionic bacteria requires two divalent metals, one (possibly Mn) being tightly combined with the protein and another which can be the same or a different metal, e.g. Mg, is freely dissociable. The two metals react at different sites and influence different aspects of the overall complex reaction mediated by a single protein. It is suggested that the bound metal combines with PEP and that Pi is linked to the enzyme via the dissociable metal. The two phosphate groups link to form a PPi bridge. As CO_2 combines with the double bond of the enolpyruvate, the PPi link with PEP is broken. The separate products—oxaloacetate and PPi—then dissociate from the protein. (See also Table 8.6 (Zn), yeast pyruvic carboxylase (82).) In systems involving ADP (and ATP) the true substrate for the enzyme is often a $1 : 1$ $Mg^{2+} : ADP$ (ATP) complex and divergence from this ratio is inhibitory. Several enzymes responsible for hydrolysis of adenosine pyrophosphate bonds are activated by Ca^{2+} and in several, Mg and Ca are mutually antagonistic or inhibitory to the respective systems. Phosphopyruvate synthetase (19) found in the leaves of tropical grasses is a key enzyme in the C_4 dicarboxylic acid photosynthetic pathway described by Hatch and Slack (1968).

Metalloproteins dependent on manganese (tightly combined with the protein) are rare. Two are noted here. Manganin (mol. wt 56 000–58 000) containing 1 atom Mn has been isolated from Virginia type peanuts. Its function is unknown. Superoxide dismutase of *E. coli* (mol. wt 39 500) contains 2 atoms Mn. The enzyme catalyses the unusual reaction $O_2^- + O_2^- + 2H^+ = O_2 + H_2O_2$, and is red purple in colour. One form of mammalian superoxide dismutase is blue and contains Cu and Zn. However in mitochondria this enzyme contains Mn, supporting the theory that the mitochondria of higher plants and animals were originally derived symbiotic bacteria.

Table 8.3 Some examples of iron-dependent proteins of higher plants, yeasts, fungi, bacteria and algae

CLASS I: haem-containing proteins (simple and complex)

Trivial name	Sources	Mol. wt and metal content, Redox value	Remarks
(27) Peroxidase	Horseradish, most higher plants, yeast, fungi	One protohaem group. Fe normally Fe^{3+} and higher oxidation states but Fe^{2+} may also be produced in some reactions	Oxidises a very wide range of substrates by different mechanisms. Typical reaction is $AH_2 + H_2O_2 \rightarrow A + 2H_2O$. Also catalyses free radical production by single e^- removal
(28) Catalase	Extremely widely distributed in plants, yeasts, fungi, algae and bacteria	Fe^{3+} with one protohaem group. Fe^{2+} produced with azide which is oxidised to NO and complexes with Fe^{2+} irreversibly	Most active catalytic protein known. Decomposes H_2O_2 but also acts as a peroxidase, as in the oxidation of ethanol
(29) Cytochrome c (respiratory carrier)	Higher plants, yeasts, fungi, algae, bacteria	13 000, 1 haem. $E_0' + 0.25$ V. approx.	Electron carriers between cytochrome b—cytochrome oxidase sequence. Not auto-oxidised. Oxidised by cytochrome a, reduced by cytochrome b—also ascorbate and other agents, e.g. $S_2O_4^{2-}$. 1 e^- transferred. Do not typically react with CO. Other c-type cytochromes have E_0' as low as -0.20 V. and as high as $+0.33$ V. Some are auto-oxidisable, react with CO and contain two atoms Fe
Other c-type cytochromes	Desulphovibrio, Chromatium, Thiobacillus	Haem linked to protein by vinyl-cysteinyl chains (2/haem)	
(30) Cytochrome f	Chloroplasts, green plants and green algae	245 000 c-type haem linkage 4 Fe $E_0' + 0.365$ V.	C-type spectrum $\lambda 554, 532, 524, 422$ nm (Soret) Not auto-oxidisable at normal pH No reaction with CO. 1 e^- transferred

Table 8.3—continued

Trivial name	Sources	Mol. wt and metal contents, Redex value	Remarks
(31) Cytochrome b_3	Plant leaves, potato tubers	$E'_0 - 0.06$ V.	λ_{max} α 567 (ox.), 559 (red.) β 529–32 nm
(32) Cytochromes b_6 b_{559}	Chloroplasts	$E'_0 - 0.06$ V. b-cytochromes have Fe protoporphyrin IX as the haem group held by covalent Fe	Cytochrome b_6 λ_{max} 563 nm Cytochrome b_{559} λ_{max} 559 nm. 1 e^- transferred Some b-type cytochromes react with CO and are prevented from reduction in the presence of Antimycin A or 4 hydroxyquinoline-N-oxide
(33) Cytochrome b_2 L + lactate dehydrogenase	Yeast	80 000. 1 haem, 1 FMN $E'_0 + 0.12$ V. 1 Mg + deoxyribonucleic acid	λ_{max} ox. (α); 560: (β) 530: (γ) 413 λ_{max} red. (α) 556·5: (β) 528: (γ) 423 N.B. The D-lactate dehydrogenase is a zinc protein (76)
(34) Cytochrome a	Yeasts, bacteria, probably higher plants	a-type cytochromes have *Spirographis*-type haem with one vinyl group replaced by hydroxylalkyl and a formyl group elsewhere. $E'_0 + 0.25$ V.	λ_{max} α 598 nm Complex of cytochrome oxidase in mitochondrial particles. Reversible oxidation and reduction of iron in a porphyrin nucleus. Extreme sensitivity to cyanide in in oxidised form, and to CO (reversible by light) in reduced form. Total of 4 e^- transferred in reduction of molecular oxygen to water

Trivial name	Sources	Mol. wt and metal contents, Redox value	Remarks
(35) Cytochrome a_3	Associated with the above as the cytochrome oxidase complex with copper (one or two atoms)	Cu atoms $E_0' + 0.29$ V. Cytochrome a_3 Fe $E_0' > + 0.3$ V.	$\lambda_{max} \propto 604$ nm. Located in mitochondria as the terminal electron donor to molecular oxygen in aerobic organisms. Linked to cytochrome a via copper (1 or 2 atoms) in which copper functions as an intermediate electron transport link
(36) Haemoglobin	In legume root nodules	17 000 1 Fe^{2+}	Probably scavenges oxygen away from the oxygen-sensitive nitrogenase in the bacteroids. Combines reversibly with molecular oxygen as in blood haemoglobin
(37) Sulphite (nitrite) reductase	E. coli, Pseudomonas sp. Micrococcus sp.	Cytochrome class a_2 (chlorin)-type haem and other haem and non-haem iron and flavin nucleotides	Highly complex proteins having several moieties under separate gene control for biosynthesis (see notes)
(38) Sulphite (nitrite, hydroxylamine) reductase	Yeast	FMN, FAD, non-haem iron	An unidentified chromophore (λ_{max} 589 nm), but a typical haem-type iron is discounted
(39) Sulphite reductase	Spinach	Possibly, a chlorin-type haem, mol. wt 84 000	No flavin nucleotides present, non-haem iron not found. No reaction with nitrite. Light absorption maxima at 279, 404 and 589 nm
(40) Nitrite reductase	Achromobacter fischeri	95 000. 0.1% Fe Two mol. of haem-c	Reduces nitrite and hydroxylamine to ammonia. Does not reduce nitrate or sulphite. No haem iron apparently observed

Table 8.3—continued

Trivial name	Sources	Mol. wt and metal content, Redox value	Remarks
(41) Hydroxylamine reductase	Spinach, vegetable marrow	Fraction I: 60 to 64 000 tightly bound non-haem Fe Fraction II: 32 000 haem	Fraction I is inseparable from nitrite reductase; irreversibly inhibited by CO. Fraction II has no nitrite reductase activity but reacts with CO (light reversible) and is associated with a b-type cytochrome absorption spectrum

CLASS II: ferredoxin-type proteins

Trivial name	Sources	Mol. wt and metal content, Redox value	Remarks
(42) High potential non-haem iron protein	Rhodopseudomonas, Chromatium (photosynthetic bacteria)	$E_0' + 0.33$ V.	Contains iron and labile sulphide but redox value is high as contrasted with the ferredoxins (below). λ_{max} 375 nm
(43) Ferredoxin bacterial	Several bacteria including Clostridium pasteurianum, Azotobacter, Micrococcus, Chromatium	Mol. wt 6000–7000 Fe 6 or 8 Fe atoms E_0' about 0.39 V. to −0.49 V.	Rapidly auto-oxidisable red-brown proteins. The most negative potential electron carriers so far isolated (equivalent to the hydrogen electrode), except 'ferredoxin reducing substance' reported from chloroplasts. 2 e^- transferred in bacterial ferredoxins. Contain equivalent amounts (mol.) of Fe and acid-labile S. λ_{max} 280, 310, 300, 390 nm lost on reduction or removal of iron
(44) Ferredoxin	Higher plants, green algae, blue-green algae, Euglena, Chlamydomonas, Anacystis	Mol. wt 12 000–15 000 approx. E^0 about −0.42 V.	Red proteins. Differ from bacterial ferredoxins in absorption spectra (λ_{max} 280, 325, 420, 455 nm), in 1 e^- transferred, and in number of Fe atoms (2/mol.) with equivalent acid labile S. 1 atom Fe reduced but the two atoms interact antimagnetically by electron spin

Trivial name	Source	Mol. wt, metal content, etc. and Flavin	Remarks
(45) Succinic dehydrogenase	Yeast Mitochondria	Fe^{2+} in non-haem protein component. Mol. wt 200 000 4 atoms Fe, 1 FAD	
(46) Nitrogenases (see also (56), Table 8.4)	C. pasteurianum Rhizobia Azotobacter Klebsiella pneumoniae	I Mol. wt 100 000 to 300 000 15 to 20 Fe, 1 or 2 Mo, 2 Mg and labile S nearly equivalent to Fe II Mol. wt 25 000 to 50 000 1 to 4 Fe and labile S. No Mo	Two protein fractions always associated and *essential together for all aspects of nitrogenase activity.* This association of high and low mol. wt fractions of characteristic composition has been found in all nitrogenase systems. Fraction I is cold labile and is sensitive to oxygen. 6 e⁻ transferred without free intermediates (see also Table 8.4)
(47) Dihydro-orotic acid dehydrogenase	Zymobacterium oroticum	Mol. wt 62 000 4 Fe as non-haem protein, with 4 Labile S, 2 FMN, 2 FAD	Oxygenase oxidation of dihydro-orotic acid. The non-haem iron protein component resembles ferredoxin

CLASS III: miscellaneous non-haem iron containing proteins with or without labile sulphur

Trivial name	Source	Mol. wt, metal content, etc. and Flavin	Remarks
(48) Nitrite reductase	Higher plants, green algae	60 to 64 000 2 atoms Fe, probably labile sulphide	Irreversibly inhibited by CO; *not* sensitive to Cu enzyme inhibitors. Chlorin haem groups appear to be present. Light absorption maxima at 280, 380 and 560 nm; brown colour

Table 8.3—continued

Trivial name	Source	Reaction	Metal requirements, etc. (Concentrations M)
(49) Rubredoxin	Clostridium pasteurianum Micrococcus aerogenes Desulphovibrio desulphuricans	6400 $E_0' - 0·057$ V. 1 Fe atom, no labile S	Can reduce hydroxylamine. Absorption spectrum with maxima at 280, 380, 490 nm oxidised, and 280, 311 and 333 nm reduced
(50) Hydrogenase	In some bacteria, e.g. Azotobacter spp. C. pasteurianum Desulphovibrio desulphuricans Aerobacillus polymyxa Also some Chlorella spp.	Fe^{2+} dissociable, or tightly bound	Generally catalyse reaction $H_2 \rightarrow 2H^+ + 2\ e^-$ Sometimes reversible (e.g. Clostridium) $2H^+ + 2\ e^- \rightarrow H_2$ but not in Azotobacter. Mostly inhibited by CO. Sometimes reversible by light
(51) Oxygenase (pyrocatecholase)	Pseudomonas fluorescens	100 000 2 atoms Fe^{3+}	Reacts with molecular O_2 (not H_2O_2) to produce ring opening yielding a dicarboxylic acid. Fe remains in ferric state. Red protein λ_{max} 450 nm
(52) Ferritin	Chloroplasts	460 000 Particles 5–6 nm in diameter with up to 23% Fe	Probably similar to animal ferritin which binds hydroxide-phosphate micelles. Fe is bound as Fe^{2+} and subsequently oxidised to Fe^{3+}, and only released after reduction to Fe^{2+}
(53) Aconitase	Some higher plants, yeast, fungi and bacteria	Fe^{2+} as a dissociable activator	

Notes on Table 8.3

The iron proteins can be classified into three principal groups. One group includes those in which the iron is combined in a porphyrin ring as shown in Fig. 8.6. Iron porphyrins are most commonly either ferrous or ferric proto-porphyrin linked by co-ordination of iron and protein, as in haemoglobin (36), b-type cytochromes, peroxidase (27) and catalase (28), or with additional vinyl-cysteinyl links, as in c-type cytochromes including cytochrome f (30), or iron in a modified porphyrin (*Spirographis* type) as in a-type cytochromes (34). The redox potentials range between -0.2 and $+0.4$ V, the potential varying partly due to the protein–porphyrin combination, but mainly by the particular iron ligand and type of bonding with the protein. Potentials for c-type cytochromes may vary widely from -0.2 (*Desulphovibrio desulphuricans*, c_3) to $+0.37$ (cytochrome f).

A few appear to contain a porphyrin ring of the chlorin type (haem d) with modified side groups and principal light absorption bands at longer wave-lengths, as reported for the sulphite-nitrite systems (37) of *E. coli, Pseudomonas aeruginosa* and *Micrococcus denitrificans*. These last complex proteins often also contain FMN and FAD co-enzymes. The *E. coli* enzyme contains, in addition to both FAD and FMN, probably two haem protein moieties, one of which resembles chlorin, and also additional iron in the non-haem form with labile sulphide groups, as in the ferredoxins (see below). The spinach sulphite reductase (39) resembles the yeast and bacterial types (38) in having light absorption peaks (or shoulders) at 279, 404, 589 (and 385) nm. It reacts with carbon monoxide, and the peak at 589 nm suggests a chlorin-type haem. There is apparently no flavin and only iron in the haem moiety. The spinach enzyme will not reduce nitrite and thus differs from this enzyme in micro-organisms.*

The L+lactate dehydrogenase (syn. cytochrome b_2) (33) of yeast contains Mg and a DNA component of uncertain affinity and also FMN. The presence of copper in the cytochrome a, a_3 complex has been established, and functions in electron transport between the two haem proteins in the complex.

The next main group includes the ferredoxins. These may be of bacterial origin (43) with several iron atoms ($2e^-$ carriers), or of plant and algal origin (44), usually with two iron atoms ($1e^-$ carriers). Both types have different characteristic light-absorption spectra, are of low molecular weight (6000 or 10–15 000) and contain acid-labile sulphide (H_2S liberated at low pH) in amounts equivalent to the iron. These free ferredoxins generally have very low redox values of about -0.42 V, at the level of the H_2 electrode. Ferre-doxin-type protein moieties are present in the complex proteins xanthine and aldehyde oxidases (57) (Table 8.4), succinic dehydrogenase (45), dihydro-

* Spinach nitrate reductase and *E.coli* sulphite reductase contain an identical chlorin with 8 carboxyl side-chains.

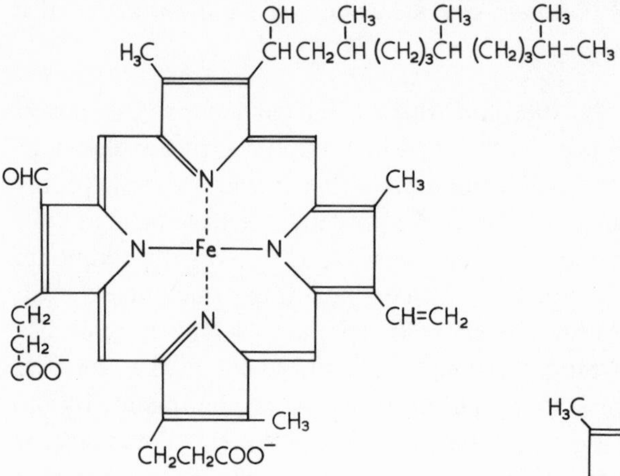

A

B

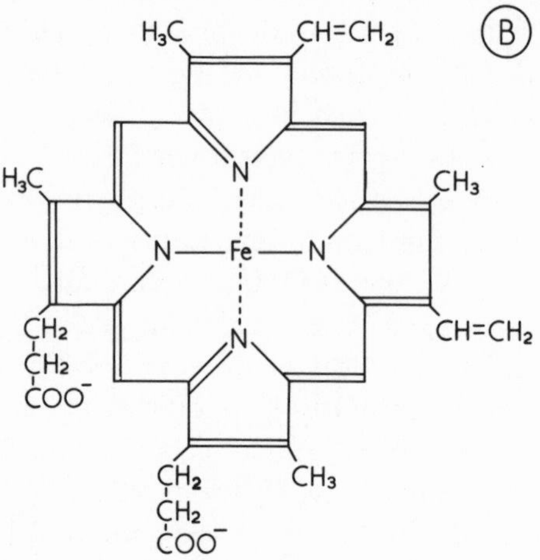

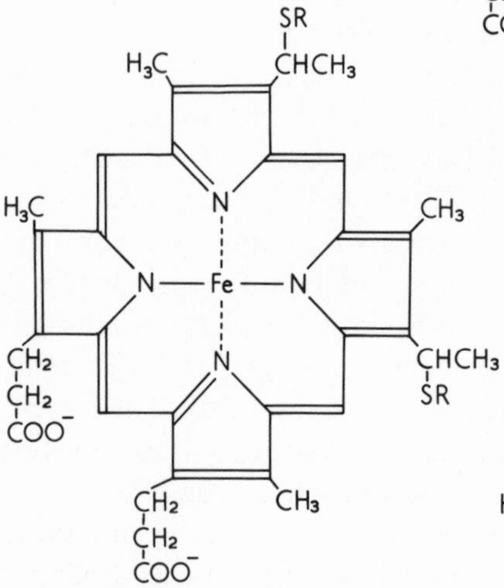

C

D

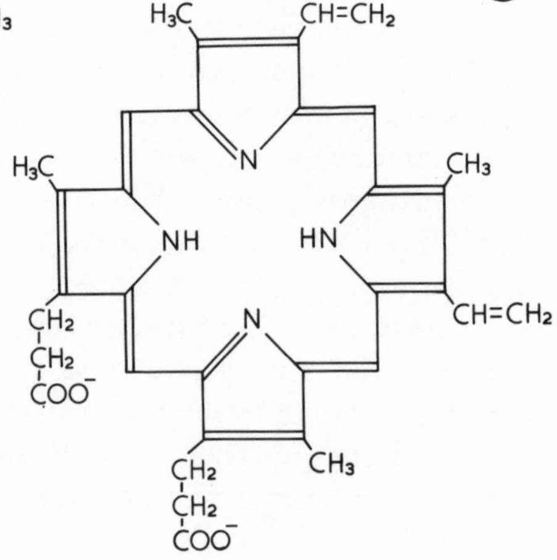

orotic acid dehydrogenase (47) and some ferredoxin-like properties are found in both of the nitrogenase fractions (46, 56) (Table 8.4). There are also other non-haem iron proteins, like rubredoxin (49), which have redox values (E_0') about 0 V or even $+0.3$ V. A selenium analogue of parsley ferredoxin has been prepared chemically. It has a similar redox potential (-0.38 compared with -0.42 V), absorption spectrum and $1e^-$ reaction.

The third group includes proteins with either dissociable or bound iron, as in hydrogenase (50), nitrite reductase (48) of higher plants and aconitase (53). Nitrite reductases have light-absorption spectra resembling somewhat those of sulphite reductases or rubredoxin and electron transport functions in the metal are not yet demonstrated.* Ferritin (52) which binds iron and oxygenase which contains ferric iron that does not undergo a valency change are other miscellaneous types.

Figure 8.6   Structure of porphyrin prosthetic groups.
  (A) Haem A: prosthetic group of class a cytochromes.
  (B) Protohaem (IX): prosthetic group of haemoglobin, myoglobin, catalase, peroxidase and class b cytochromes.
  (C) Haem C: prosthetic group of class c cytochromes.
  (D) Protoporphyrin (IX): prosthetic group of cytochrome b_6.

* Nitrite reductase has the same carboxylated side chain chlorin haem as bacterial sulphite reductase (37).

Table 8.4 Proteins containing molybdenum and sometimes iron

Trivial name	Source	Mol. wt, metal content, etc. and Flavin	Remarks
(54) Nitrate reductase	Escherichia coli	1 000 000 1 Mo and 40 Fe	Non-haem iron of unidentified type. Accepts electrons from b-type cytochrome. A similar complex occurs in Pseudomonas aeruginosa
	Micrococcus denitrifricans	165 000 1 Mo, 2 non-haem Fe and 4 labile S	First case of labile S in nitrate reductase
	Neurospora crassa	220 000 Mo and Fe	NADPH, FAD, cytochrome b557 and Mo in electron transport sequence to nitrate. Also reduces cytochrome c in presence of FAD and possibly another metal carrier
	Chlorella fusca	Mo only	NADH and Mo, but FAD is a stabilising component.
	Chlorella pyrenoidosa	Mo and Fe in cytochrome b557	Apparently different electron donation from C. fusca
	Soybean	Mo only	NADPH or NADH, FAD and Mo. Flavin essential for activity
	Spinach	About 240 000 Mo only	NADH specific and Mo. FAD may be absent or unnecessary

	Source	Composition	Notes
(55) Sulphite oxidase	Liver	115 000 2 b-type cytochromes, 2 Mo	Apparently no flavin components and no non-haem iron
(56) Nitrogenase Fraction I (see also (46), Table 8.3)	Clostridium pasteurianum, Rhizobium japonicum, Azotobacter chroococcum, Klebsiella pneumoniae	100 000 to 3 000 000. 15–20 Fe (non-haem). 1 or 2 Mo (2 Mg) and labile S nearly equivalent to 3–4 Fe. (Fraction II contains Fe but no Mo).	All sources so far examined yield the two separate but mutually dependent proteins varying slightly in mol. wt. Both jointly catalyse ATP hydrolysis, reduction of $N_2 \to 2NH_3$, or H_2 evolution by a reductant, e.g. reduced ferredoxin, dithionite, or activated hydrogen
(57) Xanthine oxidase and Aldehyde oxidase	Micrococcus lactilyticus, Milk, rat liver, chicken liver	300 000 (xanthine oxidase) 280 000 (aldehyde oxidase) 8 or 4 Fe, 2 Mo, 1 or 2 FAD	Similar enzymes have been found in Aspergillus nidulans. Xanthine and aldehyde oxidases both contain non-haem iron, with absorption spectra resembling bacterial ferredoxin
	Pig liver	1 Fe, 1 Mo, 2 FAD	

Notes on Table 8.4

There are three classes of molybdenum proteins. These are the nitrate reductases (54), the nitrogenase fraction I component (56), and the molybdo-iron flavoprotein oxidases (57).

Nitrate reductases may contain only molybdenum (as most probably occurs in higher plants, green and blue-green algae) or contain additionally haem or non-haem iron. In fungi, a cytochrome b 557/9 component is also present. In *Escherichia coli* where the mol wt is about 10^6 a non-haem iron protein component is found. This may also occur in the nitrate reductase found in *Rhizobium japonicum* bacteroids, since iron materially influences activity and is reported to be incorporated during formation. Many nitrate reductases require FAD or else contain it and most have a NADH/cytochrome-c reductase and non-specific diaphorase activity, in addition to being able to accept electrons from a reduced viologen donor instead of from NAD(P)H, $FADH_2$, a reduced cytochrome or reduced naphthoquinone. Some are membrane bound and some are repressed and/or inactivated by oxygen or ammonia, and all are probably induced by nitrate. In bacterial systems formate dehydrogenase is an associated activity which requires Fe, Mo and Se for formation and the Se is present in this enzyme in *E. coli*.

The nitrogenase fraction I proteins (molybdoferredoxins) are similar in nearly all respects, regardless of source. The molecular weights range between 120 000 and 270 000. There are 10–20 Fe atoms and equivalent labile sulphur. One Mo atom and sometimes also apparently associated Mg is present. Light-absorption spectra resemble bacterial ferredoxins (43). These proteins are cold-labile (denatured at $0°C$) and sensitive to oxygen. The fraction II components (46) contain no Mo, only Fe and labile sulphur, and have mol wts of about 25 000 to 45 000. Two molecules of fraction II are optimally functional with one of fraction I in *Clostridium pasteurianum in vitro*. Flavins do not appear to be components of nitrogenase proteins, but flavodoxin or ferredoxin are physiological electron donors, and electrons are donated non-physiologically from reduced viologens or dithionite.

The third class includes xanthine and aldehyde oxidases (57) of animal origin. These contain non-haem iron and labile sulphide, molybdenum and either FMN or FAD or both. Sulphite oxidase (55) of liver contains two b-type haems and two atoms Mo/mol, but apparently no flavin components and therefore represents perhaps a fourth class of molybdoproteins.

These enzymes show complex electron transport reactions with several possible mechanisms depending on substrate and oxidant. Like several nitrate reductases (54) they are activated by phosphate (or arsenate or silicate).

The molybdenum is less firmly bound than in the nitrate reductases or nitrogenase. In some ways their properties are a combination of many features of nitrate reductases and nitrogenase. The molybdenum moieties of all these proteins may have important common features.

Table 8.5 Some copper proteins of higher plants, yeasts, fungi, bacteria and algae, etc.

Trivial name	Sources and colour	Mol. wt, Cu and E'_0	Remarks
(58) Polyphenol oxidase, catecholase	Potato, banana, tobacco, tea (Pale blue or yellow green)	100 000. 4 Cu^+/mol	Substrates are o-diphenols oxidised to o-quinones; sometimes react with p-diphenols. Tea and tobacco leaf enzymes have no cresolase or p-diphenolase activity. Oxidation is by removal of 2H atoms to produce water and not by free radical mechanism (see Laccase, 60)
(59) Cresolase Tyrosinase (monophenolases)	Potato (Yellow green) Mushroom (Colourless) Neurospora (Colourless)	119 000. 4 Cu^+/mol 33 000. 1 Cu^+/mol	Cresolase activity is closely associated with many polyphenolases. Two sites on one protein is the generally accepted explanation, but inhibitor tests suggest closely related proteins may be involved. p-Cresol is hydroxylated to o-diphenol. Free radicals are not produced. Tyrosinase oxidises DOPA and other o-diphenols to quinones. The Cu^+ copper does not undergo valency change
(60) Laccase	Rhus succandanea (R. vernicifera) (Japanese Lac tree) (Blue) Polystictus versicolor (Polyporus) (Blue)	110 000. 4 Cu^{2+}/mol E'_0 + 0·415 V. λ_{max} = 610–14 nm 57 000. 4 Cu^{2+}/mol (Both proteins contain Cu^{2+} in two forms with differing bonding)	Reversibly bleached during action; indicates changes of Cu valency, possibly of only one Cu^{2+} atom. Substrates are ascorbic acid, p-phenylenediamine, o-diphenols, p-diphenols in complex polymerising and heterocyclic product reactions. Also oxidises m-diphenols. Removal of single H atoms forms polymerising free radicals but H atoms give water. Quinones are produced by reaction between free radicals to yield quinone and diphenol by disproportionation

Trivial name	Sources and colour	Mol. wt, Cu and E'_0	Remarks
(61) Ascorbic acid oxidase	Cucurbita pepo, Squash, and many other higher plants (Blue)	146 000. 8 Cu atoms 6 Cu^{2+} active ($Cu^{2+} \rightleftharpoons Cu^+$) 2 Cu^+ inactive Cu^{2+} may be of two forms	Specific for ascorbate. Mechanism is probably by free radical formation of mono-dehydroascorbic acid and disproportionation to diketogluconic acid. Possibly of respiratory importance in seedlings but also very widespread in plants. The 'unreactive' Cu^{1+} atoms may produce H_2O_2 in place of water and so cause inactivation
(62) Diamine oxidases (see also Galactose oxidase (66))	Pea seedlings (Pink) and other plants (especially Leguminosae) Fungi	73 000. 1 Cu^{2+}/mol No valency change	Putrescine, etc. Oxidised to amino aldehydes which may cyclise. FAD or pyridoxal phosphate may be present in many animal amine oxidases, but probably absent from plant enzyme. Hydrogen peroxide is produced
(63) Plastocyanin	Green algae Blue green algae Green plants Probably all photosynthetic organisms containing chlorophyll (Blue)	11 000–20 000 depending on source 1 or 2 Cu/mol $Cu^{2+} \rightleftharpoons Cu^+$ $E'_0 + 0.37$ to $+0.42$ V.	A pronounced u.v. absorption spectrum for phenylalanine and tyrosine as well as bands at 597 (blue colour) and 790 nm is characteristic of the blue plastocyanins. Generally regarded as 1 e^- transport factors for donation to chlorophyll a or P700 systems
(64) Umecyanin	Horseradish root (Blue)	14 600. 1 Cu atom/mol	λ_{max} 610 nm $\varepsilon = 3.5 \times 10^3$ mol cm^{-1} $Cu^{2+} \rightleftharpoons Cu^+$ reversible but not auto-oxidisable Oxidised by O_2 in presence of laccase
(65) Stellacyanin	Rhus vernicifera	27 000. 1 Cu^{2+} λ_{max} 604 nm, also 448 and 845 nm	Similar properties to laccase but only a single Cu^{2+} atom in a highly strained ligand field

Table 8.5—*continued*

	Trivial name	Sources and colour	Mol. wt, Cu and E₀	Remarks
(66)	Galactose oxidase	Dactylium dendroides	75 000. Cu^+, Cu^{2+}, $(Cu^{3+}?)$	
(67)	Caeruloplasmin	Blood (Blue)	151 000. 8 Cu/mol $Cu^{2+} \rightleftharpoons Cu^+$ Four pairs of sub-units λ_{max} 605 nm	Oxidises *o*- and *p*-diphenols to quinones and oxidises ascorbic acid. Three types of Cu combination revealed by ESR binding and exchange studies. Cu^{2+} in 2 binding states (two each) and either 4 Cu^+ or 2 Cu^{2+} pairs; may resemble fungal laccase
(68)	Haemocyanin	Squid (Purple-blue or green-blue)	613 000–950 000. Cu^+ Possibly 25 Cu/mol	Respiratory pigment of certain molluscs and crustaceans. Cu^+/O_2 complex found
(69)	Azurin, possibly a nitrite reductase	Bordatella (Blue)	14 000. 1 Cu^{2+}/mol	U.V. absorption spectra resemble plastocyanins in relation to phenylalanine and tyrosine content. Functions are not certain. May be associated with nitrite reductase (see Chapter 7); and as electron donor to *Pseudomonas* cytochrome oxidase which has no Cu component
		Pseudomonas aeruginosa (Blue)	16 000. 1 Cu^{2+}/mol λ_{max} 625 nm	
		P. denitrificans (Blue) P. fluorescens (Blue)	15 000. λ_{max} 600 nm	
(70)	Ribulose-diphosphate carboxylase	Spinach	560 000. 1 Cu^{2+}/mol, also requires Mg^{2+}	Discovered by cyanide inhibition, analysis, and ESR spectrum. The copper is tightly bound to the protein
(71)	Superoxide dismutase	Spinach Wheat germ	32 000 2 Cu, 2 Zn	Broad light absorption at 680 nm and also for phenylalanine in uv

Cytochrome oxidase (Cytochrome a_3). See section on Iron Proteins (34, 35) (Table 8.3)

Notes on Table 8.5

There is a wide diversity of properties among the copper proteins. Some are intensely blue, e.g. plastocyanin (63). The intense blue colour ($E = 10^3 - 10^4/$ litre atom Cu/cm at 590–610 nm approx.) is associated with a special type of co-ordination of the copper as Cu^{2+}, probably by sulphur in cysteine and other nitrogen ligands in which there is a partial transfer of an electron from the copper (Cu^{2+}) to the protein to produce a resonant charge transfer complex. Some contain one Cu atom, others have as many as six or eight, e.g. ascorbic acid oxidase (61), but not all of these are functional. In some enzymes, as in ascorbic acid oxidase (61), some copper atoms undergo reversible valency change, while others in the same molecule do not. In some, the metal is Cu^+ (tyrosinase (59)); but in others, Cu^{2+} (diamine oxidase (62) and galactose oxidase (66)), and there is no valency change. Some Cu proteins are pink (the pea seedling amine oxidase (62)) and some have unusual ultra-violet absorption spectra with intense absorption due to phenylalanine, e.g. plastocyanin (63) and azurin (69) (bacterial blue copper protein). In some, e.g. laccase (60) there are also two types of Cu^{2+} (Type I and II) distinguished by their ESR spectra in terms of ligand interaction with the protein, by hyperfine splitting of the ESR spectrum, and by their different contributions to the depth of blue colour, which is mainly associated with Type I. Other Cu^{2+} atoms form Cu^{2+}—Cu^{2+} ion pairs which do not show an unpaired electron.

Substrate specificity covers a very wide range of compounds including carbohydrates, amines, phenols and ascorbate. Most have fairly high redox (E_0') values around 0·37 to 0·42 V and molecular weights range from 10 000 to 150 000. Most, including ascorbic oxidase (61) and polyphenol oxidase (58), yield water when H is removed by oxidation, but diamine oxidase (62) produces hydrogen peroxide. The haemocyanin (68) forms a reversible complex with molecular oxygen. Plastocyanin (63) is an electron transport protein in chloroplasts and copper links the electron transport sequence in the cytochrome a-a₃ complex (34, 35) (Table 8.3). Ribulose diphosphate (70) carboxylase is the exception in this group as it does not mediate electron transport, but the Cu atom is essential for activity.

Table 8.6 Some zinc proteins of higher plants, yeasts, fungi, bacteria and algae

	Trivial name	Source	Mol. wt and Zn	Remarks
(72)	Carbonic anhydrase $CO_2 + H_2O \rightleftharpoons$ $H_2CO_3 \rightleftharpoons HCO_3^- + H^+$	Parsley	180 000. Six sub-units of 29 000; 6 Zn/mol; 0.21%	Comprises 1% of soluble parsley leaf protein. Co can be substituted for Zn in the erythrocyte enzyme which then is blue.
(73)	Alkaline phosphatase	Escherichia coli	89 000. 4 Zn/mol; 0.28% Two Zn at each of two sites	Zn binds sub-units in association. Co can be substituted for Zn. Cd replaces Zn but enzyme is then inactive. Mutant form produces Zn-free inactive protein which is activated by adding Zn in vitro. Different Zn binding sites have very different Zn binding affinities
(74)	Protease (hydrolysis of peptide bonds)	Bacillus subtilis	31 000. 1 Zn/mol; 0.2%	Zn removed by EDTA; substituted by Co or Mn at low efficiency
(75)	Phospho-mannose isomerase Mannose-6-PO_4 $\rightleftharpoons$ fructose-6-PO_4	Baker's yeast	45 000. 1 Zn/mol; 0.15%	Contrasts with other phospho-hexose isomerases, e.g. phospho-glucose isomerase, which depend on Mg^{2+} in a dissociable system
(76)	D-Lactate dehydrogenase Lactate + NAD$^+$ $\rightleftharpoons$ Pyruvate + NADH + H$^+$	Brewer's yeast in aerobic media	96 000. 3 Zn/mol; 0.2%	FAD is also part of the system. Apoenzyme is found in vivo in absence of Zn. Co can substitute for Zn in vivo in Zn-deficient cells. Co (25% V_{max}) or Mn (10% V_{max}) can replace Zn in EDTA-treated enzyme. Co decreases K_m for lactate from 1.7 to 0.15 mM; Cd inhibits
(77)	L-Lactate cytochrome c reductase	Yeast	Zn + FAD	Distinct from the D-lactate enzyme, and quite different from cytochrome b_2 L + lactate dehydrogenase of yeast

Trivial name	Source	Mol. wt and Zn	Remarks
(78) Alcohol dehydrogenase $EtOH + NAD^+ \rightleftarrows$ Acetaldehyde + $NADH + H^+$	Yeast	Four sub-units of 36 000. 4 Zn 0·18%	Zn may bind sub-units and also NAD. Ternary complex with EtOH is controversial. Co can replace Zn *in vivo* or *in vitro* giving active blue-green enzyme. Protein may bind extra Zn up to 40 atoms/mol. and 15 NAD
(79) Aldolase *type II* Fructose-1,6-$(PO_4)_2 \rightarrow$ glyceraldehyde-1-PO_4 + dihydroxy-acetone-PO_4	Yeasts (*Candida* and *Saccharomyces*); fungi; blue-green algae and bacteria	Two sub-units 40 000 (or single 68 000). 2 Zn/mol; 0·15%	Co or Mn can substitute for Zn after removal by EDTA. K^+ (dissociable) is also required. *Type I* aldolases have ε-amino lysine active site with Schiff's base function; contain no Zn and do not require a metal. They occur in higher plant and animal cells. *Euglena gracilis* and *Candida utilis* have both *I* and *II* types and plants deficient in Zn are reported to have low aldolase activity
(80) Glutamic dehydrogenase Glutamate + NAD^+ + $H_2O \rightleftarrows$ α-Ketoglutarate + $NADH + NH_4^+$	*Neurospora crassa* Pea seeds	Probably Zn (NAD specific form). Liver enzyme. Four sub-units of 250 000; 4 Zn/mol	Dialysis with EDTA inactivates. Restored by Zn, Ca, Co or Mn, but metal may not be removed from the protein. NADP specific forms may not contain Zn
(81) Thermolysin	Thermophilic bacteria	37 000 Zn and Ca	Zn essential for catalytic activity in peptide hydrolysis; Ca maintains stability at elevated temperatures
(82) Pyruvate carboxylase	Yeast	Bound Zn 3 atoms/mol; 600 000 and dissociable Mg	Growth in the presence of Co results in part replacement of Zn by Co. Removal of the bound metal inactivates the enzyme. Chicken liver pyruvate carboxylase contains Mn instead of Zn

Notes on Table 8.6

All the zinc-dependent enzymes are metalloproteins, the metal being very closely associated or covalently bonded to the protein. However, in several, the metal can be removed by treatment with EDTA or *o*-phenanthroline which chelate competitively. The apoprotein may then react with cobalt, cadmium, manganese and sometimes nickel, with decreased or even increased activities, or changes in ratio of dual activities, e.g. esterase and hydrolase in carboxypeptidase. It is interesting to consider why these substituent metalloproteins are not produced *in vivo* either to some extent or even in greater amount than the physiologically preferred metal protein, under normal growth conditions. Nevertheless, it has been shown experimentally that yeast cells grown with a low zinc medium which has been supplemented by cobalt produce a blue-green cobalt alcohol dehydrogenase (78). D-lactate dehydrogenase (76) is similarly produced with cobalt in place of zinc. The cobalt enzyme has a lower K_m for lactate. Although the cobalt alcohol dehydrogenase is blue-green and the cobalt analogue of mammalian carbonic anhydrase is blue with a very complex absorption spectrum, the pancreatic carboxypeptidase cobalt analogue is pink (λ_{max} 515 nm). In the alkaline phosphatase of *E. coli*, different Zn atoms have either catalytic or structural functions and are chelated with differing degrees of stability.

Index

(Page numbers in italics refer to Plates)